The
MICKEY HERSKOWITZ
Collection

ALSO BY MICKEY HERSKOWITZ
One With the Flame: Carrying the Olympic Torch Across America
The Legend of Bear Bryant
This 'n' That with Bette Davis
Catcher in the Wry With Bob Uecker
The Camera Never Blinks: Adventures of a TV Journalist with Dan Rather
The Golden Age of Pro Football
Cosell with Howard Cosell
Confession and Avoidance with Leon Jaworski
Back in the Saddle Again with Gene Autry
Self-Portrait with Gene Tierney

Series Editor, Carlton Stowers

The MICKEY HERSKOWITZ Collection

Introduction by
DAN RATHER

TAYLOR PUBLISHING COMPANY
Dallas, Texas

Copyright ©1989 by Mickey Herskowitz

Published by Taylor Publishing Company
1550 West Mockingbird Lane
Dallas, Texas 75235

The columns included in this collection originally appeared in
the *Houston Post, Parade, Gameday,* and *Southern Living.*
Reprinted by permission. All rights reserved.

Library of Congress Cataloging-in-Publication Data

Herskowitz, Mickey.
   The Mickey Herskowitz collection / introduction by Dan Rather.
   p. cm. — (The Sportswriter's eye)
   "The columns included in this collection originally appeared in
the Houston Post"—T.p. verso.
   Includes index.
   ISBN 0-87833-635-4 : $14.95
     1. Sports—United States. 2. Sports. 3. Newspapers—Sections,
columns, etc.—Sports. I. Title. II. Series.
GV583.H48 1989   88-28635
070.4′49796′0973—dc19   CIP

Printed in the United States of America
0 9 8 7 6 5 4 3 2 1

To the memory of Jack Gallagher and Steve Perkins, the kind of writers who would pull you out of a ditch.

Introduction

The first thing to know about Mickey Herskowitz is what a great storyteller he is. Always has been.

This is how I know. In the late 1950s, in Houston, I was supplementing my reporter's paycheck by calling the play-by-play on radio for minor-league baseball and college football games. Mickey was getting his start in the sports department of the morning paper.

His stories always had a beginning, middle, and end. They had a narrative flow. He put you on the scene and made you feel you knew, really knew, the people involved.

I said to myself then, and have often said since, "This guy is one helluva storyteller."

In the nice way that these things sometimes happen, readership turned into friendship and in time collaboration. Years later Mickey helped me assemble a book of personal stories about broadcast journalism, called *The Camera Never Blinks*.

My wife Jean thought it should have been subtitled *And Mickey Never Sleeps*. The reason was that Mickey, despite his unflagging good humor, was so meticulous about details and so caring about the project as a whole. It was never too late—in his mind, at least—to make a correction, to change a word, or to insert a better phrase in a lagging sentence that had already seen five rewrites. Nor did he ever think it was too late to say, "This chapter just doesn't have it. Let's start over."

This attention to craft is a key to his achievement as a writer. There is another thing, more subtle. It is a detachment and sense of perspective that one always finds in sports copy written by the best, a realization that there are other things happening in the world, more important by far than sports, that there are greater joys than winning a game, and more significant human tragedies than losing.

As a sports columnist, Mickey has tried especially hard, I know, to be a sensitive observer. His stories address the reader directly. These moments of connection occur in such thoughts as this one, in the middle of a magazine piece about a much maligned golfer, J.C. Snead, nephew of Sam Snead: "The J.C. Snead story ... is interesting because it brushes the line between writers and the people they cover, and goes to the heart of the contract that exists between writers and you, the reader. Have we treated these people fairly and without favor, and as fully dimensional figures? Do we owe them more sympathy, or none?"

Because he is uncomfortable as an advocate or a take-no-prisoners critic ("Like Houston fans, it takes a lot to make me boo"), Mickey goes for the funny bone or the heartstrings, rarely for the jugular. About as caustic as he gets is to poke fun at the futility of the local pro teams, via such backhanded compliments as this: "The Houston Astros held Sandy Koufax to a three-hitter last night."

The comings and goings, the entrances and exits, are part of what engages our interest in sports. Mickey saw Paul (Bear) Bryant's first season at Texas A&M, Cassius Clay's first fight and Muhammad Ali's last, Casey Stengel in his heyday, and scores of Houston Astros and Houston Oilers traded away to form championship teams elsewhere.

He did some coming and going of his own, leaving his newspaper work from time to time, but returning to it each time with more books to his credit.

Daily sports reports, columns, magazine stories, and books. No American writer, sports or otherwise, has consistently turned out more quality work than Mickey Herskowitz over the past thirty years or so. And the basic reason—I keep coming back to it—is that he is such an amazing storyteller.

When *The Camera Never Blinks* was published, I discovered one of the hazards of the business. In the retelling, two people who had been an influence in my early years were overlooked. One was a judge named Spurgeon Bell, the other a former University of Houston football coach, Hal Lahar. This happens, in publishing as elsewhere—a friend goes unacknowledged. The usual response, if any, is to write a note of apology and wait for the next crisis. In this case, I mentioned my regrets to Mickey. Using our conversation and what he could find in our notes, Mickey wrote a magazine article about the relationships and turned a loss into a gain.

Typical. Mickey rarely wastes his own time, and he never wastes the reader's. What follows in this book, dear reader, is the work of one of the great storytellers and yarnspinners of our time. Read it and cheer.

Dan Rather

Contents

Preface / xv

Touching All the Bases / 1

OH, WHAT A GAME! / 2
FROM ASPROMONTE TO RYAN / 5
ALWAYS A LAUGH AROUND CASEY / 11
ASTROS WIN TITLE—FINALLY / 14
ASTROS RUN OUT OF INNINGS / 18
THE ASTROS' LONGEST DAY / 22
A PAIGE OUT OF HISTORY / 25
BEST PLAYERS, WORST HABITS / 28
NAME-DROPPING IN THE MAJORS / 31
FAN LETTER REVIVES MARIS MEMORIES / 34

From the Greatest to the Latest / 37

ALI'S IDLE THREATS / 38
SUGAR RAY ASSUMES ALI'S ROLE / 41
LULL BETWEEN LEGENDS IS OVER / 44
TORA! TORA! TORA! / 47
GLITTER COUNTS, BUT PUNCHES DON'T / 50
FLORIDA WITHOUT ORANGE JUICE / 53
TYSON KEEPS APPOINTMENT / 56
ALI'S ANSWERED THE LAST BELL / 58

CONTENTS

The Rockets' Red Glare / 63

GAME OF THE CENTURY—TWENTY YEARS LATER / 64
LEMONS GIVES 'EM WHAT THEY WANT / 68
BOSTON'S ONE-MAN SHOW / 71
LAST OF NBA'S GREAT MINI-STARS / 74
FREE ADVICE FOR RALPH / 77
BRINGING THE DUNK DOWN TO EARTH / 79
COOGS LOSE A GREAT GUY / 82

Football Follies and the Circus Maximus / 85

END OF AN ERA / 86
BIG LOU APPEALS TO THE PLAYERS / 89
IT WAS BUM'S FAULT / 92
THE HARD WORK COMES FIRST / 95
ALOHA, OILERS!!! / 98
THE RETURN OF THE SNAKE / 102
A QUIET GOODBYE FOR JOHNNY U. / 105
SUPER MEMORIES FROM SUPER BOWLS / 108
SUPER BOWL SHOWTIME / 112
BIGGEST OF THE BIG / 114
NEW ORLEANS IDEAL FOR RAIDERS / 117

CONTENTS

Off the Field / 121

DIAGNOSING SICKER AND SICKER SWC / 122
THE GREEK'S COMEBACK ODDS / 125
WAIST-DEEP IN DISHONESTY / 128
SYMPATHY BECOMES SCARCE / 130
MASTERS OF THE MEANINGLESS GESTURE / 133

The Write Stuff / 135

APRIL BROUGHT YOU ROCKETS, EL TORO / 136
THE TEXAS SPECIAL / 139
THE FIRST LADY OF SPORTSCASTING / 142
STILL WANDERING AFTER FORTY YEARS / 145
THE CHALLENGE STILL MATTERS / 148
WORDS OF WISDOM FROM WILL / 152

The View From the Press Box / 155

THE UBIQUITOUS ONE / 156
BIG DADDY OF THE WISHBONE-T / 159
COSELL TACKLES THE CINEMA / 164
SWEPT OFF HIS FEET / 167
BEST STORIES ALSO RAREST / 170
GENDER-GAP HEROES / 173
LOCKER ROOM QUOTABLES / 176

CONTENTS

The Tyler Rose, the Ryan Express, and The Bear / 179

WELL WORTH THE WAIT / 180
SIMPLY DOIN' WHAT'S RIGHT / 183
NO TEARS, NO FEARS, NO REGRETS / 186
OF NO-HITTERS AND HOMERS / 190
RYAN BACK WITH CINDERELLA / 193
A MAN OF STYLE AND POWER / 196
ONE MAN: BRYANT / 199
THE RECORD AT LAST / 204
A FINAL TRIBUTE / 208

With a Little Help From My Friends / 211

HE'S STILL GOT THAT SWING / 212
FIVE HUNDRED WAYS TO WIN OR LOSE / 217
THE PLEASURE OF HIS COMPANY / 220
UECKER GETS A HIT—FINALLY / 223
SPITZ STILL SMOOTH / 226
BACHELOR BO NO MO' / 229
BUBBA WHIPS POVERTY / 234
NAMATH ERA ENDS QUIETLY / 237
A BONUS FROM BERRA / 240

CONTENTS

Letters From Lefty / 243

SPRING TRAINING / 244
HOLDING OUT / 247
IN THE BULL PEN / 250
RATING THE FANS / 253
SOME FORGETTABLE MOMENTS / 256
LEFTY SAYS GOOD-BYE / 259
BACK HOME AGAIN / 262
GOOD-BYE, DIAMOND JIM / 264

Index / 267

CONTENTS

Preface

I have two memories of a hotel in San Francisco, the first year Houston fielded a baseball team in the major leagues.

The hotel management had prepared a special welcome for the team on its first visit to the city. Unaware that the previous night's game had gone into extra innings and that our flight had arrived in the wee hours, a basket of juicy red apples went around to each room at seven in the morning.

There was a disturbance at the door to one room, occupied by a first baseman named Norm Larker. The basket had gone flying into the hallway. The bellman, on his hands and knees, retrieved its contents.

At 1 P.M., rested and refreshed, Larker called down to the front desk and announced, "I'm ready for my apples now."

On the last night of that season, I found myself in the bar of the hotel seated next to Loel Passe, of the team's radio crew. Word had just reached us that Al Helfer would not return the next year. It had not been a good year for Helfer, once ranked with Mel Allen and Red Barber as the top men in his field. On occasion, Loel's unabashed cheerleading drove him from the booth. The news meant more airtime for Loel, but his reaction was unselfish.

"I'm going to miss Big Al," he said. "Ol' Loel learned a lot from Big Al." He took a sip of his drink and then added, "Of course, Big Al learned a lot from ol' Loel, too."

A year later, Helfer retired from broadcasting altogether.

As someone once said, a little knowledge is a dangerous thing. Houston fans in every sport have grown more educated since the pioneer days of the Houston Colt .45s, and where, you are free to ask, has it gotten us?

If you patrol the sports beat long enough, you are going to brush up against a fair amount of weirdness, much of it your own.

PREFACE

There was the time I left an important photograph behind in a cafe in College Station and didn't realize it until I walked into the *Post* sports department ten minutes before the deadline for photoengraving. An Austin writer, a guest in the same booth, took it home and used it in his paper's next edition. He was kind enough to give me a credit line: "*American-Statesman* Photo by Mickey Muffit."

The hardest thing for a writer is finding someone else to blame. The first time I wrote about Gene Autry, the owner of the California Angels, I referred to his horse as Trigger. A few days later, I received a postcard with these hand-printed words: "Dear Sir. Boy, are you stupid. Any eight-year-old kid could tell you Gene Autry's horse is named Champion. Roy Rogers' horse is Trigger." The kid signed his name and then, so I would not miss the point, wrote under it, "Age 8."

It is a matter of record that the *Post* no longer allows me to write the daily fishing report when the outdoor editor is on a trip or recovering from a hangover.

My ignorance of all matters related to fishing was seen as an advantage . . . right up until the day I wrote that one of the camps had reported a record catch of what I understood the man to say were "gasstops." I thought it was an odd name, even for a fish. (At least twenty people told me the next day that the fish is called a gafftop.)

None of this is quite what I had planned to write. I had started out thinking about the events I have seen and covered, the spectacles of sport.

Instead, I remember covering the closed-circuit telecast of an exhibition between Muhammad Ali and a Japanese wrestler named Inoki. Incredibly, this odd entertainment drew a nearly sellout crowd to the Astrodome. "This is a travesty," one writer said, "and there are 40,000 travestites here watching it."

A few years ago, I wrote about sports now and then, as opposed to not at all. Then I returned to my newspaper readership on a more regular basis, three times a week. Being back in that forum pleased me, because the people who inhabit the sports world—which has been our world—are an unending source of delight.

You have been fine readers and we have learned from each other. I'm ready for my apples now.

Touching All
the Bases

OH, WHAT A GAME!

MARCH 18, 1984

A confession is in order. Football is a fan's game, one that brings out either the beast or the child in most of us. Baseball is a writer's game. There is time to take notes, to think, to compare. The way time passes at a ballpark is special. It is boring at times, but most people who go to ballparks are not afraid of being bored. TV producers never will understand this.

Part of the appeal of the game is the fact that a good career tends to last ten to twelve years. The fan is there all the time. So he sees, in effect, a birth, a flowering, an aging, and a death. It's a life story. And not all the stories are happy ones.

It is immensely sad to consider the cases of J.R. Richard and Mark ("The Bird") Fidrych, both brought down in the high noon of their careers. J.R. is back in Houston's camp, on a minor-league contract, still trying to recapture the magic three years after a stroke almost killed him.

Fidrych is flat gone from the scene, the memory fading of the sizzling rookie year that made him a national hero, almost a kind of comic-book character.

Then there was Mike Ivie, whose problem was in his head—for most athletes the very worst place. Many scouts thought Ivie would make a terrific catcher. But he developed a mental block against throwing the ball back to the mound. He flung the ball into center field. He bounced it in the dirt. At times he couldn't let go at all.

Imagine the colossal irony of a catcher not being able to get the ball back to the mound. As the late Casey Stengel once said, "The catcher is the most important player on the team. If you don't have a catcher, the ball will roll back to the screen on every pitch."

Baseball touches us so deeply because it is essential American corn. There is Lou Gehrig, dying of multiple sclerosis, telling a Yankee Stadium crowd, "I consider myself the luckiest man on the face of the earth."

And there was Willie Mays, standing in the center of another New York diamond, making his retirement speech: "Willie, say good-bye to America."

Spring training is an anachronism, of course. It dates back to a time when there was little else going on in the country, least of all in sports, and especially in the South. Spring training was a way of filling the void, preparing the fans up n'awth for the start of the season, and raising a little cash. The crowds they drew in the spring sometimes determined whether the teams made a profit for the year.

Every spring it is tempting to fall into the do-you-remember game. Have a handful: Steve Bilko, Diamond Jim Gentile, Greg Goosen, Carroll Sembera, Walt ("No-Neck") Williams. But names are just that—empty shirts with lettering on the back, without a sense of teams and seasons.

For years the Detroit Tigers were my favorite team, a loyalty I have never been able to explain to anyone's satisfaction, including mine. It just happened. Sitting on a bench in Florida one spring, I confided to Al Kaline that the Tigers were my adopted team.

I told him how, as a boy, I had known from memory the records of Hal Newhouser, Hank Greenberg, Hoot Evers, and Virgil ("Fire") Trucks. When I finished, Kaline asked, "You ever see any of 'em play?"

I said no. He tapped his bat against the dugout steps, then nodded and walked to the batting cage to take his cuts. It was a weird conversation but it had to do with making heroes out of people you never met, who worked in cities you had never seen.

A spring delight was the chance to visit the people who play in the seventy-five-year-old-and-over softball league in St. Petersburg, on teams called the Kids and the Kubs. They were wonderful, with few concessions to their ages. Some of the complaints were not unlike ones in Little League. These senior citizens always were crabbing that the coach didn't play them enough at their best positions.

The league has existed for fifty years, and over that span five players had dropped dead during games. One, an eighty-three-year-old, had fallen dead reaching for his first baseman's glove as someone threw it out to him on the field.

"We all crowded around," recalled a man named Jack Wernz. "We were extremely sympathetic to each other's ailments and pains. Everyone felt badly that Lee was dead, but no one felt frightened. And no one felt badly about how he had died."

They stopped the game until the ambulance had driven slowly off the field and into the street, carrying their friend. And then they continued playing. There was no siren. A few blocks away the New York Mets were playing a game, and the fantasy of spring training was unbroken.

FROM ASPROMONTE TO RYAN

APRIL 6, 1986

Many springs ago, the Astros were playing the Los Angeles Dodgers in what is commonly known as the Grapefruit League. The public-address announcer was Orland Sims, who worked in the team's publicity department.

The next batter was a Dodgers rookie infielder named Luis Alcaraz, but when Sims made the introduction it came out as "Alcatraz." Scattered laughter rose up from the crowd.

In the press box, Orland turned to the writers for support. "Do you think," he asked, "that I should say no man is an island, but for him we'll make an exception?"

In this same spirit, you are urged not to ask for whom the bell tolls in April. It rings for all twenty-six teams in the major leagues, as loudly for the least of them as the best.

The Houston Astros enter this season, their twenty-fifth, hoping to rejoin the ranks of the upwardly mobile. Over the years, they have changed names, stadiums, spring-training homes, and managers, Hal Lanier being the ninth and latest. He replaced Bob Lillis in a move that represented a break with the past, real as well as symbolic.

Lillis was a Houston original, one of the players selected in the expansion draft. As a player, coach, and manager, he had been a continuing presence on the team. Now the cord has been cut.

In the beginning there was Apache Junction, in the Arizona desert, where Geronimo's warriors once roamed. That was in 1962, a silver anniversary ago, and the team was called the Colt .45s.

There has been some loose talk over the years about the Astros having been born with a curse. Possibly it was not wise to train in the shadow of a place called Superstition Mountain, where Indian spirits and the ghost of an old Dutchman were said to guard a lost gold mine.

No one takes such legends seriously, of course. We only know that the Colt .45s did not suffer any bad luck until the first inning of the first exhibition game they ever played. Al Heist, their best outfielder, stepped in a hole and broke his ankle, ending his career.

Harry Craft was Houston's first manager and the biggest name in the cast was Bobby Shantz, the onetime glory tot of the old Philadelphia A's, who had pitched under Connie Mack.

In the so-called "premium" phase of the draft, Houston selected four players for $125,000 apiece: Turk Farrell, who threw a high fastball and liked a fast highball; Hal Smith, a catcher who helped Pittsburgh win the 1960 World Series; Al Spangler, a promising outfielder from the Milwaukee Braves; and Joey Amalfitano, a young second baseman who had been unable to break into the Giants' lineup.

For twenty-three players, the new franchises had paid the staggering sum of $1.8 million. When he heard what Houston had paid for him, Amalfitano quipped, "I'm worth more than I thought I was. I may have to increase my insurance." Later, Joey heard from so many insurance agents he had to get an unlisted phone number.

Opening at home, the Colt .45s sent three left-handers against the Chicago Cubs—Shantz, Dean Stone, and Hal Woodeshick—and swept the series. It was a giddy way to launch a franchise. Reality sank in rather quickly, but they hung on to finish eighth in a ten-team league, ahead of the embarrassed Phillies and the last-place Mets.

The hopeless Mets created a mystique while losing 120 games, encouraging the laughter of the crowd and sometimes joining in.

For most of their years the Colts/Astros were never consistently good enough to be heroic, or bad enough to be funny. Mostly they were just different.

The trend was established in 1962, when Judge Roy Hofheinz got the inspired notion of decking them out in blue cowboy suits on road trips, with matching hats and boots. The idea was apparently to advertise the fact that the team played in Texas.

TOUCHING ALL THE BASES

People kept mistaking them for the Sons of the Pioneers, and finally the players voted not to wear the outfits and the Judge gave up.

Don Nottebart pitched their first no-hitter in 1963, but the one that would become their most historic was recorded the next year by Ken Johnson. He lost to the Reds 1-0 on his own throwing error in the ninth inning. No pitcher had ever before lost a no-hitter.

By 1964, the franchise was on the move. That spring, they switched their training base from Arizona to Cocoa, Florida. In 1965, they celebrated the opening of the world's first indoor, multipurpose sports stadium—the Astrodome. The Big Bubble was that year's hottest sports story. We sort of woke up one morning and found ourselves all under the same roof.

Joe Garagiola, the ex-catcher-turned-sportscaster, took one look and declared, "It's like falling out of *Mechanix Illustrated*. If they'd add a cemetery you'd never have to leave."

It was so spectacular they had to open it twice, against the Yankees in a preseason series and then, for real, against the Phillies. Mickey Mantle hit the unofficial first homer. The one that counted came on opening night. Richie Allen of the Phillies connected with a man on against Bob Bruce for the game's only runs.

For the only time in their existence, the Astros drew two million fans. A million more paid a dollar each to follow a tour guide through an empty stadium.

The Dome was not exactly unflawed, a fact that added to the mystique. The outfielders couldn't see the ball in the daytime because of the glare of the sun through the skylights. And when they painted the ceiling, to eliminate the glare, the grass died, leading to a discovery called Astroturf.

That year, 1965, the Astros peeled off a ten-game winning streak, an occurrence so unthinkable that their opponents accused them of tinkering with the air-conditioning currents, causing the air to blow out when the home team was at bat. Ah, if only winning had been so simple.

Robin Roberts, who had known greatness in Philadelphia, had lost his fastball but not his pride when he joined the Astros that season. He pitched shutouts in his first two starts. Bob Aspromonte hit the first indoor homer—called a domer—for the local team, and Willie Mays collected his 500th.

In their first fifteen years, the Astros signed some bright and exciting young players who went on to do wonderful deeds, become All-Stars, and play in the World Series—always for other teams. The list included Joe Morgan, Rusty Staub, Jimmy Wynn, Jerry Grote, pitcher Mike Marshall, and one or two others too painful to recall. At nineteen, Staub was a cleanup hitter in the majors, the symbol of the team's future. He hit .333 in 1967 and a year later they traded him.

But the Astros kept searching. Larry Dierker signed on at eighteen, stayed around to pitch the 1,000th game played in the Astrodome, and celebrated his twelfth season in Houston with the first no-hitter of his career, against Montreal.

Don Wilson and Bob Watson joined the club as rookies in 1966. Wilson would pitch two no-hitters, strike out eighteen Atlanta Braves in one game, and die young, in an accident at home.

Watson scored baseball's millionth run and received an award from the Tootsie Roll Company. Don't ask who kept count; just be proud it was an Astro.

In 1966, the Astros got hot, stayed in the pennant race until midseason, and made the cover of *Sports Illustrated.* Sonny Jackson and Joe Morgan were shown turning a double play. It was a nice, almost poetic touch when Morgan returned to Houston in 1980, to help his old team win a Western Division title.

The Astros had been in the league ten years before they had a season in which they won more games than they lost. The breakthrough came in 1972. Sensing a shot at the pennant— oh, Impossible Dream—the Astros in August replaced Harry Walker as manager with the legendary Leo Durocher. They finished second.

In 1973, they were hovering around .500 again, and at the end of the season Durocher was gone. But Cesar Cedeno had bloomed as a big-league star, hitting .320 with twenty-five homers and fifty-six stolen bases. But Cedeno did not turn out to be Houston's savior, no more than Rusty Staub had.

While the Astros were seeking a franchise player, players who had won their fame in other cities came and went: Shantz, Roberts, Pete Runnels, Nellie Fox, Johnny Temple, Don Larsen (who pitched the only perfect game in World Series history as a Yankee).

Then there were the wild and crazy ones—Bo Belinsky, who

quit the team one spring so he could spend more time on the beach with a former Playmate of the Year; and Doug Rader, the free-spirited third baseman who, during a radio interview, advised Little Leaguers to eat bubble-gum cards. Not the gum, the cards. "They have lots of good information," Rader said, "about hitting and pitching."

Your mind sweeps back over the years, and what you find is not so much a history as a variety show.

There was a rookie named Walter ("No-Neck") Williams, whose head seemed to grow right out of his shoulders. When a writer asked if Williams had received a bonus, catcher John Bateman piped up, "Yeah, Paul Richards said if he made the club, he'd buy him a neck."

A few of the boys had a nice touch with a phrase. A relief pitcher named Russ Kemmerer, when told he was being sent to the minors, complained, "How can they cut me? I was hitting .280."

And still sharp is the memory of Belinsky, at his first Houston news conference, raising a wineglass and proposing a toast: "If music be the food of love, by all means, play on."

Training in Cocoa, in the spring, they were on the doorstep of the space program. One morning, from the windows of the team bus, they could look across the Indian River and see poised in its gantry the rocket that would carry America's first astronauts to the moon. It was Bateman, the craggy catcher, who broke the silence. "It makes our exhibition game with Kansas City seem insignificant," he said.

Some had style, some wit, and a few even could play baseball. The Astros took a more serious turn—they became respectable, and then contenders—in the late 1970s. The franchise had passed from the hands of Judge Hofheinz into the temporary stewardship of the team's creditors, and then (in 1979) to a group headed by John J. McMullen.

The Astros had finished last in 1975, a mere 43 1/2 games out of first place. Bill Virdon was hired as manager in the final month of the season to start pulling the team out of the depths.

It all came together briefly in 1980. The Astros went into the marketplace to sign Nolan Ryan, baseball's strikeout king, and bring back Morgan. For one of the few times anyone could remember, the Astros had a set and healthy lineup. Cedeno, Enos Cabell, and José Cruz played up to their top form. Terry

Puhl was a rising star in right field. Craig Reynolds at short and Alan Ashby behind the plate made major contributions, and Art Howe played everywhere.

By midyear, the pitching staff may have been the equal of any in the majors—Ryan, the dominating J.R. Richard, Joe Niekro, and Ken Forsch were the starters, with Joe Sambito the stopper out of the pen.

It was a wildly exciting year with flash eruptions along the way. At the height of the pennant race, the Astros lost Richard, who was felled by a stroke. His loss, at the crest of his powers, affected the team for seasons to come.

But in 1980, the Astros hung on, and Vern Ruhle came out of the spare-parts pile to pick up the slack on the mound. They won the Western Division, needing a one-game play-off to beat the Dodgers.

They led the Phillies in the fifth game of the National League play-offs, going into the eighth inning. The Phillies won it in the tenth, 8-7.

The Astros returned to the play-offs in 1981, in a season split by a player strike. This time, they won the second half of the season but lost to the Dodgers in a series to determine the division champion.

There were upheavals off the field and more unhappy medical bulletins. Tal Smith was fired as general manager, followed by his successor, Al Rosen, replaced this winter by Dick Wagner. Sambito's Houston service ended with an arm injury, and a wild pitch nearly ended everything for Dickie Thon, who had come into his own as a hitting shortstop. Thon is still coming back from the eye injury that wasted his 1984 season.

Meanwhile, Ryan, from down the road at Alvin, picked up his fifth no-hitter and his 4,000th strikeout. And another youth revival was underway, featuring Bill Doran, Mark Bailey, and Glenn Davis.

The Astros would like to shake their tag as a hard-luck team. So 1986 is another season, another reason, to keep trying.

ALWAYS A LAUGH AROUND CASEY

OCTOBER 1975

In his heyday with the New York Mets, Casey Stengel appeared in Florida one spring with his hair dyed a strange, youthful shade of henna. It was a wild sight, that hair, above that wrinkled, biblical face. The New York writers could hardly wait to tell you about it.

"Have you seen Casey?" they braced each new visitor. "He looks like Dorian Gray's UNCLE."

So it went with Charles Dillon Stengel, cut down last week in the prime of his life at the age of eighty-five. They talked about his gift for mangling the language. Well, Casey wasn't meant to be understood. Like Shakespeare, he was meant to be enjoyed, to be shared, to be experienced.

He was gnarled and cantankerous and he could be hard on inexperienced ballplayers. But he believed in the miracle of being young. "I'll tell you about youth," he once said. "Look how big it is. They break a record every day."

In the quality that really counts—in being truly alive to the wonders of the world, large and small—he was eternally childlike. His memory was prodigious. Once he recalled a moment that had taken place nearly fifty years before, when Casey was playing right field for Pittsburgh.

That day a shiny new red fire engine was to be shown off at the ballpark. In honor of the occasion, a mock house had been erected of two-by-fours in center field. At the proper moment, the house was set afire and the fire engine was supposed to dash out and douse the flames.

"Only they forgot to measure the bull pen," recalled Casey. "The engine was too big. They couldn't get it through the gate."

So the house burned merrily, finally tumbling upon itself. When it had burned to the ground—and still no fire engine.—Stengel could stand it no longer. "I filled a glass with water in the dugout," he said, "and I ran out like Charlie Chaplin and SHOOSH! I threw the water on the fire. It was almost out anyway. And you know something? The fire department was mad as hell at me."

He was part clown and part genius. He managed the Yankees to ten pennants, but he proved his greatness in 1962 when he saw his expansion Mets lose 120 games. Not once did Casey go back to his hotel room and try to hang himself.

The truth never frightened him, as it does so many others in sports. In the second year of the Mets, when better things were expected, he stormed into his office after an opening-game loss and slammed down his cap. "The attendance was robbed," he said. "We're still a fraud."

The team he created out of rejects and misfits and his own humor went on to win the World Series for Gil Hodges. It wasn't the same team, of course, but their legend and his are inseparable.

There isn't much to add to the eulogies already written and spoken, except for a personal impression or two.

He was at heart a teacher, even of the writers who crossed his path only two or three times a season. In his company you always learned, even though it may not have been related to the questions you had asked. He was a joy to hear and to watch. His legs were so lumpy it looked as though he were smuggling walnuts in his stockings. He walked like Popeye the Sailor and he even made umpires laugh.

One of my favorite Stengel stories involved the time Lindsey Nelson, the Mets broadcaster, attempted to describe a game from the gondola that hangs suspended from the roof of the Astrodome. The gondola, which resembles the basket of a hot-air balloon, and has been used as a photo deck for certain events, was lowered during a pause in the infield drills, and Lindsey, with an assistant, clambered aboard. Then, the cables hoisted them back toward the ceiling, high above second base, as the crowd cheered their ascent. It was like a scene from *Around the World in 80 Days*.

As the game was about to begin, Stengel met at home plate with the Houston manager and the umpiring crew to review the ground rules. "All right," said Casey, "what about my man up there?"

"What man?" asked Tom Gorman, the chief umpire.

"My man Lindsey, up there," he said, pointing, "in that cage under the roof."

All eyes were raised, as if expecting rain. Tom Gorman scratched his head and decided that, since any ball hitting the top of the dome was in play, any ball hitting Lindsey Nelson should also be in play.

Casey was pleased. "Well," he said, beaming, "my man is a ground rule. That's the first time my man was ever a ground rule."

He was funny and unpredictable and unsinkable. When he turned eighty-one, someone asked what his plans were. "To tell you the truth," he said, "what I'd like to do is become an astronaut."

It is fashionable to say that successful people, in any field, could have been whatever they wanted. But you could not picture Casey Stengel being anything else but what he was. The greatest showman baseball ever knew.

ASTROS WIN TITLE— FINALLY

OCTOBER 7, 1980

LOS ANGELES—Forget those comparisons to the *Titanic*, the *Hindenburg*, the Crash of 1929, the fainting Phillies of 1964, or the Incredible Shrinking Man. Laughter could be heard on Sudden-Death Row Monday and it came from the Houston Astros.

After waiting through nineteen years, three excruciating days, and nine unplanned innings, the Astros celebrated the first title in their history, silencing at last the Dodgers and their infernal noise machine—silenced them good, 7-1.

Obviously, there was a madness to Houston's method. How else can one explain the fact that the Dodgers had caught them at the wire, trailing by three games on Friday and three runs on Sunday. Perhaps the Astros merely wanted to give Joe Niekro a chance to win his twentieth game of the season. The Polish prince certainly deserved it. He's a splendid fellow, grateful and witty and too little recognized as a pitcher of importance.

Or possibly the Astros were simply setting up the Dodgers, seeking the perfect way to break their hearts and pay them back for past abuses and the colossal earache the L.A. fans caused them.

Or maybe the Astros, unaccustomed as they are to prosperity, needed to feel the wall against their backs—needed to know that they had run out of room and time and reprieves.

"The way things turned out," said Nolan Ryan, "you'd have to say this was an appropriate way to end it. This is the way our whole season has gone."

True enough, the Astros have won the game they absolutely had to win throughout this, the year of their lives. And they only had to beat the Dodgers once. They just didn't figure on doing it the day after the regular season had ended, in the fifth tie-breaking play-off in National League history. You expected them to come out Monday as loose and relaxed as a steel rod. Their voices were so low Sunday, after their third one-run loss in a row, they sounded as though they were broadcasting a golf match.

On the field before Monday's encore performance, Tal Smith, the Houston general manager, turned to a writer who had been present at the team's creation. "Did you ever think," he asked, "back in Apache Junction, that someday you'd be seeing anything like this?"

"Tal," the writer responded, "as recently as *Friday* I didn't think I'd be seeing anything like this."

The Astros might have gone down in flames and found themselves a place in baseball's book of legendary failures. Already, observers were recalling the collapse in 1964 of the Phillies, who blew a 6½-game lead with twelve to play. But the Astros simply kept their composure and they played their kind of game. The Astros win with guerrilla warfare. They're at their best when they pester the opposition, hitting them not with heavy artillery, but with a bow and arrow.

So they scored twice in the first on two errors, a stolen base, and a single. They finished off the Dodgers in the fourth, scoring three runs on one hit, four walks, and stealing two more bases. The Dodgers needed three pitchers to get out of the inning, and six for the game, which ended 7-1. The Dodgers had used up a pocket full of miracles. This time they reached in and found only lint.

Houston errors had kept the Dodgers in two of the games, and home runs had won all three—by Joe Ferguson, Steve Garvey, and Ron Cey. The Astros won't win many games on pure muscle, but this was a day when they could and did use all of their resources. Art Howe popped a two-run homer in the third, just to prove that they could hit something other than an Astro double—which is a single and a stolen base. They even got to show off their own high-five handshakes.

"We've been criticized for the way we play," said Howe, who had three hits and drove in four runs. "We're not the big bombers—but we use what we have and we don't quit."

When the Astros flew into Los Angeles for Friday night's series opener, one newspaper referred to them as "the faceless Astros."

They have faces. They just weren't all that keen to show them the past few days. Now they're headed for Philadelphia, for their first exposure to the National League play-offs. The rest of the world may soon discover that they aren't just a bunch of guys named Joe.

Of course, there is nothing wrong with the Joes they have—namely Niekro, Morgan, Sambito, and Cruz. Niekro was simply masterful as he let the Dodgers down on six singles to collect his twentieth win for the second consecutive year. "You have to give him credit," said Steve Garvey. "He had the burden of the season on his shoulders."

The Dodgers made a monumental try at catching lightning in a Dixie cup, spurred on by the sellout crowds that gave them standing ovations again and again during the series. But seldom have so many made so much noise for so little reason as Monday. After all, when you talk about impossible dreams and adversity overcome, the Astros are contenders, too. They came back from last year's tepid finish, when they wound up 1 1/2 games behind the Reds. And they overcame the physical and emotional midsummer loss of J.R. Richard. And they rallied to stay in the race each time it appeared that one more defeat would bury them.

In a way, Howe symbolizes this team. He almost quit baseball in 1976 when the Astros, after obtaining him from the Pirates, sent him back to the minors. He has been haunted by injuries, including two broken jaws. He was a part-time first baseman this season until Manager Bill Virdon put him in the lineup to stay for the stretch drive.

Howe was asked when Virdon told him the position was his. He said, "I wish I could say he did, but he didn't. I just started playing every day. Then I read in the paper that I had the job."

The tall, low-keyed, balding veteran was at the center of the lunatic celebration taking place in the Astro clubhouse. The champagne the Astros stored four days ago might have gone flat, for all anyone really knew. A lot more of it covered the floor and was poured over assorted heads than went down any throats. At one point Howe and Niekro doused each other, then embraced and for a weary, jubilant moment touched heads. Then Howe and Rafael Landestoy ran at each other, more champagne went spraying, and the scene wound up with a high five.

The weekend sequence had left the mind reeling—not to

mention the Astros. "My wife is with me," said Howe, "and last night in our room she was crying. She kept saying, 'You've got to win, you've got to win.' I said, 'Hey, don't worry about it. I'm trying to get my mind off it.'" He grinned and added, "Now I'm ready to think about it."

He was asked how he felt about facing a rested Steve Carlton at Philadelphia Tuesday. "I'd much rather face a rested Steve Carlton," said Home Run Howe, "than be at home watching it on television."

ASTROS RUN OUT OF INNINGS

OCTOBER 13, 1980

This is the fifth or sixth beginning this story has had. I've lost track. My favorite was the one about the Houston Astros winning the National League pennant with three runs in the last of the seventh inning Sunday night, with Denny Walling, hitless in the play-offs, getting the big hit, a tiebreaking single, and later scoring on Art Howe's triple.

Those are just details and they do not seem terribly important now. The main thing is that you would have loved the way the story began. It had pace and a poetic phrase and a touch of humor. I was saving the biblical reference for the second paragraph. It struck just the right note.

I thought about writing the story anyway, and claiming that I had to leave the Astrodome at the end of the seventh because my goldfish died and I didn't catch the final score. But I figured the editors would notice.

The Houston Astros didn't win the pennant Sunday night and stories do not always begin the way we want them to begin. The Astros fought back twice to tie the Philadelphia Phillies and once to go ahead, and they finally ran out of innings and ran out of rallies, and the Phillies, who do not exactly roll over like a puppy either, won the game and the play-offs and the pennant.

The score was 8-7 in ten innings, the fourth-straight overtime game in this wild, dizzy, and often dazzling series. By a margin of one run or six outs, take your choice, the Houston Astros are now officially the second-best team in the National League. Of course, you will find it easier to sell stocks in the Kremlin than to get the Astros, or their fans, to accept that judgment.

The team in the other dugout had waited thirty years to return to the World Series, having done so last in 1950, before the

Houston franchise and most of the players in this game had been born. Reasonable and unprejudiced people would find it hard to begrudge the Phillies their victory, coming back as they did for five runs in the eighth, after it appeared that Nolan Ryan had them at his mercy.

There were not many reasonable or unprejudiced people in the crowd of 44,802 fans, who screamed and implored and demanded and clapped, and, at the end, wept real tears for a Houston team that died hard and late.

They saw one of the great games ever played in a big-league ballpark. Actually, what it was, was the longest-playing cowboy-and-Indian scene since John Wayne filmed *Stagecoach*. First one, then the other, hung out the window, fingers around the throat.

The game, the thrills, the improbable plays and unlikely heroes went on and on. Twice the Astros had runners thrown out at home on bang-bang relays. The Phillies used twenty players, a play-off record, three more than the Astros employed. Terry Puhl collected four hits, for a total of ten in the series, another record.

It was as if the teams were afraid to let the season end, knowing that one of them had to lose.

The odds didn't favor the Phillies. They had to win two out of three in the Astrodome. They had to beat Ryan, who was throwing fastballs clocked at ninety-seven miles an hour, with gusts up to ninety-nine. And they had to overcome at least one self-inflicted jinx. In this series, no team had taken a lead into the sixth inning and held on to win. The Phillies led after five, 2-1.

Then Alan Ashby, out of the lineup with an injured rib, pinch-singled to tie the score, driving in Denny Walling, who had reached second when Greg Luzinski dropped his high liner in left field.

If it is any consolation, the county can drop any immediate worry over the condition of the Astrodome roof. The bubble survived its greatest test when the Astros scored three in the seventh to take a 5-2 lead. The noise of the crowd bounced off the girders. There even may have been a little levitating going on.

At that moment, in the press box, two writers held a conversation, which is what writers do best when they aren't drinking.

First writer: "I blew the story. I should have gone to Alvin [Nolan Ryan's home] and talked to the townspeople about the game."

Second writer: "You can still do it. They're all here."

Suddenly the Phillies had the bases loaded on a single, a hit off Ryan's glove, and a bunt single by Greg Gross. Then Pete Rose worked the count to 3-and-2 and drew a walk, forcing in a run. And Ryan was gone.

When the inning was over, the Astros had used Joe Sambito and Ken Forsch and the Phillies had scored five runs on five hits, one a two-run triple by Manny Trillo. No pitcher had ever so overpowered a team as Nolan Ryan did Sunday night and gone to the shower trailing, 7-5. He struck out eight.

In the Houston clubhouse, quiet as a tomb, Sambito said it for the team: "Based on how this series went, and how this game went, no one will ever convince me that one team is better than the other. I'm proud to be an Astro.

"I was hoping Nolan would finish the game. You know what kind of year it has been for him. You get six outs away and you have what seems to be an insurmountable lead, well, as a pitcher I feel for him."

The Phillies won it with a run in the top of the tenth off Houston's fourth pitcher, Frank LaCorte, on doubles by Del Unser and Gerry Maddox. The run was so routine it would have been an anticlimax if it had not settled so many earthly matters.

The Astros had left runners on base in each of the first eight innings, including six in scoring position, until Dick Ruthven retired them in order in the ninth and tenth. He was appearing in relief for the first time since 1975, coming on as the sixth pitcher in a line of succession dating back to rookie Marty Bystrom.

Earlier, Ruthven had vowed to go home if Manager Dallas Green passed him in favor of the rookie. If he had any class, that is what he would have done, or at least the Astros wish he had. And he should have taken Pete Rose and Manny Trillo and Bob Boone, who had a two-run single and made two big plays at home, with him.

But as Dandy Don Meredith is so fond of saying, if ifs were candy and buts were nuts we'd all have a merry Christmas. Houston won't be as merry as it might have been.

In the Astro clubhouse there were tears and lowered heads

and the sound of silence, but no excuses. "Winning today would have been what this season has been all about for us," said Sambito. "How many times have we come through when we needed the unattainable, when we were nearly out of it?"

Alas, one less time than they needed.

THE ASTROS' LONGEST DAY

OCTOBER 16, 1986

To begin with, there is no truth to the rumor that extra security had to be provided at the Astrodome for the umpires: nine armed optometrists. The umpires did not decide the game, and from there you can go either way. "They earned it," Nolan Ryan said of the triumphant New York Mets. "We didn't give it to them."

The Houston Astros lost what was simply the longest and the greatest October baseball game ever played, and if you have not personally experienced rigor mortis, there is no way to understand exactly the scene in their clubhouse Wednesday night.

This sixth game of the National League Championship Series was not planned as a contest to see who could claim the heart most broken, although one fan kept flashing an appropriate sign: ANYONE KNOW CPR?

The 45,718 fans who filled the Astrodome will have to argue their own cases. But there was Bob Knepper, pitching a two-hit shutout for eight innings and nothing to show for his labor but an early vacation he did not want.

There was Billy Hatcher, whose bases-empty homer with one out in the fourteenth tied the score 4-4 when hope seemed lost for the second or third time and whose single drove in the first of two runs in a sixteenth-inning rally that almost made you believe the Ghostbusters had finally arrived.

And there was Kevin Bass, Houston's most consistent player all year, a rising star, who came to bat with two out and the tying and winning runs on base and missed the last pitch of the game.

"You can't hold that team down forever," said Jim Deshaies, Houston's twelve-game winner but a missing man in the play-offs. "We had our best hitter at the plate at the end. K.B. is the guy you want up there in that situation. He's done it all year. [Jesse] Orosco just threw him a hellacious pitch on 3-and-2."

TOUCHING ALL THE BASES

We flash back now to the bottom of the sixteenth. Catcher Gary Carter has gone to the mound to talk to New York's fourth pitcher, southpaw Orosco. Carter is telling him they are going to play mind games with Bass. "We are not going to give him anything but sliders," Carter decides. "All sliders. But I want Jess to shake his head or something, so maybe he'll think another pitch is coming."

With the count full, Bass is thinking exactly what Carter is thinking. "I'm not stupid," he said. "I kind of figured it [another slider] was coming. I just couldn't hit it."

If you want to know what actual, physical pain sounds like, you needed to hear the voice of Bass when he was asked to describe his feelings about the season, the series, and the game.

"I don't think you want to hear my feeling," he said. "I'm not in a very nice mood. I made the last out. What happened during the season doesn't matter. What matters is now." Then he yanked on a shoelace, looked up, and corrected himself. "No, not now, either. We lost. They're going on, and we're not. It's as simple as that."

Oh, that it were so simple. The New York Mets won the National League pennant in six games, and there was nothing ordinary about any of them. Of course, in this one the Astros left themselves a winter's worth of second guesses. They battled the Mets from lunch to dinner, jumping in front with three runs in the first off Bob Ojeda. And that was all the scoring until the ninth, when the devilish Lenny Dykstra delivered a long fly that fell behind Hatcher for a pinch-hit triple and ignited New York's three-run rally.

Dykstra, whose homer off Dave Smith won game three, singled in another run in the sixteenth. Ray Knight had driven in the tiebreaker with his first hit of this longest day, then scored the run the Astros couldn't recover on a wild pitch by rookie left-hander Jeff Calhoun.

Both teams collected eleven hits. But in ten of their sixteen innings, the Astros went down in order. Twice, they had runners picked off third and another thrown out at second, and a season-long vacancy came back to injure them: no seasoned left-hander in the bull pen.

To a man, the Mets considered this a game they had to win, even though they were the ones with the luxury of a 3-2 edge. The reason was obvious. Waiting out there like a toxic cloud, in the event of a seventh game, was Mike Scott, who had allowed them one run and struck out nineteen in two complete wins. "Our back was to the wall," Manager Davey Johnson said. "We didn't want to face Scott."

Added Carter: "We just felt like this was the game we had to win. Scott has just killed us. But we knew we had to get into their bull pen. Knepper was on the corners all day."

In Houston's twenty-five-year history, the Mona Lisa of losing efforts had been the last of the five-game play-off against the Phillies in 1980. Nolan Ryan was a sympathetic figure in defeat then, and now: We learned a day later that he had pitched four splendid innings on a sprained ankle Tuesday, leaving a 1-1 game that the Astros lost two innings later.

"This was as gut-wrenching a series as 1980," Ryan said. "The tension and the excitement were about the same. It's frustrating to lose, but I'm proud of my teammates. They didn't quit."

The Ghostbusters were there. But they either went to the wrong clubhouse or left early, and the Houston Astros will be sending their regrets, for the second time in twenty-five years, when the World Series opens.

A PAIGE OUT OF HISTORY

MAY 31, 1981

Just in time to give us a breather from the class warfare of baseball in the 1980s, television has arranged to transport us to another time and another world. There may be hope for television yet.

Don't Look Back, the film biography of the legendary Leroy ("Satchel") Paige, airs Sunday night over ABC, and the title—in its unedited form—might serve as timely advice for the players and the owners as they engage in their annual haggle: Don't look back . . . something might be gaining on you.

Try as we might, we can find no connection between the saga of Satchel Paige and baseball's current labor unrest. Which is only one reason we are able to recommend this entertainment to you.

There are no hidden messages, nor is there a subtle plea for a return to simpler and more romantic times. We do not mourn for bathtub gin or penny candy or the Great Depression, when merchants paid the help something like seventeen cents an hour and would have worked them around the clock, except that they had a tendency to fall down about 10 P.M. on Saturday night.

Really, the message is whatever you want it to be, whatever you wish to make of a remarkable character who spent more than fifty years flinging a baseball, and along the way accepted rejection and hardship as part of the territory, the way today's players accept artificial turf and six-figure paychecks.

Much has been made over the fact that cranky ol' Gaylord Perry is still hanging in there, at the age of forty-two, winning games for the Atlanta Braves. When Satchel Paige was forty-two, he was one year away from his rookie season with the Cleveland Indians.

When Bill Veeck signed him out of the Negro leagues in 1948, to beef up a leaky Cleveland bull pen, *The Sporting News* howled that it was a publicity stunt. "Many well-wishers of baseball," J.G. Taylor Spink wrote in an editorial, "fail to see eye to eye with the signing of Satchel Paige, the superannuated Negro pitcher. To bring in a pitching rookie of Paige's age is to demean the standards of baseball in the big circuits."

"I demeaned the big circuits considerable that year," Satchel would later recall. "I won six and lost one." He helped pitch the Indians into the World Series.

In the office of the baseball commissioner, the birthdate of Paige is listed as July 7, 1906. That piece of information has been anything but notarized. By this time, it is doubtful that even Satchel knows his actual age. Still, if you accept that date, he would have been forty-six when he won twelve games for the forlorn St. Louis Browns. He made his last appearance on a big-league mound in 1965, pitching three shutout innings for Kansas City against Boston. He would have been fifty-nine.

The late Turk Farrell, the only Houston pitcher who was ever good enough to lose twenty games in one season, was a Phillies farmhand in Miami in 1958, when the club signed Paige as a free agent. Turk once recalled how the young dudes would torment the old-timer by putting dead fish in his shoes and nailing his uniform to the ceiling. But Satch always had the last laugh.

"He would warm up by putting a silver gum wrapper on home plate and pitching for it," said Farrell. "In Columbus, Ohio, there was a knothole in the outfield fence. A hitter got $5,000 if a homer went through it. Satch said he could hit it from twenty feet. The guys laughed. He missed it five times. Then the betting started and Satch hit it three in a row."

A few years ago, the Atlanta Braves hired Paige as a combination coach, trainer, and resident philosopher. He was an authentic baseball treasure, an antique, and the players looked at him as though he had stepped out of the King Tut exhibit.

An old friend paid him a visit at the Atlanta ballpark one day, a Hall of Fame pitcher named Dizzy Dean. In 1934, on a winter tour of mostly minor-league cities, Satchel beat Dean four games out of six. That year Dean had been a thirty-game winner in the majors. Satchel was still barnstorming for $100 a game, and sleeping on his suitcase in the clubhouse in towns in Dixie.

Hank Aaron asked Dean if Paige could really throw, asking the question just to hear how Dizzy would react. "Could he throw?"

TOUCHING ALL THE BASES

repeated Dean. "Could he throw? Is a pig pork? You bet he could throw. Lissen. He was quick. Me and him would pitch in exhibitions and it sounded like firecrackers going off. Warming up it was like double-barreled shotguns. Boom, boom, that's all you'd hear. Cotton came out of the mitts. We'd saw the bats off . . . right at the top."

Paige is approximately seventy-five now, still active as a minor-league pitching coach and P.R. man for the Springfield Redbirds, in the St. Louis farm chain. He no longer talks about making a comeback, but in other ways he is, according to reports, little changed by time.

He still has that long, splendid face, and a memory that astonishes you. No one knows what feats he would have accomplished in the twenty years he was barred from the big leagues because of the color of his skin. Dean and Bob Feller, two fair judges, called Satchel "The Greatest Pitcher Who Ever Lived." He probably won a thousand games, or more, in the black leagues and logged more miles than anyone can calculate on buses that rattled across the landscape.

Satchel used to boast that he could tell by the vibrations of the road what town he was approaching. Even today, he says, "I can come within fifty miles of predicting when a motor is gonna need an overhaul."

He seldom showed any emotion, but loved company. Talking to him was nearly as good as getting to watch him pitch. He would talk to anybody. If a holdup man pulled a gun on Satchel and asked him what he had, he would have told him, "I got bloopers, loopers, and droopers. I got a jumpball, a screwball, a wobbly ball, a hurry-up ball, a nothin' ball, and a bat dodger."

In a way, Satchel Paige came out of an era as rich as it was sad. He had everything but money and opportunity. His career in white baseball lasted less than six seasons, prompting him to say, "My train got to the depot ten years too late." He had hoped to be the first black to break the color line, a distinction that went to Jackie Robinson. That was one of the few public regrets he ever voiced.

One might argue that his train actually got to the depot twenty years too soon. Today he would have an attorney, an agent, and a tax problem. If anyone is entitled to do some looking back, it is Satchel Paige.

BEST PLAYERS, WORST HABITS

JULY 8, 1984

This is that lovely, languid time of year when baseball's All-Star balloting leads to many friendly arguments, and an occasional stabbing.

All-Star teams are wholesome and romantic and pure. They were created for the little boy who lives in each of us, except those of us who are little girls.

The players are viewed without flaws. The small boy does not know that the best third baseman in the league is human, that he yells at his wife, eats with his fingers, doesn't pay his parking tickets. The small boy doesn't care.

But for those of you who prefer to take the game sugarless, we are pleased to reprint at this time a different All-Star selection, the All-Depraved team, as chosen by Bill Veeck and other Chicago historians. One of baseball's most inventive promoters, Veeck gave us the exploding scoreboard, midgets, Satchel Paige, and the last years of the St. Louis Browns. The man is qualified.

Left field. Babe Ruth could do it all, off the field as well as on. As Veeck recalls, "He was a drunk, a braggart, a glutton, a brawler, a prolific lover. Ruth went to Hollywood once to appear in a movie. The status symbol among movie stars that year was whether they had gone to bed with Ruth. He gave dozens and dozens of them status."

Yet, he had enough strength left to play for twenty-one years and hit 714 home runs. If he hadn't spent so much time playing baseball, no telling how many records he might have set.

Center field. Ty Cobb was the all-time batting king: .367 for twenty-three years. As for goodness, decency, and sportsmanship, one observer wrote, "Cobb was the meanest, most hate-filled man ever to play the game. And his temperament became no better off the field." He would get in knife fights. He once got cut up but still played the next day.

Right field. Paul Waner was always sipping from a Coca-Cola bottle in the dugout. One day, while he was batting, a new batboy snuck a long swig. The kid woke up with a crashing hangover. Between belts from the Coke bottle, Waner hit .333 over nineteen years.

First base. Hack Wilson usually played in the outfield, but this move would have made it less far to stagger to the dugout. Veeck remembers, "I walked into the locker room one morning and Wilson was soaking in a tub with three fifty-pound blocks of ice. They were trying to get him sober enough to play. He did— and hit three homers. He also picked a fight with a fan, hoping to get arrested. He didn't want to stand out in the hot sun with a hangover."

Second base. Rogers Hornsby has the National League's highest lifetime average (.358). He did not smoke or drink and seldom brawled. So what's he doing on this team? Horses and women. Every team needs versatility.

Shortstop. One of the greatest of all fielders was Rabbit Maranville. Says Veeck, "He once staggered out of the team hotel and got in a fight with a cabbie. He lost. So he picked a fight with the next cabbie and lost. He fought three more of them and they all beat hell out of him. So I asked him what he was doing. He said, 'I'm trying to find one I can whip.' " Maranville played until he was forty-two. Had he led a clean life, he might have lasted until he was thirty.

Third base. Those who knew Jimmie Foxx (534 homers, .325 average) were never sure if he was sliding into a base or just falling over. Veeck says, "He once bought a restaurant and showed up for the grand opening four days late."

Catcher. The cops in Queens once phoned Veeck at 3 A.M. They had Rollie Hemsley, the great catcher, in jail for drinking and brawling. Veeck got him out, took him back to the hotel, and put him to bed. Three hours later, the police in Brooklyn called and said they had Hemsley. Veeck got him out again and stayed with him until game time. Had Bill minded his own business, Rollie might have set a record by being arrested in every borough in New York in one day.

Pitcher. The legendary Rube Waddell loved pitching, fishing, and drinking. When he died, they found him in a gin-filled bathtub with three drunken trout.

Manager. Who else but Billy Martin? He drinks, snarls, bullies, throws dirt on umpires, and punches out marshmallow salesmen in hotel bars. With these leadership qualities, it's no surprise that he is the best manager not now in baseball.

NAME-DROPPING IN THE MAJORS

JULY 10, 1983

At the end of a magazine interview with Lanny Wadkins, a writer suggested that his was a splendid name for a golfer. There was an almost audible click as the comment sank in.

"You into names?" asked Lanny, with a grin, recognizing a fellow collector when he saw one. "My favorite now is this new kid with the Mets, Darryl Strawberry. With a name like that you know he has to be great."

The really satisfying part of this addiction is that it doesn't actually matter. The athlete doesn't need to be great, although the pleasure would be so much sweeter. But he is starting off with a terrific advantage just by virtue of having the right sound, the right ring. This quality may not replace having the right stuff, but to the true namephreak it is close.

For the purpose of today's sermon, we will limit ourselves mainly to baseball names, because they are endless and timeless and they appear almost every day in the box score. This is not to imply that there are not wonderful names in other games. Football gave us Bronko Nagurski and Big Daddy Lipscomb and Doak Walker.

But the best names in football nearly always belong to the receivers: Fair Hooker, Lynn Swann, Golden Richards, Lance Alworth. There is music here. Alworth was doubly blessed with one of the pure nicknames of sport, "Bambi," a tribute to his grace and style. His coach at San Diego, Sid Gillman, once said, "If Lance played the piano, he would sound like Artur Rubinstein."

It must have been nice to have played for a coach who knows how Artur Rubinstein sounded. Yes, someday we will do a column devoted entirely to football names.

But this is about baseball, except for this next paragraph about golf. There are athletes whose names are perfect for whatever their sport is, but we cannot imagine them competing at anything else. Arnold Palmer. Kel Nagle. Byron Nelson. Ben Hogan. They speak to us of green acres and the hush of a waiting gallery.

But baseball names are not elitist. They are universal and democratic, even republican. The Houston Astros have had their share. Not great names, mind you, but a few that stick to the ribs. Turk Farrell. Al Heist. If you were an outfielder, wouldn't you want to be an Al Heist? We still feel badly that Mark Lemongello didn't make it big, or Merritt Ranew. We had terrific hopes for Cesar Geronimo. The name Rusty Staub held up well, but in too many other places. Of them all, our favorite was a lumbering catcher who came here at the end of his career, Gus Triandos. We always imagined that in Greek his name meant 3-and-2.

And that is the point. In no other activity are there so many names that are either playful or descriptive or perfectly aimed. Take Atlanta's Brett Butler, the name most suited to a city made famous by a motion picture.

I am not sure why names are so important to baseball, but they are, and that fact tells us something about ourselves, but I don't know that answer either. A song was written, years ago, composed entirely of baseball names. It was called "Van Lingle Mungo," after a Brooklyn Dodger pitcher of another era.

Of course, myth and history are on the side of the New York Yankees. No team can approach them in quality or depth, beginning with Babe Ruth, the most epic name in our sporting folklore. The Japanese in World War II were said to launch attacks screaming, "To hell with Babe Ruth." Can you picture the Russians coming at us, yelling, "To hell with Dan Fouts?"

Joe DiMaggio is so deeply ingrained in our consciousness that when we noticed we hadn't seen him around lately, back in the 1960s, his name started an entire nostalgia boom. But the Yankees keep coming at you: Lou Gehrig, Scooter Rizzuto, King Kong Keller, Yogi Berra, Mickey Mantle. *Yogi* and *Mickey.* All you have to do is read the words and you can see their faces.

The true fan doesn't need any heavy research to compile his lists. The problem is to hold them down. It is like drowning in an encyclopedia. Any halfway-devoted baseball nut can rattle off an All-Star team composed of their favorite flavors (Strawberry, Lemongello, Juan Bonilla) or nine players who sound like a fish or nine players nicknamed Red.

TOUCHING ALL THE BASES

And there is the continuing argument: Are they making names today like they used to do? In the good old days their salaries went up in pennies, but in retrospect the workmanship seemed oh, so much better. Ty Cobb. Tris Speaker. Rogers Hornsby. Grover Cleveland Alexander. Nobody names their kids Honus Wagner or Pie Traynor anymore.

Of course, there is no reason to apologize for the likes of Enos Slaughter, Duke Snider, or Sandy Koufax. Some names beg to be paired: Boo Ferris and Ferris Fain; Dizzy Dean and Dazzy Vance. Vida Blue was a terrific name. And we got our money's worth out of Ferguson Jenkins, who sounded like a bandleader, and Harmon Killebrew, who sounded like a circus strongman. Roberto Clemente had a nice beat, and so does Rod Carew. Hank Aaron suggested the crack of a bat.

Short names are attractive in a special way. Mel Ott, Ron Cey, Pete Rose, Nellie Fox, Joe Foy. They seem to offer power, hustle, or cuteness, and fit easily into headlines.

Do you remember Clint Hartung? That may have been the most promising name a rookie ever had. It was a Hall of Fame name. The postwar New York Giants weren't sure if he would make it as a pitcher or a hitter. He made it as neither. The high spot of his career came as a pinch-runner, in the 1951 play-offs. He was on base when Bobby Thomson hit his historic homer to beat the Dodgers.

The most exciting name to come along in two decades belongs to the Dodgers: Fernando Valenzuela. He sounded like a whole country, and he pitched with a fearlessness beyond his years. His pitch was the screwball, made famous by Carl Hubbell, the kind of name capable of striking out five great hitters in a row in an All-Star game.

Some names get better with age: Nolan Ryan and (until this year) Gaylord Perry. Some live forever: Cy Young. In the end, they give the sport a sense of fulfillment and emotion. And that, fans, is the Dale Long and Chris Short of it.

FAN LETTER REVIVES MARIS MEMORIES

MARCH 15, 1981

COCOA, Florida—The human mind works in strange ways, when indeed it works at all. The other day an item appeared in an area newspaper that reminded us that this was 1981, the sort of thing the trained journalist often notices.

The item consisted of a letter from an irate fan, as many fans are in these troubled and expensive times. But this one was complaining because the name of Roger Maris had been omitted from a list of VIPs appearing in a charity golf tournament. The editor replied that Maris could have an apology, if he wanted one, but that Roger had been in these parts for twelve years, working eight counties as a beer distributor, and therefore qualified as home folks.

So now you know not only whatever happened to Roger Maris, you know that twenty years is just a speck of sand in the hourglass of time. It was twenty years ago this season—if there is a baseball season—that Maris put on the most remarkable one-year performance of the past half century to break Babe Ruth's record of sixty home runs.

You reflect that fame came almost overnight to Maris, who never wanted to be a special person. No player ever accomplished so much and enjoyed it so little. As he closed in on Ruth's legend, the buildup engulfed him. He tried to blend in with the scenery but it wasn't easy, and Maris began to lose ground.

Bob Cerv, who later played briefly with the Houston Astros, was his roommate the year Maris pursued Ruth's ghost. Roger was a loner, not a very social person, and the fame and the media crush that came with it almost did him in. He stayed close to his hotel, avoiding nightclubs and tourist sights.

Once, their wives joined them in Kansas City and the Cervs and the Marises went to an art museum. Someone asked Roger how it was. "They had a lot of old pictures in there," he replied.

Maris was resented because he had the irreverence to challenge the record of baseball's foremost hero, but he had none of the gaudy color that the nation had come to expect of its idols. He was uncomfortable in the spotlight, where Ruth had reveled in it.

Roger was too nervous to enjoy the cheers when he heard them and he never learned to ignore the boos that followed when the cheering stopped. As the home runs mounted, so did the pressure; he went after the record with a sullen intensity, and his hair started falling out.

The newsmen and television reporters were at him constantly. He had to answer more questions than a suspect at a bank robbery. And at times he was treated with about as much courtesy. Once a Japanese editor sent a list of eighteen questions to the Associated Press in New York, asking that Maris answer them all.

After hearing five or six, Maris blurted out, "This is driving me nuts."

The AP reporter replied, "That's the next question. They want to know how you're reacting to all this."

A writer traveling with the Yankees asked Maris if he played around on the road.

"I'm married," snapped Roger.

"I'm married," said the writer, "but I still play around."

"That's your business," said Maris, walking away.

There were several ironies in the saga of Roger Maris, and not the least of them involved Mickey Mantle. As the fans of New York turned on Maris, and rejected him as unworthy of Ruth's legacy, they embraced Mantle, and lavished upon him the respect and adoration that for unexplained reasons had been rationed in the past.

Of course, part of it had to do with the fact that, if Ruth's record had to fall, the fans wanted it to be at the hands of Mantle. His record, his style, his great talent made him acceptable. Maris was regarded as a .270 hitter, and he swung with rhythm and grace, not Ruthian strength.

The year the Babe produced his sixty homers, his teammate, the gallant Lou Gehrig, connected for forty-seven. Maris got his sixty-one in 1961, and Mantle bagged fifty-four, and between them they eclipsed the Yankee gods of another era. It was the grandest two-man show over one extraordinary season that baseball had ever seen.

For most of the summer and down the stretch it was Maris and Mantle racing the legend of Ruth for the home-run title of all time. Then Mantle gradually faded. The day he stroked number forty-eight, Mickey turned to Roger in the locker room and said, pointedly, "I got my man. The pressure's off me."

For Maris the pressure never ceased. In Chicago, a writer asked him if he really wanted to break the record, inasmuch as Ruth was a great man and all. "Maybe I'm not a great man," said Maris, honestly enough, "but I damned well want to break the record."

And so he did. His detractors point out that Maris had four more games than the Babe, but it isn't added that Ruth never saw the depth of pitching that Maris did. The Babe never faced such bull pens, nor did he play at night, when the percentages are against the hitter.

Irrespective of his personal problems, the achievement of Maris cannot be overlooked. It was beautiful irreverence. Today he says, "I hardly made anything out of it at all. When the trouble came I wanted only to stay out of the public eye." You get a sense of Roger's confusion when you realize that he got to a point where he no longer cared about money. He was like the mouse who didn't want the cheese, he just wanted his tail out of the trap.

When the 154th game of the regular season rolled around—Roger's last chance to beat the record without an asterisk—the Yankees were playing in Baltimore, Ruth's hometown. Maris had fifty-eight homers and needed two more to tie Ruth under the establishment rules. He lined out. He homered for fifty-nine. He lined out again. He dribbled a Hoyt Wilhelm knuckler back to the mound. The Baltimore crowd stood on its feet and cheered his effort. This was Babe Ruth country and Maris had won them over. A few days later he hit sixty and sixty-one and, in his own mind, the record was his. Never mind the asterisk and the diehards and the Roaring twenties. Roger Maris had given a new baseball generation something for their own memories . . . the glory of their own times.

From the Greatest to the Latest

ALI'S IDLE THREATS

MARCH 1971

NEW YORK—The line is from *Julius Caesar,* Act IV, Scene 3: "There is no terror, Cassius, in your threats."

Not any more, there isn't, not now, not again, maybe never. To a country accustomed to aw-jeewhiz-I-was-lucky heroes, Muhammad Ali, the former Cassius Clay, always did the unbearable. He backed up his brags. This time he did the unforgivable and the unforgettable. He did not back them up.

And so, like insurance adjusters after a great fire, the experts gather now to appraise Joe Frazier's victory in what may well rank as the most extravagant sporting event of this age.

Frazier promised that he would shut the mouth of Ali, and he kept his word, closing that great natural wonder—a kind of Grand Canyon of public speaking—with a vicious, grenadelike left hook early in the fifteenth round.

Ali went over on his back like a large hooked sailfish, and flopped there for a moment, until his unquenchable pride and enormous courage yanked him to his feet. Instantly, the left side of his face was swollen the size of a small cantaloupe. Twice more during the round, Frazier touched up that sensitive target. You could see pain in Ali's eyes, and he winced and his face had the look of ashes, but he wouldn't go down again.

It was thought at the time that his cheekbone might have been broken. X-rays early the next morning showed that it wasn't, but Muhammad will talk—when he talks—with a jaw that won't open wide for the next several days. There has to be some irony in that.

So the great gold rush is over, and all the waiting and the wondering, all the boasts and threats and hair-tonic commercials. Joe Frazier emerges as an awesome fighter, a guy whose endurance and capacity for punishment stagger you. He may, as many claim, possess just one punch, but for Joe one is enough.

FROM THE GREATEST TO THE LATEST

He is no counterfeit champion.

As for Ali, nothing he ever did or said in victory so became him as the way he accepted defeat. He did it bravely, refusing to quit, getting up from a fearful, injuring blow that left his world quite vacant.

He fought with tricks and skill and cuteness, but his legs failed him. He allowed himself to be pinned constantly against the ropes, you understand now, not to taunt Frazier but because his legs did not feel obligated to get him out of there.

For forty-three months he had kept in shape largely by outrunning the U.S. marshal. There is no need to pity him now, of course. The long inactivity, the crises he stirred, were at least partly of his own making. He took his stands in the bright sun of publicity, which he courted and exulted in, and he invited—and enjoyed—the role of a martyred fighter.

Ali fought Monday night in the fresh, arrogant, slashing way that has always been his style. But this time the punches didn't slash, they simply landed splat on the willing features of Joe Frazier. The freshness withered. The arrogance cooled.

Yet in defeat, he won grudging admiration from some of his most consistent critics. One of them was Joe Louis, the great old champion who had insisted all along that Frazier would win.

I was interested in the reaction of Louis Tuesday, the morning after, in the light of a cool, gray day.

"Clay, to me, showed a lot of courage," said the man who may have been the most popular champion of all time. "I had the idea that Clay didn't have the guts. Generally, when a guy talks so much about himself, you think he's using that as a substitute for courage. But last night he proved I was wrong."

Louis added that he admired Ali—a name he doesn't use—more now than ever before and, surprisingly, indicated that the unfrocked champion would probably win a rematch, one that is surely coming.

"If Clay had two more fights under his belt," he said flatly, "he would have beat Frazier. You can't just take a layoff for three or four years and make it against a good fighter."

Louis was asked how he would have attacked Smokin' Joe, had he been in the tasseled shoes of Muhammad Ali.

"I would have met him head-on. Clay didn't have the power to stand toe to toe with him. But Clay would have done it three and a half years ago, because he was in condition to do it. Last night he had to skip around, to save his strength, to think about going fifteen rounds."

This may have been the most dramatic and the most emotional fight since Louis himself fought Max Schmeling, the second time, in that famous morality play of more than thirty years ago.

The setting in New York was not to be believed, borrowing from the best-known works of Boris Karloff, Cecil B. DeMille, and Humphrey Bogart. By early evening a light, swirling snow had begun to fall as the pedestrians hustled in and out of doorways.

Earlier, threats on the life of Frazier had been received by telephone and by mail. Madison Square Garden was heavy with tension. Security could not have been much thicker at Fort Knox, which is probably where this fight should have been held. The place was flooded with police, and tickets had to be displayed at five different checkpoints before one could reach one's seat, where one could at least be jostled sitting down. A few minutes before fight time, tickets were being scalped for $800, more than Frazier earned in his first pro bout.

The wildly costumed crowd of 20,000-plus included so many celebrities, they could have held the Academy Awards. There were dozens of stars whose names you wished you could remember, and most of the women at ringside looked like Tuesday Weld.

Ali gave them a show, a sometimes infuriating show, shaking his head to assure the crowd that a Frazier punch had missed its mark, keeping up a stream of what Joe called "ghetto talk," and twice disdainfully waving off his opponent as they turned toward their corners. At times he used his long reach to hold off Frazier, as though at the end of a broom.

Maybe it was part of his act, or maybe he simply could not afford to fight Joe on Joe's terms. At the end, after the judges had made it unanimous for Frazier, he told the winner, "You're a real champ."

It must have hurt him to say those words, in more ways than one.

SUGAR RAY ASSUMES ALI'S ROLE

SEPTEMBER 20, 1981

The day after Sugar Ray Leonard reestablished himself as the crown prince of fisticuffs, Muhammad Ali flew to New York to announce he would begin his fifth or sixth comeback, we forget which, against someone named Trevor Berbick in December.

You could not ask for a clearer, more poignant example of what is happening today in the canvas jungle.

A welterweight title fight grossed more than $35 million, and though Ali is only a parody of himself now, he still counts great. The king isn't dead. He is only out of a job.

Four times Ali held the heavyweight championship, the biggest prize in the perspiring arts. He had it taken from him once, lost it twice, and abdicated once. When he emerged from exile at the age of thirty-nine, Allah punished him for it, unless you want to give the credit to Larry Holmes, a competent fighter but not one you would describe as royalty. So now Ali again is plotting his return to power, pretending he is needed to restore order and mercy to a troubled kingdom. He hears the people calling.

Sadly, the call is a wrong number. The fact is, we had begun to believe it would never end, and perhaps Ali still thinks that way. But his time has passed and, to the surprise of many, boxing has survived and so have the blockbuster gates.

And that is the real significance of Leonard's heroic win over Thomas Hearns, in a stadium built on the parking lot of a Las Vegas gambling emporium, Caesar's Palace. We ask you, where else but in America can a fight in a parking lot draw 25,000 people? You will see some swell fights in a parking lot, but people paid $500 for ringside tickets to this one and no complaints were heard later.

FROM THE GREATEST TO THE LATEST

All of which seems to suggest the welterweight class is now the showcase of the sport, and Leonard is the most popular and entertaining of its creatures.

Ali may continue to fight, against the advice and wishes of his friends and most of his fans. If it isn't Larry Holmes or Trevor Berbick, possibly he will wind up fighting Sherlock Holmes or Trevor Howard. But there is no need to feel sympathy or embarrassment for him. Ali knows what he is doing. He is not one of those innocents who will take a hit on seventeen when the dealer has a six showing. If he wants to take a licking, and keep on ticking, let him. If the suckers want to join him for another multimillion-dollar ride, why shouldn't he take them along?

We owe Ali that much. Through his travels a generation of schoolkids learned a little about world geography. He took us to Lewiston, Maine, to Kuala Lumpur and Kinshasa, Zaire, where Ali identified himself as a favorite son. For Ali every fight was a kind of homecoming. If he fought in Stockholm, he would tell the natives he was of Scandinavian extraction.

It can't be the money that still propels Ali. He likes it, of course, just as he likes chocolate fudge cake. But he hungers more for the center of the stage, the bright lights, the commotion, the high he gets from taking a senseless match and turning it into box office.

The Leonard camp used to pay Ali's expenses to ensure his presence at the fights of Sugar Ray, whose trainer, Angelo Dundee, groomed Ali. They didn't do so this time, which may be taken as a sign of Leonard's belated declaration of independence, or a sign of weariness with Ali's act. Or it may mean nothing at all. Ali can certainly afford to pay his own way. But he was almost visibly excluded from the ceremonies, even to the point that the ring announcer had to be reminded to introduce him. There may be a message in there somewhere, about time and fame and new heroes rising to elbow aside the old.

Man and boy, Ali has been among us now since the Olympic year of 1960. During that period he has entertained us and outraged us and astonished us. He never ducked a fighter. No one ever questioned his courage—he fought with a broken jaw for eight rounds against Ken Norton—and he always fought clean. No interviewer ever walked away from Ali with an empty plate. He changed his name, his religion, his wives, his attitudes. What never changed was his outlook on boxing. For all his crises, for all the devil he stirred and all the trouble he brought upon himself, he never lost his love for the sport or his dedication to it.

Leonard is very much like Ali in one quality. He approaches his big fights with a feeling close to joy. And he takes the feeling into the ring with him. He looks like a man who enjoys his work.

Sugar Ray is close to towering over his division as Ali did his. You tend to doubt that Hearns can beat him in a rematch, now that Sugar Ray knows he can take what Hearns can throw. Or, at least, what Hearns can throw and land.

Once, Hearns caught him with a straight right, and Sugar Ray's head snapped back. But he didn't stagger or stumble and he never lost his rhythm. If not for the fact that he was still blinking his eyes the rest of the round, you would not have guessed that he had been hurt.

In that sense, boxing is a sport of illusion. Fight fans are notorious for going nuts over punches that miss. The reason is that many times, depending on your angle, the blow appears to connect. Motion-picture companies have turned this trick into a way of life. A fighter will swing from the heels, and miss completely, or the blow will glance off so lightly it would not break a nun's glasses. And still the roar will go up somewhere in the arena, and the reaction is almost as good as the real thing.

There is no question about the punches Sugar Ray landed that stirred the crowd. With all due respect for the other soft drink he endorses, they were the real thing. And so is Sugar Ray.

LULL BETWEEN LEGENDS IS OVER

NOVEMBER 23, 1986

LAS VEGAS—Mike Tyson did not exactly wade into Trevor Berbick Saturday night. What he did was launch himself like a missile out of an underground silo, and down crashed Berbick, taking with him the post-Ali lull in heavyweight boxing.

This was a mythmaking, record-breaking, head-shaking Mike Tyson who knocked out Berbick in the second round to become at twenty the youngest champion in the often-strange history of the heavyweight division.

Tyson, the ghetto kid, an ex-delinquent from Brooklyn, saw Berbick offer himself up as a short-range target, what the new champ labeled "a blessing in disguise." But there was nothing about this victory that could be considered unconcealed.

Tyson was everything his fans thought he could be as he was winning twenty-seven consecutive fights, exploding upon the heavyweight scene as no one has done since the young poet called Cassius Clay came out of the Olympics in 1960 to turn pro.

Clay became the legend known as Muhammad Ali, and he was in the crowd Saturday night to watch Tyson bludgeon the man who retired him in December 1981. That represented one of Berbick's three distinctions as a fighter and temporary champion: He was the last man to beat Ali, the first to go fifteen rounds against Larry Holmes, and he decisioned Pinklon Thomas to claim one-third of the world's heavyweight crown.

And when was the last time a fellow defending his title went into the ring a 4-1 underdog?

Such was the faith in Tyson, the sense that there is something different, that the outcome seemed almost ordained.

FROM THE GREATEST TO THE LATEST

There will be no stopping Tyson, who will meet the winner of the Tim Witherspoon and Tony Tubbs contest on his way to unifying the title. For now he is the fractional champ, the grandest child prodigy the sport has known, eclipsing Floyd Patterson, who was five weeks short of his twenty-second birthday when he won the title from Archie Moore in 1956.

Ol' Arch was also in attendance to watch the coronation, among a stargazing audience of 8,200. The introductions took longer than the fight. So did the interview in the ring after it was over, after Tyson set up Berbick with a right hand behind the ear, and then just wasted him with a left hook to the temple. Later, Tyson described the punch as "murder."

It was fascinating to watch Berbick's body try to respond to his brain, but his brain wasn't home. He hit the canvas, rolled into the ropes, got up once, wobbled, went down again, stumbled halfway across the ring in an effort to get up, and then almost pulled the referee down with him.

The bout was over, officially in 2:35 of the second round. But Berbick was never really in it, not from the moment Tyson's first punch, a wicked left, caught him flush on the cheek. Or maybe even earlier, before the opening bell, when Mike tapped his gloves together and beckoned for Berbick to come to him.

Berbick did, which was a fatal error in judgment, as the loser woefully acknowledged: "I wanted to prove to myself I could take his best shot and I got caught. I fought the wrong fight."

The bulky chap known as "The Fighting Preacher" did not have a prayer. As the crowd filed out of the Hilton Pavilion, he was so stunned that he had to ask one of his handlers what round the fight ended.

In winning his twenty-eighth in a row, twenty-sixth by knockout, Tyson was almost untouchable. He said Berbick landed only one decent blow: "He snuck in an uppercut on the break."

In those two explosive rounds, Tyson threw an amazing 106 punches to thirty-eight for Berbick. And after the fight he had all the good lines, such as:

"My goal was to throw every punch with a bad intention."

"I was throwing hydrogen bombs .... I refused to leave the ring alive without that belt. Now I want all three."

And, responding to a question about how the title, and the fame and riches that go with it, might change him: "I'm just a twenty-year-old kid, and I'm going to remain one until I get older . . . . I can't be the champion forever. When it's gone I'll still have to be a person."

The reporters in the press interview room applauded when he said that, and it is a quote you may want to file and refer to a few years from now. Many others have made similar vows, on their way to multiple marriages and bankruptcies.

But Mike Tyson may be the one who beats the odds. His late trainer, Cus D'Amato, who also groomed Patterson, had discovered him in a school for troubled kids at thirteen or fourteen, and told him, "Stay with me and someday you'll be the heavyweight champ."

Cus had seen something in him besides the body shaped like an anvil. He had seen his character and intensity. And Saturday night, in a city where quick knockouts are the rule, so did the rest of us.

TORA!
TORA!
TORA!

JUNE 27, 1976

The United States and Japan have been at peace now for thirty years, and you certainly couldn't disprove it by what happened Friday night in Tokyo.

While a standing-room crowd of 47,000 watched on closed-circuit television from the Astrodome, the bout to decide the Bossling Championship of the World ended in a tie. After fifteen rounds of exquisite boredom, Muhammad Ali, the boxer, and Antonio Inoki, the wrestler, were awarded a draw. Saving face is a fine old Japanese custom.

In this case nothing could have been more fair, or more poetic, with the possible exception of putting both of them in jail.

The weird entertainment proved nothing about sports, or boxing or wrestling. It only proved that Inoki's legs are longer than Ali's arms. As the night wore on, the greatest fear was that Inoki would develop a cyst on his tailbone and the match would have to be stopped.

He would slam himself to the floor, somewhat like Chevy Chase, the comic on NBC's "Saturday Night Live" who imitates President Ford, and then he would chase Ali around the ring, scooting along on his rump. You got the feeling that Inoki was confused. This time it wasn't his face that needed to be saved.

His strategy was to lash out at Ali with his feet, wicked karate kicks, while Muhammad walked around him as though he were a swamp. Ali danced and mugged and called him names—you're a girl, you're a coward, and, at least once, he used a hyphenated word that made global television history, and does not translate into Japanese. On occasion, Ali kicked back; short, impatient jolts to the ankle, a fair imitation of a fight between two angry five-year olds.

There was one hilarious scene when Ali literally climbed the ropes as if they were a vine, and just hung there, like a man being attacked with a machete, pedaling his feet to avoid Inoki's slashing legs.

When Inoki entered the ring, as tall and strong and as handsome as his storied American opponent, one thought struck me: Where have I seen that chin before? Chuck Connors? Randy Matson? Edmund Muskie? Tank McNamara? It was roughly three acres of chin, a gorgeous chin, and the saddest part of the night was that not once did Ali make contact with it. What a waste. One good right hand to that chin and it would have sounded like a waiter dropping a tray of glasses on a tile floor. To miss that chin is to visit northern Arizona and miss the Grand Canyon.

Yet, incredibly, in fifteen rounds Ali threw only two punches, both light left jabs. The fact was that Ali, aware of the danger in Inoki's kicks—it is a great way to get a kneecap broken—stayed out of range.

That tended to reduce the threat, but it also made it impossible to deliver a solid punch. Ali blew his best chance when the two men shook hands to start the final round. He should have nailed him right then.

As if the contest itself wasn't goofy enough to summon up memories of the Mad Hatter playing croquet on the lawn with a flamingo, the audience had to cope with the two clowns doing the commentary on television. Fortunately, most of it couldn't be heard. But there they were, in the midst of all this nonsense, playing it absolutely straight, analyzing the action in a really serious way. It was like trying to analyze the annual cow-chip throwing contest in Oklahoma.

One of them kept saying, "I don't like the looks of Ali's left leg. It is badly swollen and we are beginning to see some discoloration. I don't know how long those beautiful legs can take those kicks."

Ali confided later that Inoki did hurt him a few times with his foot sweeps, and once "when he kneed me in the privates." At one point Ali was fouled, but, gracious sportsman that he is, he raised a hand to urge the crowd to remain calm and unheated. The crowd continued to pick its teeth and yawn.

A few cynics began to suspect rather early that the evening was not entirely on the level; that it was, shall we say, a piece of theater. They concluded this when, in the preliminary, Andre

FROM THE GREATEST TO THE LATEST

the Giant, who is seven-foot-four, picked up heavyweight boxer Chuck Wepner, held him above his head, whirled him around the ring, and dumped him into the seats. Whereupon a free-for-all broke out. We did not see a little ol' gray-haired lady beat on the mat with an umbrella, but that doesn't mean she wasn't there.

Observing the ease with which Andre handled Wepner, our colleague, Jack Gallagher, who is a student of the classics, said he was reminded of King Kong and Fay Wray. But Fay probably put up more resistance.

So now we come to the higher, moral question: Were the fans bilked? Were they ripped off? Not in Houston they weren't. Leaving aside the fact that Ali and Inoki both made enough millions to start their own religions, the fans got the rarest gift in sports today: a bargain. They were offered two events for less than the price of one.

It was a splendid move by the Astros' management. Projecting a gate of 23,000, they doubled that, made money, gave the fans a break, and provided a film crew with the crowd shots it needed for a movie to be made here. Tickets for standing room were still selling at 9:30. But the fans who waited until then missed all the action, four Houston home runs, in an 8-6 loss to the Reds.

As for the nightcap, it was the kind of show that was so bad you brag to your friends about being there. Yet in a curious way it was fun. Ali established again that he is the most remarkable showman of his time. It was possible to say that Inoki is an athlete, not a freak. And no one should have been deceived about the fight for the world bossling title.

"This is a travesty," decided one witness, "and there are over 40,000 travestites here watching it."

GLITTER COUNTS, BUT PUNCHES DON'T

APRIL 19, 1987

Any number of heated arguments have broken out, and one or two polite stabbings, over the outcome of the Hagler-Leonard tiff. A solid week later, the debate goes on.

For those of you whose TV sets do not receive Home Box Office, and for those who do, just consider this another tape delay.

We have the answer for you: Hagler was stiffed. Sugar Ray won it on showmanship.

Leonard fought the classic "Las Vegas" fight. He gave them a laser-and-light show, a little circus with slot machines and 200 topless dancers, his bolo punch, and his roadrunner footwork. He was swift and graceful and poetic, and his performance had the added advantage of not requiring Marvin Hagler actually to be in the ring with him. Sugar Ray would have looked just as impressive working on the light bag.

I have watched the delayed telecast a half-dozen times now, heard the judges defend their cards, heard Sugar Ray explain how he "stole" three or four rounds and the fight.

What he did, he said, was to retreat until the final half minute, then close with a flurry of punches to excite the crowd and sway the judges.

Larry Merchant, the HBO boxing analyst who asks the most intelligent questions of anyone in TV sports today, put it to the judges: "Do you think people tend to pay more attention to the fighter who is doing the unexpected?" Say, as in the case of Leonard, whose very survival had been the focus of so many prefight essays.

Again, there was a split decision. One judge said absolutely,

FROM THE GREATEST TO THE LATEST

another said he didn't agree, and a third didn't understand the question.

Forget the statistics: how many hundreds of punches Hagler threw, and how many Leonard landed, most of them on Marvin's arms. If you want to call Sugar Ray the new noogie champion of the world, okay, but don't try to convince us that he really won the fight.

The most convincing stat is this: Not the most, but the only meaningful punches in the entire twelve rounds were thrown by Hagler. Sugar Ray did not connect with a single blow that left an impression on Marvin.

What Leonard did best was wrap both gloves around Hagler's neck, or the back of his neck, and give a yank. The referee provided the lyrics that went with this tune, "Don't hold, Ray, don't hold." But Ray continued this tactic throughout the fight and was never penalized for it.

Leonard also hit Hagler below the belt twice—one was pretty close to being what I would classify as "meaningful"—and three times he threw punches after the bell.

But two-thirds of the judges and a little more than half the crowd and TV viewers, if the surveys can be believed, only had eyes for Sugar Ray. They did not seem to notice that when Hagler took one on the chin, cheek, temple, or nose, his head never moved.

Those who favored Leonard gave him high marks for defense and ring generalship (tactics). Hard to argue with that conclusion. If you believe that the best offense is a good defense, then Sugar Ray made Hagler look like a fool.

In fact, all Hagler had to do was stop chasing him, just stand there, and Leonard would have been exposed: a guy creating an illusion.

Leonard won because neither fighter hit the deck and he was the underdog. You may argue that he deserved it, just by going the distance after nearly five years of inactivity. And while the view here is that the call was raw, let no one cheapen what a staggering athletic feat Sugar Ray achieved.

Not much in boxing surprises you. But it is hard to remember a fight that left opinion so divided, or so many to question the honesty of the outcome or the effort of the fighters.

The punches of Hagler seemed to lack the explosion of old. But we find it hard to believe he didn't try. He was simply outwitted.

FROM THE GREATEST TO THE LATEST

Marvin got taken, as many of us did, by the stories about this sweet-talking, half-blind kid making one more grab for glory.

It was indeed hard to pick Sugar Ray, in the face of so much speculation that he and his head might leave the ring on separate conveyances. And, of course, he worked that angle just fine.

You could tell that this was not the first time Sugar Ray had played Las Vegas.

FLORIDA WITHOUT ORANGE JUICE

SEPTEMBER 17, 1978

Let's face it. Muhammad Ali without Howard Cosell is like Florida without orange juice, Philadelphia without a ghetto, or Saint Patrick's Day without a parade.

This is not to suggest that Cosell made Ali—or even the other way around. After all, Dr. Johnson would have been a success without Boswell. If there had been no Ernie Pyle, World War II still would have been famous. And Elizabeth Taylor would have been beautiful without Richard Burton—or, for that matter, Nicky Hilton, Mike Todd, Eddie Fisher, or her most recent husband, John Warner.

But in sports, at least, there has been nothing quite like the symbiotic relationship between Ali, The Greatest, and Cosell, The Man Who Grates. As Howard has acknowledged, together they simply make great show biz.

A scene flashes to mind from the long and marvelous oral biography of Ali that led into the telecast of his rematch with the neglected Leon Spinks. A younger Cosell, his hair unflecked by gray, his suit black, his face whiter than white, looking somehow like an amiable Dracula, asked Ali a question that brought a quick and testy reply.

"You're being extremely truculent," needled Howard.

"Whatever truculent means," snapped Ali, "if that's good, I'm that."

And now we know, maybe have always known, that Muhammad Ali can be whatever he wants to be: funny, charming, outrageous, exasperating, hungry, sleepy, or impossible. Against Spinks he was brilliant, relentless, and serious. At no time did he resort to burlesque, although twice he showed Leon—and the crowd—a touch of the old Ali Shuffle.

FROM THE GREATEST TO THE LATEST

Today you ask yourself, was there ever a bigger anticlimax than the announcement that Ali had won a unanimous decision, losing no more than four rounds on any of the judges' cards? Long before the result was official, Spinks had wedged through the adoring mob around Ali to congratulate him, and they had touched foreheads, an odd but gentle moment.

Then there was Cosell, fussing over his microphone, not sure it was even on, but still sending, like the wireless operator on the *Titanic*. He fought off the rabble and reminded Ali of his vow to retire; we had seen his last workout, his last fight, his last triumph.

"You're going to stick by your word and retire, right?" Cosell challenged him.

And in his own direct and forthright way, Ali replied, "I don't know yet, Howard."

Didn't you feel it? Didn't you know it would happen? Couldn't you see it coming? The fight would go fifteen rounds and Ali would make a fool out of Leon Spinks; and Howard Cosell—in maybe the best performance of his career—would become the first television announcer to describe the winning of the heavyweight title for the third time by the same man.

And we didn't really think the Prince of Islam would quit, did we? It is the autumn of 1978, and Ali has been entertaining us for half of his life. It has been eighteen years since he emerged from the depths of Kentucky to enrich professional boxing with his fists and his imagination. At thirty-six he is still very much the circus horse who smells the sawdust.

One needed only four rounds to realize that it was Ali's fight, and another wild promise fulfilled. In the first round he missed badly. Even in the next three he seemed to flinch when Spinks unleashed one of his reckless, flailing charges, backing him into the ropes. Ali looked as though he was afraid of getting his nose caught in the gap where Leon's teeth used to be.

But then you saw Ali begin to score, and he grew before your eyes. Ali's left uppercut brought Spinks out of his crouch; the champion—we kept forgetting that Spinks was the champion—never got a clean shot at him. By the eighth round Ali was way ahead. By the tenth Spinks was no longer running and leaping. He was trotting, like an actor coming onto a stage with a tennis racket in his hand. In Round 12, the ring microphone picked up Ali's voice: "It's all over, Leon."

FROM THE GREATEST TO THE LATEST

Who really expected Ali, at his age, to put on such a show? Not I, said Cosell. And surely not Leon Spinks, who won the title after seven pro fights, but lost the public's good will with his bizarre behavior, all those traffic arrests, getting high with a little help from his friends.

Ali did not so much turn back the clock as fight it to a standstill. The puffiness was gone from his face. He looked lean and taut. Cosell thought he might be overtrained, tired. But Ali was just right.

Meanwhile, Howard let out all the stops. He quoted Bob Dylan. He compared Ali to Henry Kissinger. And his narration of Muhammad's career was a work of art. Sample: "It was nice to be in England . . . now that spring was there . . . and the test-tube bleeder that was Henry Cooper went early, this time."

When and if Ali retires, the most interesting new face in boxing may be Mike Rossman, who won the light-heavyweight title in a slashing upset of Victor Galindez, in the semifinal event at the Superdome. Who knows? That crowd of nearly 80,000 in New Orleans, and the millions at home, may have seen the changing of the guard.

Rossman numbers among a species that has been vanishing like the golden condor. He is a white contender, billed as "The Jewish Bomber." There has been speculation in the past that he wasn't really Jewish; Max Baer once wore the Star of David on his trunks for box-office reasons. But if any proof was needed, it came when Rossman's mother rushed into the ring and kissed him. You could almost hear him saying, "Please, Mama, not now."

TYSON KEEPS APPOINTMENT

JUNE 29, 1988

ATLANTIC CITY—If Mike Tyson ever stopped to smell the flowers, would the flowers be afraid?

Animal, vegetable, mineral, or mutation, there is nothing on the horizon today that does not bow to the prowess of this twenty-one-year-old terminator.

To begin with, Tyson does not pause to smell the flowers. Nothing can keep him from his appointed rounds, which usually means one round or less, as when he hammered Michael Spinks into a defenseless blob Monday night in a minute and thirty-one seconds.

Those who had predicted an upset by Spinks were groping the next morning to explain this mental overload. Some had tilted toward Spinks simply on the grounds that he has no mother-in-law.

Really, there is no slick way to explain how the fight that should have been the toughest of Mike Tyson's career turned into his wildest mismatch. A minute and thirty-one seconds. Donald Trump takes longer than that to knot his necktie. Don King can't clear his throat in a minute and thirty-one seconds.

A security guard told me that Tyson passed him on his way to the ring at 11:21 P.M. (Eastern time). He passed him on the return trip at 11:35, an interview with the TV folks accounting for most of the delay.

The humiliation of Michael Spinks could not have been more complete if Tyson had tossed him off the pier at Atlantic City. Here was a fellow who had been undefeated in thirty-one fights, who had ranked among the best of all light-heavyweight champions, and who had never known what it was like to be knocked down.

Tyson floored him the first time with a left hook to the head, setting up the flurry that finished him off. "It doesn't take a

FROM THE GREATEST TO THE LATEST

very hard punch to take a guy out," said Spinks. "You hit a guy on the right spot and he's gone. He hit me in the right spot."

Spinks is smart, he can move, he can hit, and his awkwardness was thought to be an advantage. The only advantage it served Monday night was that Spinks looked more comfortable than the average semi-conscious fighter as he sprawled at the feet of Mike Tyson.

The shrewd observer noted that Tyson wore no socks.

Yes, the emperor wore neither socks nor robe, a fashion statement that means whatever Mike wants it to mean. He was naked except for his trunks, his gloves, and his fierce and consuming dignity.

As Tyson keeps reminding us, he has been groomed since the age of thirteen, since his first meeting with the late Cus D'Amato, to be what he is: the undisputed heavyweight champion.

The theme of the bout was "Once and For All," and whatever the issues, they will not need settling again. Not for Spinks, who will wisely decide to retire, and not for Tyson, who said in a moment of sulk that the fight might be his last.

Hey, if you had to work a minute and a half to earn $20 million, wouldn't you be worried about burnout, too?

It was, of course, the richest fight ever staged, and the most remarkable feature was the fact that Spinks collected $145,000 a *second* without landing a single punch.

It was not Tyson's power alone that demolished Spinks, and the thirty-four opponents before him. It is his constant pressure, his reluctance to give them any air. If he demonstrated anything new Monday night, it was a confidence stronger than ever.

"I've read in the papers that I'm cocky and arrogant," he said. "But I'm not. All I've said is the truth, that I'm the best there is, that no one on this planet can beat me."

For sure, no names leap into mind, certainly not Frank Bruno or Carl Williams or Evander Holyfield—although you have to be intrigued by a fighter named either Evander or Holyfield.

Somewhere out there in this vast and bountiful country, a thirteen-year-old kid is lifting weights with his teeth and pumping up. In ten years, when Mike Tyson is going on thirty-two and perhaps losing a little of his wallop, that kid has a chance to be the next heavyweight champion of the world.

ALI'S ANSWERED THE LAST BELL

DECEMBER 13, 1981

In a moment of soft reflection, Muhammad Ali once confessed that his endless babbling and posturing was a device partly to hide his fear—his fear of losing.

In more recent years, the voice grew lower and slower and somewhat slurred, but still he continued to fight, and to talk. But now he was trying to tame a more elusive fear, a fear of age, of creeping obscurity. Not for him the sounds of silence.

Pity that Ali never understood how little he had to fear. His place, his fame, his respect were assured many years and dozens of fights and millions of words ago. He leaves boxing with a history almost too incredible to accept.

Once, he recalled how he stood on a street corner in Los Angeles, yelling at people as they passed by, promoting his next fight with Jimmy Ellis. "These three college girls came up to me," he said, "and they asked, 'Are you Cassius Clay?' I said yes, and all three of them showed me $30 tickets. They said, 'We never been to a fight in our life, but we will be there to see your big mouth on the floor.' "

He has not been Cassius Clay for seventeen years. He has not been Muhammad Ali, as we knew him, for at least three, when he recaptured his title from Leon Spinks, the toothless tiger. His last performance of quality against a really worthy opponent came five years ago, when he defeated Joe Frazier in Manila with a will and a vigor not easy to forget.

And now he has lost to someone called Trevor Berbick, which sounds like the name of a newscaster on the BBC. The novelty has long since worn off. Precious few are the fans who still enjoy seeing Ali lose, seeing his mouth on the floor.

Berbick joins a list that includes Frazier, Ken Norton, Spinks,

FROM THE GREATEST TO THE LATEST

and Larry Holmes. And this is where the story must end, with Trevor Berbick, who revealed his sense of history by refusing to go into the ring until he knew his money was in the bank.

This retirement will stick. Ali may not want it this way, a month short of his fortieth birthday, but he has fought his last fight and hustled his last crowd. He cannot go back to Kuala Lumpur, San Juan, Frankfurt, Dublin, London, or Tokyo, where he once fought a kick-wrestler. The Japanese have threatened to raise the sticker price on Datsuns if he tries it again.

Larry Holmes was right when he said, "Ali can't keep pulling rabbits out of a hat. There are no more rabbits." It was also Holmes who said, before their fight in Las Vegas, "His ass is grass and I'm the lawnmower." Right again. All Berbick did was edge the curb.

It is no longer possible to get sentimental or weepy over Ali's last fight. There have been too many of them. He asked for it, he got it. The first time he retired—for two days, I think it was—after his dramatic knockout of George Foreman, many of us spilled our hearts all over the typewriter keys in tribute to the man who had been the most engaging and provocative fighter of this century.

We would look back on those pieces as our First Annual Muhammad Ali Retirement columns. We have lost track of which number this one is. But I promise you, it is the last. No more. Do you hear us, Muhammad? Now get out of here, you knucklehead.

No writer followed Ali more faithfully, or got closer to him, than Jerry Izenberg, out of Newark and New York. Jerry was at ringside in Detroit, pounding out a story on the Hearns-Cuevas fight, two weeks after Ali had signed to challenge Larry Holmes, vowing to win the heavyweight title for the fourth time.

Jerry felt a tap on his shoulder. He looked up and saw Ali towering over him. "Who you picking?" Ali demanded. "Be a man. Tell me the truth. Me or Holmes?"

"Holmes," said Jerry, and then he went back to work, racing his deadline.

There was another tap, and this one was even more insistent than the first. "What if I lost all this weight?" said Ali. "What if I turned the clock back twenty years? What if I looked the way I looked when I stepped in the ring with Sonny Liston? Who would you pick then?"

FROM THE GREATEST TO THE LATEST

"Still Holmes," came the quick reply.

Ali looked at him and he smiled. He said, "Lissen, be careful. Don't get fooled." And then he winked.

As he tells the story, Izenberg sighs, a wistful, not quite sad sigh. "Sometimes," he said, "we'd be better off knowing a lot less than we do. I wish I could have winked back at him."

Ali winked at all of us for most of two decades. When he fought his first professional fight, the president of the United States was Dwight David Eisenhower. NASA was still struggling to get a rocket off the launching pad; the things had an annoying tendency to blow up or to tip over on their side and fall to the ground with a loud thunk. Two of the countries where Ali later fought did not even exist.

He took us on an outrageous romp through sports, from his Olympic gold medal in 1960, to his bizarre victory over Sonny Liston, and his three-and-a-half-year battle against the draft and the government. His legal case may be studied long after his fights and his poetry are forgotten.

He always had an answer, an angle, or a cause. Where money ranked on his personal list isn't certain, but he made enough of it in his time to finance the arms race. From the Holmes fight he took away a check for $8 million. After taxes and expenses, he was able to put enough in tax-free bonds to assure him an income of $60,000 a month.

"Holmes is fighting for a car, a house, and a swimming pool," he said before the fight, drawing the moral lines. "I am a kamikaze, fighting for Allah. I pray to be successful in Allah's cause against the hypocrites and infidels."

It isn't for the pagans to question the powers of Allah. But Holmes won easily. Allah did not get much glory, but Ali got the tax-free bonds.

He was embarrassed in the ring by Holmes and he lost to Berbick in what may best be described as a polite minuet. Now it is over. Finished. Done. His courage will never be questioned, only his judgment. By going on, Ali accepted a great risk, that he would be remembered more for his carnival magic than for his speed and classic defensive skills. He is like one of those irrepressible salesmen that Dagwood Bumstead is always battling. We can't shut the door because of his hand, his foot, his knee. In truth, Ali and the media used each other. He never sent a writer away hungry.

FROM THE GREATEST TO THE LATEST

Izenberg wrote and coproduced a documentary about Ali, the best ever made about him, and I looked at it again after his loss to Trevor Berbick. He comes across, as he always does, as a combination of Jack Johnson, Sugar Ray Robinson, and Don Rickles. His mind is like the cloverleaf on a freeway, and sometimes he loses you on the turns, but at one point he said all that needs to be said about his career:

"There comes a time," Ali admitted, "when you have to know that nothing is forever. In life you have to travel from here to here. In order not to grow old you have to die young. So what do you accomplish? Some people stay in one city all their life. Some people never help nobody. Some people are a trouble to society. So what did I do in traveling from here to here? What did I do from the age of twenty-two to thirty-nine?"

He paused, then offered his own one-word summary: "Unbelievable."

The Rockets' Red Glare

GAME OF THE CENTURY— TWENTY YEARS LATER

JANUARY 21, 1988

That same night, the annual boat show was being held in the Exposition Hall, across the street. One customer wandered into the Astrodome, noticed very tall people in short pants warming up on a hardwood floor, and asked an usher, "Where are the boats?"

"You're in the wrong place," he was informed. "This is the Houston-UCLA basketball game."

The man turned on his heel and stalked out.

"I didn't come here," he growled, "to see some stupid basketball game."

Too bad about him. All he missed that night—January 20, 1968—was the game that changed college hoops forever. Houston versus UCLA. Elvin Hayes versus Lew Alcindor. It was the night they raised the roof, the night basketball came of age in the oil-and-cactus belt.

Some 52,693 fans didn't miss it, the largest crowd ever to see two teams trade buckets. Two years earlier, the Cougars had played in a high-school gymnasium that seated 2,500 fans.

The irony was clear: The Cougars would be drawing in one night what they recently had in a year. Now the record for basketball attendance, pro or amateur, would be broken in the first match of national importance ever held in a state where football was king.

Every seat in the building had been sold out ten days before the game. What drew them was a matchup between the first- and second-ranked teams in the land. In Houston, the buildup to the game had begun in June; students and fans could talk of little else. Some confessed that the game was too big for them, but they hoped to grow into it.

The challenge for the Cougars was as clear as lacquer. The question was not whether UCLA had the best basketball team in the country, but did it have the best of all time?

The Bruins had not lost in two seasons, not in forty-seven games, a streak that included a victory over Houston in the NCAA semifinals the previous spring. If the Bruins of Coach John Wooden were not invincible, they were doing a dandy imitation of a team that was.

Houston was poised to give them a test—a gut check, to use the idiom of the locker room. The upstart Cougars were unbeaten since their last encounter, winning their first sixteen games in 1968, while Coach Guy Lewis issued constant sanctions against mentioning "That Team" by name.

"We've been ripe for an upset," he said, "because we can't get our minds off UCLA."

He had slipped, and mentioned "That Team," but the Cougars kept winning.

To add an odd twist to the story, the Bruins would in one respect own the home-floor advantage. Since basketball had never been played inside the Astrodome, a portable floor had to be borrowed, not an easy task in the shank of a season. The one they found belonged to the Los Angeles Sports Arena, where the Lakers had played before their recent move to the Forum in Inglewood.

The one-ton surface was trucked to Houston in two days. The Bruins had played three games on it, the Cougars none.

So the teams would collide in a stadium built for football and baseball, with a floor shipped from California. The seats were so far from the court that many of the fans in the upper levels brought binoculars or opera glasses.

Of course, the phantom of this opera was one Lew Alcindor, later known as Kareem Abdul-Jabbar. From the moment he appeared on the floor, the seven-foot-two Alcindor was the focal point of the crowd. Curious Texans gawked and followed his every move. They seemed surprised to find that he had two arms, two legs, and lived out of water.

A series of medical bulletins had preceded his arrival, the result of a scratched eyeball suffered a week earlier.

THE ROCKETS' RED GLARE

The huge crowd had come to see not only the battle for the top spot in the polls, but also the duel between Alcindor and Elvin Hayes. The "Big E" was Houston's game plan. At six-foot-nine, he gave away five inches to Lew. But Hayes was as strong as a water buffalo, and the Cougars were willing to pit his strength against Lew's grace.

Quick! Find your seat. Suck in your breath. The game is about to begin, January 20, 1968, exactly twenty years ago today.

The whirring noise in the background may have been James Naismith spinning in his grave. This was as far as you could get from the humble beginnings of the sport the good doctor had created out of a peach basket and an inflated bladder.

The standing-room crowd had spilled into the aisles of the Astrodome. The noise was like sticking your head inside an airplane engine. On the green carpet that bordered the portable floor, UCLA cheerleaders performed a wild Watusi.

Was it "The Game of the Century," as many later said and wrote? Actually, it was not billed at the time as an equal battle of titans. The Cougars of Houston were heavy underdogs. Coach John Wooden was the Wizard of Westwood. Lew Alcindor was the greatest of many great players he had coached. The Cougars were a distant second in the polls, a team hungering for this kind of showcase, this kind of showdown.

Suddenly, the ball was in the air and the trappings of the game were forgotten. Here was Elvin Hayes hitting a jumper for the game's first points. Hayes would live off that turnaround jumper for sixteen years in the NBA. On this night, he would introduce it to a national television audience.

The shooting of Hayes would keep the Cougars ahead most of the first half. During one stretch, the "Big E" sank three in a row from inside and the Cougars led 37-28.

In the Lew Alcindor era, UCLA had never before trailed in a game by as many as nine points. Alcindor appeared unsure, distracted. The Bruins were behind at halftime for only the second time in his career, 46-43. Gibraltar was crumbling.

The pace slowed after intermission. To deny Lew the ball, the Cougars used a 1-3 zone, with Hayes taking Alcindor man for man. With twelve minutes to play, Hayes and guard George Reynolds both had four fouls.

The Bruins, pressing the entire floor, responded to the

challenge. Mike Warren's jump shot from the top of the key tied the score at 54 with ten minutes on the clock.

They would be tied twice more, but UCLA would never lead. With just under two minutes to go, Hayes hit from the corner and Don Chaney sank a two-hander. Houston was up by 69-65.

Lucius Allen cut it to two with a driving layup, but he missed a free throw and Hayes rebounded. Houston had to run seventy-two seconds off the clock to put away the win.

Moments later, Alcindor wrapped himself around Houston's six-foot-ten Ken Spain to break the stall. Spain missed at the foul line, UCLA recovered and started working the ball inside. Now Spain fouled Allen, and the UCLA playmaker converted both shots to tie the score at 69.

The tension inside the Astrodome seemed enough to lift the whole place off the pad. With twenty-eight seconds left, Hayes was fouled by Jim Nielsen. He buried them both and Houston led by two.

The Bruins wouldn't get off another shot. Allen's pass for Warren was tipped by a teammate and sailed out of bounds. Here came Hayes dribbling across midcourt, a little display of élan aimed at those observers who had been gushing about Alcindor's dexterity.

Then he passed to Reynolds, who held the ball the last three seconds, then gave it a joyful heave toward the spidery ceiling.

The performance of Hayes was the stuff of legend. The senior from the tiny Louisiana hamlet of Ruston dominated the game, scoring thirty-nine points with fifteen rebounds, five blocked shots, and four assists.

Alcindor played forty minutes and was clearly off his form. The fans shrieked and whistled at his every miss, and he obliged them by hitting only four of eighteen from the field. He finished with fifteen points and twelve rebounds, bothered no doubt by the eye injury that had sent him to the hospital a week earlier.

In ninety-nine games at UCLA, this would be the only loss Lew ever suffered, and it ended the Bruins' forty-seven-game winning streak.

College basketball would move to another level, of bigger arenas and bigger coverage. And the image would linger, twenty years later, of a packed Astrodome, Elvin Hayes hitting the jumper, and the scoreboard lights frozen forever at 71-69.

LEMONS GIVES 'EM WHAT THEY WANT

JULY 27, 1980

As a championship coach, an appraiser of talent, and a student of human behavior, Abe Lemons listened quietly to the account of a friend's recent travels with the Houston Astros.

Spellbound might be too strong a word. But Abe was attentive.

The friend was Don Sanders, whose position as a stockbroker with E. F. Hutton enables him to support his addiction, which is sports. Sanders is an investor in the Astros, a live-or-die booster of the Texas Longhorns, and an incurable tennis nut. The order of interest depends on: (a) which team is in season, and (b) how his tennis game is going. Over the years it has improved to a point where he was once able to carry Bobby Riggs to straight sets before losing.

In any contest to select Houston's most passionate sports fan, Sanders would be rated so strong that Jimmy the Greek would give him a first-round bye.

A few weeks ago, Sanders joined the Astros on a road trip to the West Coast. One night in San Francisco, he entertained a party of ten, including Nolan Ryan, Joe Sambito, Craig Reynolds, Terry Puhl, Denny Walling, Joe Niekro, Vern Ruhle, Alan Ashby, and Don Leppert, the third-base coach.

Now, in other years, if that many Astros had gone into town in force, the city authorities would have called out the National Guard. But this Houston team is different. After a seafood feast on Fisherman's Wharf, Sanders marched them several blocks, up and down hills, to find an ice-cream parlor that made chocolate sundaes with fudge so thick you had to spoon it with a bayonet.

Then more blocks, up and down more hills, to a shop featuring what Don promised were "the best chocolate chip cookies in the world." Earlier, he had sent an unmarked bag to the hotel rooms of Manager Bill Virdon and each of his coaches. The reaction was interesting. Leppert, pointing out that "there are a lot of weirdos in San Francisco," refused to eat any until he found out who sent them. Virdon hesitated, then ate the whole bag. "If they're going to get you," he said, with a shrug, "they're going to get you." It is the mark of leadership.

This was the kind of night that would have made an old-timey ballplayer weep. The Astros were a curious sight, parading along in more or less single file, like an overgrown Boy Scout troop looking for exotic rocks, or whatever. They did not even knock over a garbage can. How does one explain such conduct to Leo Durocher, who once said, "You don't play the game on milk and gingersnaps."

For the moment, at least, the Astros are proving Leo wrong.

Abe Lemons listened to the story of Don's exciting night in San Francisco, and shook his head. "People don't want to hear about cookies and fudge sundaes," said the Texas basketball coach. "That's the kind of stuff that will send you next door."

Folksy and homespun are the words most often used to describe Lemons. But there are shrapnel fragments of wisdom in nearly everything he says. Abe appears to have made a lifelong study of what people do want to read and hear. "A writer asked me," he said, "what was the happiest time of my life. I told him it was when I was coaching at Pan American College. Later, somebody asked me why I didn't say right now, at Texas. I told him people don't want to hear that, even if it's true. Sounds too self-serving. They want you to say something different, or nostalgic. They want you to talk about your first paper route."

Lemons and his assistant, Barry Dowd, were in town for the coaching clinic and All-Star Games. Abe had been reading about the problems of J. R. Richard, the hints that maybe his tired muscles were in his head, not in his arm, or that J. R. was exhausted from thinking too much about Nolan Ryan's salary. Abe was sympathetic to the troubled Houston pitcher, and suggested that he might need more understanding and less criticism.

"I don't think it's money that gets a pro athlete in a box today," he said. "It's pride. It's the fact that they think they will go on forever."

An athlete is tugged in many directions—by his manager or coach, by his family, his friends, the press. He soon finds himself in an orbit all his own, out of radio contact with the planet Earth.

Abe Lemons used to receive frequent letters from the father of one of his players who spent much of his time on the bench. The father lectured the coach about misusing his talent—he once sent him a pamphlet on personnel management—and about his failure to enforce more rules. "If I had any rules," Abe wrote back, "I would have had to kick your son off the team because he was the first one I caught drinking."

In time the young man decided to transfer to a smaller school. For the purpose of our story, let's call it Peaceful Valley Tech.

Lemons wished him well, but said, frankly, "I think you're stupid for leaving Texas. You could have played here. But you'll be able to think about that when you take your kids to homecoming at Peaceful Valley."

Basketball in the state may have been given a lift the other day when the courts struck down a ban against high-school athletes attending summer camps. Abe is not sure how soon or how much the ruling will help, but in general he is pleased. "I like it mostly because the superintendents are against it," he said. "You know what they're doing, don't you? They're saving the taxpayers' money. That's right. They're afraid if they let the kids use those gymnasiums in the summer, the floors will wear out. It's just like our Gregory Gym. It was built around 1920. Why, just two or three years ago we had to re-sand the floor."

When Abe Lemons talks, even E. F. Hutton listens. Don Sanders nodded, and passed him a plate of chocolate chip cookies.

BOSTON'S ONE-MAN SHOW

OCTOBER 26, 1986

With all due respect to the Raiders and the Oilers, the Mets and the Red Sox, and anyone out there throwing, hitting, kicking, or bouncing a ball, the most distinctive athlete in America passed through Houston Saturday night.

His first name is Larry, and he is, as headline writers cannot resist reminding us, a Bird of a different feather.

Not since the Yankees and DiMaggio do the names of a team and a player blend so surely and instantly in the mirror of our minds.

His skills on a basketball court, and the confidence that supports them, send opposing fans into spasms of envy, fear, and loathing. To patrons of the Houston Rockets, the Alfred Hitchcock flick, *The Birds,* is a horror story about the Boston Celtics.

But you can mark it down now. By the time the self-styled "Hick from French Lick" retires, he will be revered in all those cities where he ruined so many appetites and trampled so many hearts. And they will know that they won't see the likes of him again.

When they start ranking the all-time competitors of sport, Bird may be the one to beat. This is the White Shadow, recalling his high-school days: "I remember we used to shoot free throws at six in the morning, before classes. There was this one friend of mine, my best friend at the time, and he would never show up. We were in the regionals that year and he missed three 1-and-1 situations in a row. We lost in overtime. I never said a word to him. I just looked. He knew what I was thinking.

"I have not talked to him since that day."

No athlete has ever outworked or outhustled or—trust us on this one—outslicked him on the basketball court. Some of his closest friends believe that there is nowhere else that Bird feels quite as comfortable, where he finds it so easy to communicate.

He practices constantly: all year, before games, even *after* games. After all his success, all the acclaim, why? Why work so hard? "It's not hard," he says. "It's fun. Pouring cement is hard."

His lawyer-agent, Bob Woolf, once spent most of a day tracking him down. He was in a pickup game at a neighborhood gym. Woolf left word for Bird to return his call; it was important.

Woolf had three requests that needed answers. The president of Harvard had invited Bird to speak to the freshman class on the value of a college education; *Time* magazine wanted to assign a photographer to follow him around; *Sports Illustrated* needed to schedule an interview for a cover story.

When Bird called, Woolf rattled off the requests. To all three Larry said no. Nothing else. Just no. No questions. No explanations. It made for a quick conversation, and when his agent said, "Okay, thanks," and started to hang up, Bird said, with just a touch of agitation, "Mr. Woolf, I thought you said this call was important."

Woolf is believed to have been the first credible agent in sports. He goes back to a day when an agent was not allowed to sit with his client in the general manager's office, and he negotiated his first contract from a hotel room one block from the ballpark. When the player needed to confer with Woolf, he stepped outside and used the phone on a secretary's desk.

So Bob has seen them come and go, hundreds of them, the greats and near-greats and ingrates. And Woolf will tell you that Larry Bird is one of a kind: "He is the least interested in publicity of anybody I have ever known. And the least selfish.

"If he had scored ninety-nine points in a game and needed one more to tie Wilt Chamberlain's record of 100, and had four seconds left to play and could score a field goal just by dribbling to the hoop, he'd pass the ball to a teammate if the guy was open. Why? Because it's the thing to do."

As a senior at Indiana State, he didn't talk to the press until the Final Four because his teammates were not sharing the attention. At last he met the media. "How's your thumb?" asked a reporter, referring to an injury he had suffered late in the season. "Broke," Bird said.

Twice he turned down a chance to visit the White House, after the Celtics won the National Basketball Association title. "Why didn't they invite the team that lost?" he wondered.

It is called character, and it is part of the reason Red Auerbach,

THE ROCKETS' RED GLARE

who created the Celtics, says that Larry plays "like he is obsessed with earning the money I'm payin' him."

Bird leaves the analyzing to others. And there are signs that he doesn't take himself as seriously as his critics. When he traveled to Israel with a team of All-Stars, he and Woolf paid a visit to the historic Wailing Wall in Jerusalem.

A friend saw a photograph of them at the scene, Larry with one hand holding a yarmulke on his head. The friend asked what the agent was doing in the picture.

"Well, gee," Bird replied, "Mr. Woolf had to do 10 percent of the wailing."

LAST OF NBA'S GREAT MINI-STARS

OCTOBER 30, 1983

Calvin Murphy said it at the very beginning of his career, when someone asked him if he felt his height was a disadvantage in a sport designed for giants: "I'll only be a basketball player a few years. I have to be a human being for a long time."

The years stretched into thirteen, fewer than he might have wished, but longer by far than the early forecasts. He became a star, a crowd pleaser, a brilliant shooter. He played in more games, scored more points, had more steals, gave more assists than any player in Rockets history. And, best of all, he got a terrific start on his post-career planning. He scored big as a human being.

The retirement of a popular athlete can be a trauma, for us as well as for them. The athlete may experience difficulty as he reenters the earth's atmosphere. The fan has a tendency to think sad thoughts, and to resent the passage of time. Careers end in different ways, with a whimper or a bang, or an injury. The career of Calvin Murphy ended with a news conference. It was a nice news conference, with cold cuts and free drinks, and a much happier occasion than a knee operation. But it wasn't the last game of his last season, with Murphy hitting a twenty-footer at the buzzer. For those who carry scrapbooks around in their heads, the one for Calvin Murphy has a page missing.

Naturally, if anyone expressed such feelings to Murphy, he tried to console them. "I understand," he said, "but you have to be a realist. I'd like to think I had two great years left. But it wasn't going to happen. There was no place for me to go but down. I didn't figure to play much. I would have been just traveling around the country watching a lot of basketball. I've done that all my life."

So now they might as well stuff Calvin and ship him off to the Smithsonian. He is, or was, one of a kind, the last of a breed, an endangered species, like the golden eagle or the snail darter.

It is, in fact, easier to picture a snail darting than to imagine the Rockets without Murphy, rising above his inches, suspended in air, banging home a jumper. Or whirling across the floor, always moving in a gear no one else seemed to have. Given the cost of talent today in pro basketball, either by the inch or by the pound, it isn't likely that teams will be willing to gamble on a five-foot-nine jitterbug, even one who ranked among the national scoring leaders at Niagara University, and in his spare time twirled the baton.

Murphy retired rather than go through a season of feeling that he was an unnecessary person. He deserved to go out with grace and respect and the Rockets tried to oblige him. Later, there will be a night in his honor, so the fans can pay their final cheers, and he will be showered with gifts and sweet words and the highest compliment a team can offer: No Houston player will ever again wear a jersey with Calvin's number 23 on it. In sports, this is the ritual closest to the way the Egyptians once buried their kings, tossing into the tomb the jewelry, wife, and servants.

Calvin's will be the second jersey retired in the history of the franchise. He follows Rudy Tomjanovich, his friend, ex-roommate, and Houston neighbor. They started out together as rookies in 1971 when the Rockets were still based in San Diego.

Superbly conditioned, and motivated always by the need to prove that his size was no handicap, Murphy has not changed visibly in his thirteen years as the pocket Rocket. At thirty-five, he is no slower, no shorter, no weaker of eye than he was in his prime. Only the game has changed. If they wish, the Rockets will be able to line up with two six-foot-eight guards, the returning Robert Reid and the rookie Rodney McCray. When you pay McCray an estimated $350,000 a year—as much as, if not more than, Murphy earned in his best seasons—you have to make room for him. In pro sports today, money talks. What it says is, play me.

The irony of his timing was hardly lost on Calvin. He ended his career the same week that Ralph Sampson would begin his. On the first day of what has been advertised as the Age of Sampson, Murphy had made up his mind to stay home. He had

THE ROCKETS' RED GLARE

not missed the opening game of a basketball season since he was eight years old, but he would miss this one. Calvin will need time to adjust to his role as a spectator.

"Right now, I'm trying to hold back a little," he said. "I'll be out later. Opening day belongs to the new Rockets. I know if I was there the crowd would want to get me involved. There will be time for that later."

The only regret he allowed himself was not getting to play with Sampson. In the three months they've known each other, the seven-foot-four tower and the Little Big Man established a kind of kidding rapport. They gave each other nicknames out of the old Jackie Gleason television series, "The Honeymooners." Sampson was Ralph Cramden and Murphy had the role of Ed Norton.

His Rocket career was not always—in fact, very seldom—a honeymoon. Calvin played on only three teams that won more games than they lost. Fitch would have been his sixth coach, and to each one of them Murphy had to prove that he could be a regular in the NBA. No man, big or small, ever played harder or proved himself more often.

Year after year the coaches would try to make Calvin a role-player, coming off the bench to provide instant firepower. But his performances were so consistent, and sometimes so astounding, that he kept playing himself into the starting lineup.

He broke the NBA record for consecutive free throws, hitting seventy-eight. He was the fourth-leading scorer among active players, behind Kareem Abdul-Jabbar, Elvin Hayes, and Bob Lanier, and seventeenth on the all-time list. He once scored fifty-seven points in a game against New Jersey.

The plight of the short man in pro basketball has been a source of concern for years to social workers and sportswriters. Calvin Murphy was one of the few players you could hold a conversation with and not feel you had to yodel. He was a joy to watch, a player who never hid his emotions. He gave new meaning to the word *feisty*, three times getting into fights with players six-feet-eight or over and winning them all. Once, the Rockets lost a game when Murphy's last-second shot rimmed the basket and fell out. He cried in the locker room.

He was beyond special. He has been unique. He has been Calvin Murphy, the last of the great mini-players.

FREE ADVICE FOR RALPH

JUNE 11, 1987

Sit down, Ralph. Watch your head. I want to talk to you not as a fan, a friend, or a father figure, but as the total strangers we are and probably will be all our lives.

We know you're busy, so let's get right to the point. I only wish you had talked to us before you decided to test your wings as a free agent. I know you have an agent, a lawyer, an accountant, maybe even your own astrologer. No disrespect to them.

But you need to hear from someone who can be truly objective about what is about to happen in your life.

They are going to come after you, Ralph. The Lakers. The Knicks. Maybe even the Celtics. Who knows about McHale's foot?

You're going to get the millions, no matter who is counting, or how. They can pay you in yen and they can count backward. It will be there. But you have to decide something bigger than money, Ralph. And we're not talking about friendship.

We're talking towns. How big a town will it take to make you happy, Ralph? Put it another way: Who do you want to be, Ralph? You want to host "Saturday Night Live?" You want your own MTV? You want to meet Madonna?

You can have it all, Ralph, from Beverly Hills to the World Trade Center, home of the original twin towers (little historical footnote, there).

But at some point a question has to be answered: Is Ralph Sampson a New York kind of guy? A Los Angeles kind of guy? If they put the money up, would you play in Indianapolis? It's a terrific town if you're going through it at 200 miles an hour.

Some of us thought you looked fine in Houston, Ralph. We just wanted you to smile more. But we remembered that splendid photograph of your graduation day, looking proud in your cap and gown, head and shoulders above your classmates.

As a Rocket, you looked forward to facing the Lakers, going

one-on-one with Kareem Abdul-Jabbar. How do you imagine it would feel to *be* Abdul-Jabbar, or at least his successor? And then to take on your old buddy, Olajuwon. If you held your own, beat him now and then, you could finally bury your critics, the ones who say that Ralph sulks; and when the games get big, Ralph gets tiny.

You kick Akeem's rear a few times and you could have your own float in the Rose Bowl parade.

But L.A.? Woody Allen once said that L.A.'s gift to humanity was the fact that it was the first city to make legal a right turn on red. Of course, Woody was a Knicks fan when the Knicks were great.

I guess it would not be hard to picture you in New York. You and Patrick Ewing could make them forget Walt Frazier and Willis Reed and the Pearl. Pearl who? Are you kidding, Ralph? Earl ("The Pearl") Monroe. Who did you think, Pearl Bailey? Minnie Pearl? You're not *that* young.

I like what your agent said: Ralph Sampson is a sensitive guy and the fact that the Rockets' management wouldn't meet his price doesn't make them bad people.

There is a sense of maturity in those words, even a hint of poetry.

Not to turn soft on you, but this is America, after all. Look at Bill Bradley, who gave the Knicks some quality years. All those brains and his suits still look wrinkled. But he turned out okay. You ever think about being a senator, Ralph? (Incidentally, may I ask you a personal question? Do you mind being called "Stick"?) You can live anywhere you want, even a condo in New York's midtown. You know who can afford those? Arab sheiks. Doctors who marry lawyers. And you.

It's like that line from the song in *A Chorus Line*—"And now life really begins. Go to it."

At some point, each of us has to decide what we want to be when we grow up. You can be whatever you want, Ralph. Any place you pick. Most Houston fans will wish you well. Some won't. They won't matter. Just one final bit of advice: This time loosen up, and have some fun.

BRINGING THE DUNK DOWN TO EARTH

APRIL 3, 1983

Purely by accident, the way great discoveries often happen, we tuned in the other day to a radio interview with Darryl Dawkins. In a calm, measured voice, Dawkins revealed that the planet Lovetron was no more—it had been closed for remodeling—and he now made his spiritual home in a place called "Thunder Under," a nautical kingdom Dawkins located 50,000 "phantoms" below the sea.

The interview with Dawkins was followed by a short, edgy, almost plaintive one with Larry Brown, the coach of the New York Nets, who looks on Darryl as a kind of wayward son. "I just want him to be a basketball player," said Brown. "I don't know how to relate to these guys who are from outer space."

Clearly, Brown would prefer the preppy, academic types such as those well-known scholars and all-around earthlings, the kids from *Phi Slama Jama,* the most famous fraternal order since *Animal House.* Heading into this weekend's date with Louisville, and with Destiny, the Cougars had been playing out of this world. Akeem Olajuwon was even playing out of this Third World, and was as near as the Cougars could come to producing an alien being.

Dawkins is not exactly a role model for the Cougars, who need no escape from reality. But there is a connection. Dawkins gained a certain notoriety a year or two ago by taking the slam dunk to artistic heights seldom imagined. Twice he shattered glass backboards, the whole fixture collapsing in what seemed like slow motion, while bemused players walked around lightly, up to their socks in broken glassware. Over and over we watched the replay on television.

Dawkins became known on Broadway as "Dr. Slam," and he

gave lectures on the Go-rilla dunk, and his most famous invention, called Chocolate Thunder. He beguiled the public with accounts of life on the planet Lovetron. We might have followed him there, eating flowers and tossing an occasional laser beam at the Russians, if not for a sad and disheartening turn of events. Dawkins did not seem to improve. Traded by Philadelphia to the Nets, he continued to flounder. His performance never equaled his act. He is six-feet-eleven and mountainesque, and yet he can't find himself. All anyone knows for sure is that if he does, it won't be on Lovetron.

Dawkins is a prophet gone wrong, but in their modest way the Cougars have carried on his work. They have reestablished the slam dunk as a celebration of college basketball. On a good night they might collect eight or ten, but never mind the stats. Slam dunks are not meant to be counted. They are meant to be seen, heard, felt, experienced.

It is hard to realize now that the dunk was outlawed by the college rulemakers for ten years. Many observers thought the ban was aimed at a UCLA sophomore named Lew Alcindor. Certainly Alcindor thought so. Joining the NBA, he changed his name to Kareem Abdul-Jabbar and dunked to his heart's content.

Curiously, his coach, John Wooden, always contended that the rule change made Jabbar a better player. He had to work harder on his shots, his coach pointed out, and he developed what became his most dangerous move, the sky hook.

Wooden never liked the dunk for another reason, feeling that it encouraged individual heroics at the expense of the pass. "Teamwork is what the game is all about," he once noted.

It still is. But you watch the Cougars—or the Cardinals of Louisville—and you conclude that the slam dunk has a new status. It is part of the bonding process. Houston's fine point guard, freshman Alvin Franklin, confided that he was expelled from *Phi Slama Jama* for a week when he blew a dunk. He was reinstated after a breakaway jam against Villanova. And Reid Gettys, a minority kid trying to make it in big-time college basketball, cracked up the entire squad when he stuffed one in practice.

The problem with the dunk a few years ago wasn't that it penalized the little man, but that it was so boring. Some seven-footer hovered around the rim like a seal balancing a beach ball on his nose, and then raised both arms and rammed it through. No imagination. One coach argued that they should put the basket on the floor so the little man could dunk it, too.

The Cougars are so diversified that in any one game you are likely to see a half-dozen versions of this art form. Patrons of the team grow faint when they describe the techniques of Olajuwon, Clyde Drexler, Larry Micheaux, and Michael Young.

When Akeem goes for it, you get a quick flash in your mind of Armageddon, and somewhere a choir seems to be singing "Rock of Ages." Drexler reminds you of the Flying Wallendas, cradling the ball gently under his arm, floating from the foul line to the hoop, and then cutting it loose in a blur of leather and net.

We have seen the windmill dunk, the hesitation, the reverse, the in-yo'-face, an assortment so rich the question is no longer how much coaching Guy Lewis does, but who does their choreography?

It isn't easy to determine when the dunk shot first appeared in basketball. The eminent historian Red Auerbach claims it was introduced in the early 1950s in a Harlem amateur league. The inventor is said to have been a gentleman named Jumping Jackie Jackson.

Jumping Jackie, according to Red, not only dunked but could skim a dime off the top of the backboard.

For years there was talk of discouraging the dunk, of raising the height of the basket, not only in college but in the pros. Today everyone does it. A six-foot-eight guard is no longer an uncommon sight, and the little man is even more an endangered species. The Rockets' Calvin Murphy, at five-feet-nine, has the spring to dunk and has done so in warm-ups. But Murphy has never tried it in a game, believing that he would get only one chance. The next time he showed up under the basket, the big men would pound him into the ground like a railroad spike.

The dunk, the slam, the stuff, has become a moment of anticipation to a college basketball crowd, like the fireworks display at Disneyland. It electrifies the crowd and insults the opposition. Sometimes, when a Cougar scores one, when the power and the sweep are just right and the iron is still vibrating, they will sneak a sideways grin at each other as they run upcourt. It is the kind of grin you can't hold back, the kind that feels good all over.

COOGS LOSE A GREAT GUY

JANUARY 22, 1986

For years, a student manager was assigned to keep twelve cups, filled with water, in a cooler next to the University of Houston bench. Chewing on his red polka-dot towels kept Guy Lewis thirsty.

Years ago, at halftime of a close game against TCU, Lewis lectured his players and sent them back out to the floor. Guy did not go with them, for reasons related to his consumption of water. Unaware that the coach had not followed them out, the team manager locked the door behind him.

When the Cougars lined up to start the second half, a quick glance at the bench told them they were a team without a coach. Meanwhile, the manager had wandered off to find a water fountain under the stands. He was refilling his paper cups when he heard a fearful racket, a pounding and yelling that seemed to be coming from the Cougars' dressing room, fifty feet away.

He walked over to the door and hesitated, the way people do when they hear a strange noise coming from a room that should be empty.

"Coach," he asked, "is that you?"

"Hail, yes," roared Lewis, in his East Texas twang. "Now get me out of here."

Rare indeed was the day anyone needed to go looking for Guy V. Lewis. You could always find him in the gym or on the Cougar bench. He has been there for thirty years, through 586 victories, and enough cups of water to float a small cabin cruiser.

But he won't be there after the 1986 season, and the sidelines will not be the same without him. He was the second coach the Cougars' basketball team ever had . . . and he played under the first.

Lewis came home from the war in time to help the Cougars open the 1946 season, their first, with a practice game against Ellington Field. He stood six-feet-three and played center, which is still the correct position for that height if you happen to be in grade school.

The game ball was a little moldy and part of the cover was peeling off. But Guy knew what to do with it. He was a fine player, one whose scoring records lasted for years.

His coach was Alden Pasche. Guy became his full-time assistant in 1953, and three years later took over as head coach.

In a sense, Guy never left school. His record is hard to fault, although heaven knows people have tried. He was criticized even when his teams reached the NCAA's Final Four, as they did five times.

But Lewis has been a great coach, because he won in different eras, with different material. He won with fast teams and slow; short teams and tall. He won with teams that were all white and teams that were mostly black. The Cougars have played run-and-gun and they have played to the tempo of a Viennese waltz. And they kept on winning.

Two or three National Basketball Association coaches found Elvin Hayes difficult to handle. They blamed it on Lewis, who handled him beautifully. His patience with Olajuwon, who came to him as a seven-foot soccer player, was the making of Akeem's career.

His teams have not suffered a losing season since Eisenhower was in the White House. His 1968 squad won twenty-eight games in a row and defeated UCLA and Lew Alcindor in the Astrodome, in one of the greatest games ever seen.

No one ever really typed him as a coach. He was not volcanic or mysterious, and he did not speak in fables. He scored high as a recruiter and an organizer. What he landed he kept and what he kept he motivated.

He took players in the quiet 1950s and the troubled 1960s and the selfish 1970s. Regardless of what went into the compactor, winning teams kept emerging from the Cougar campus.

You wonder if the fans of the school ever realized how lucky they were to have Guy Lewis represent them. After thirty years—really, after forty—they are about to find out.

Football Follies and the Circus Maximus

END OF AN ERA

DECEMBER 5, 1976

You try to imagine Arkansas without Frank Broyles, or Texas without Darrell Royal, and it is like trying to imagine "White Christmas" sung by anyone other than Bing Crosby. I am not sure it can be done.

When the news broke this week that Broyles would retire as the Arkansas coach after his team's last game against Texas, and Royal might join him, you had to be struck by a sense of irony.

Royal had come into the Southwest Conference twenty years ago, Broyles a year later. Between them they had dominated the league. In eighteen of those years, their teams had won or tied for the title. They were the only head coaches to start and finish the 1960s.

How fitting if they went out together.

But how wrong the stage, how strange the setting, this game that meant nothing. No unbeaten season, no championship, no bowl invitation. Nothing except the remembrance of glories past. Yet what a very special game, if it was indeed to be the last of these two distinguished careers.

In a way, it was more of a shock to picture Broyles stepping down than Royal. There was no adjusting Darrell's flame. It always burned with the same intensity. His thermostat had no low or medium controls. Broyles seemed to spend himself less, was looser and less sensitive.

Part of Frank's charm, part of his style, was a tendency to make so much of his success seem accidental. In the early 1960s, one of his favorites was a young player named Jim Grizzle, a defensive end whose first start was unforgettable. Against TCU, Grizzle was out of position on the opening three plays of the game. All he did was break up a pass, spill the quarterback for an eight-yard loss, and cause a fumble, which he recovered.

"After we studied the film," said Broyles, "and compared what Grizzle was supposed to do as opposed to what he did, we decided we wouldn't try to coach him any more."

FOOTBALL FOLLIES AND THE CIRCUS MAXIMUS

When Arkansas pulled itself together in the last 100 seconds to beat Texas in 1965, in the first of the famed "Big Shoot-outs," Broyles gave the credit to Jim Lindsey, a senior halfback, for inspiring the drive that won the game, 27-24. "Jim Lindsey is the one who rallied our team," he said, "not me. I was a babbling idiot."

Frank had a great deal of company. The Texas-Arkansas series just did that to you. The games were usually close, decided late, and almost always played for important stakes. The rivalry was heightened by the fact that the coaches genuinely admired and enjoyed each other. There was no meanness in them.

Before the teams met one year in Austin, Broyles had a message for the press. The Razorbacks would be flying home to the hills about the time Royal held forth at his traditional postgame service at the Villa Capri Motel. "Sorry I can't stay for the press conference, fellows," Frank assured them, "but anything Darrell says goes for me."

Their relationship withstood the bitterest of losses. Texas had won fifteen games in a row when the Hogs upset the Horns in 1964, with the help of an eighty-one-yard punt return by Ken Hatfield. Later, Royal was saying, "Frank and I have had a good rivalry. Anything he tells me I know to be true. I trust him and have confidence in him."

"Darrell," broke in a friend, "that's where you made your first mistake."

"Well," said Royal, grinning, "he did tell me that Hatfield had a charleyhorse."

They have been not only great and successful coaches, but superb representatives of college football and its finer instincts. Once they were the Young Turks of the Southwest Conference. Suddenly, in a fingersnap, twenty years have flown by. If you work for the gas company, twenty years on the same job may not seem extraordinary. But in football it qualifies you as an institution. At the least, the government should name an aircraft carrier after you.

For us ink-stained wretches, Broyles and Royal have been a joy, enriching our Saturdays and filling our great white spaces. Royal said he wanted his team to play "as though they were planting the flag on Iwo Jima." He gave us: "Three things can happen when you pass and two of them are bad." And his most famous of all lines, explaining that he did not believe in getting tricky when a big game arrived: "We'll dance with the one who brung us."

Broyles once described football as "a great laboratory of teamwork." To demonstrate that coaches do read something heavier than Batman comics, or textbooks entitled *Ramifications of the Three-Point Stance,* he would on occasion toss out such quotations as: "Whosoever shall humble himself, shall be exalted." Frank gleaned that nugget from the Book of Matthew, after Arkansas had lost to LSU one year in the Cotton Bowl.

As we used to say on the farm, even a blind hog finds an acorn every now and then. I think that means we all get lucky sometimes. The suspicion here is that Texas and Arkansas are about to find out how lucky they have been.

BIG LOU APPEALS TO THE PLAYERS

JULY 7, 1974

When lovable Lou Rymkus was a howling, rawboned tackle for the Cleveland Browns, he alone among the veterans would pay attention, socially, to the rookies. After practice, Lou would invite five or six of them to a bar where the owner gave away free cigars to the Cleveland players.

"As soon as we got the cigars," remembers one of the rookies, a chap named Don Shula, "Rymkus would collect them for himself, then go off to another table."

Once, the rookie in professional football was regarded as a kind of nonperson. Under the friendliest of conditions, what the veterans felt toward him was contempt. He represented all the wrong things: money he had't yet earned, new styles, and, meanest of all, his very presence meant that an older fellow— a pal—had lost his job.

One of the swell ironies of the current NFL player strike is the new prominence of the rookies, who are being romanced and threatened by both sides. They are being picked at, and quarreled over, like children in a custody case. You can be sure, of course, that both sides have the best interest of the rookie at heart. Have a candy bar, little boy. Have a cigar.

Lou Rymkus sees what is happening today to a game that had been his lifetime, and he feels disgust, confusion, and a little redness around the ears. He sat down this week and dashed off a letter to Bill Curry, the president of the player's association, with copies to his old friends around the league, and on newspapers, and in Congress. Writing letters has become an exercise for Lou, one of the ways he tames the hurt and the frustration he feels deep in his bones from being out of pro football.

The letters used to come in from places like Detroit and Baltimore, where he would work as a line coach or a scout, while he waited for someone to call and offer him a team of his own, and give him back his life. For a time the letters even carried the postmark of a town in the Louisiana outback, where Lou took a job coaching a high-school team, because it was as close as he could get to the job he really wanted.

Ever since he was a small boy in a crumbling section of Chicago, all he thought about was becoming a great head coach. There aren't many cornball stories like that anymore. Back in the 1930s, Big Lou went to see all those stirring movies that starred Pat O'Brien, the ones that usually ended with the alma mater booming in the background and the theater audience sobbing. He played at Notre Dame, the shrine, and he went on to a fine career in the pros at Cleveland, with Lou Groza and Otto Graham and Marion Motley. That crowd.

Then he made it, for one brief, shining moment. He was hired by Bud Adams to create the Houston Oilers, and his team won the championship, and he became the American Football League's first Coach of the Year. They can't take that away from him. It was 1960, and a year later, he was fired. Some said he tried to be tougher than he was. Others said that he simply talked himself out of his job. Yet no matter how long the Oiler line of succession gets, it will always begin with Lou Rymkus.

But Lou still cares about the game, and he follows it closely, and he gets worked up enough to write passionate letters to those who have custody of the sport. The dreams of a lifetime do not perish easily.

It just unhinges him to hear the modern player talk about freedom issues and social amenities, when Lou can remember playing for $2,000 a year and watching his salary go up in pennies. Freedom? "To have a championship team," he reminded Bill Curry, "you *must* have rules and discipline." And he bemoaned the attitude of today's player, "who wants to retire before he even reaches camp. Football is secondary in his mind. He wants the big bonus, the job, and other benefits before he hits the field."

Lou expressed the wish that the strike will be settled soon, before the sport is scarred forever. More than that, be wishes

FOOTBALL FOLLIES AND THE CIRCUS MAXIMUS

both sides could return to the day when every issue did not wind up on a conference table, across which lawyers quoted Latin to each other.

Pro football has changed since the funky fifties, of course. So has the country. Those were the days when the national anthem made you feel warm and good all over, even the part about bombs bursting in air, and a coach could tell a player to get a haircut without the American Civil Liberties Union getting into it.

A certain give-and-take existed then that is gone forever. One year, after a disappointing season, Bobby Layne insisted on taking a $2,500 cut in his next year's contract at Detroit. The Lions knew it was no stunt, no grandstand play. Nor did it embarrass the management to accommodate him.

But you can't blame Lou Rymkus for deciding that the game is no longer Everything. "Bill," he concluded his letter, sadly, "there are a lot of people in pro football, but not many pros."

IT WAS BUM'S FAULT

AUGUST 1981

Hi, I'm Tyrone Dumptruck of the Houston Oilers, and I'm here to set the record straight. People keep asking me, "Ty, how come you guys folded up in the play-offs last year like a slab of pita bread? Was it just lousy coaching, or what?"

Lissen, this isn't easy to talk about. Most of the time we don't talk about it. We just wink or nod or nudge each other with our elbows. But if you want to be a pro you got to stand up for what you believe. A fair question deserves a fair answer. I'm not gonna pass the buck.

It was Bum Phillips's fault.

All of it. Everything. Whatever went wrong last season and even our two losses this summer. The Oilers do not make a special effort to win preseason games, a tradition we got from Bum. Of course, he made an exception in our case a couple of weeks ago when we played the Saints. That's another thing about Bum. He can be sneaky.

Let's face it, under Coach Phillips the team had no discipline, and our offense was as predictable as cafeteria food. We won eleven games last year, eight of them by six points or less. How predictable can you get?

Some fans think discipline is what you do in the fourth quarter, but that can't be right because the Oilers won seven games that were not decided until the final two minutes, and everybody knows we lacked discipline.

You should have seen our team meetings. Guys would show up late, come and go without getting attacked, and talk without raising their hands. It was like a Marx Brothers movie. All we needed was a duck flying around the room.

Most NFL coaches keep a gun on the desk. If a player's attention wanders, the coach fires a warning shot through his legs. I mean, they take the game seriously.

FOOTBALL FOLLIES AND THE CIRCUS MAXIMUS

When the Oilers traveled, we were on our own, almost like grownups. Bum trusted us. We didn't even take along a bail bondsman. We were the only players in the league whose phones weren't tapped. How can you respect a coach like that?

I know, I know. People keep saying how we seemed to have fun playing for Bum. Sure, we liked him. We even pretended to like country music and chili and gumbo. Sometimes we even pretended to play real well. But all the time we knew we were not reaching our full potential because we had no discipline. No curfews. No bedchecks. Our little hearts were breaking.

Take San Angelo. *Please.* Ha, ha, a small joke. But the head coach sets the example for everybody, and Bum ran a very relaxed training camp. The whole town reflected it. The place was practically Sin City. Beer, pool, disco . . . name your action and you could find it.

San Angelo was closed this year when we reported to camp. The 7-Eleven stores only stayed open until nine. For amusement we drove out to the Wholesome Bakery on the highway and smelled the hot bread. We let our whiskers grow, went to bed early, and now we feel mean and strong.

Look, I don't want to put pressure on the new staff, but if they give us any coaching at all—I mean, if they can teach us to count to three or something—I don't see how we can lose a game. No kidding. This team is studded with talent like a ham with cloves. Always has been. Bum just didn't get it out of us. We've got character, too, and loyalty. We got a thing about loyalty.

You probably are thinking about now, "Hey, Ty, c'mon, gimme a break. The Oilers were dogmeat for ten years until Sid Gillman and Bum came along. You guys went to the play-offs the last three years, which no other team did. And each time you lost to the team that won the Super Bowl. Doesn't Bum deserve any of the credit?"

Hey, this is a football team, not a charity hospital. Are we supposed to thank him just because he made us respectable and popular? *Wake up, America.* I'm telling you the way it is. Pro football isn't pretty.

Bad-mouthing your old coach is a dirty job, but someone has to do it. I remember last season, when we lost to the Steelers and Earl Campbell only carried the ball fourteen times, some of us told the press, "If you got a horse, you got to ride him." Later, after Earl had carried the ball thirty times, we said, "You can't run the guy that much and not wear him out. And the other team knows what's coming."

At least we didn't criticize Bum behind his back. We said a lot of the same things then that we are saying now, except that we didn't use our names. If any of it sounds petty, self-serving, or ungrateful, that's tough. For three years we covered up the fact that we were getting outcoached, and it isn't easy when you keep making the play-offs.

Along with his other weaknesses, Bum had a heart as soft as rice pudding. He once let a player miss a practice without being fined so the player could attend his mother's funeral. How do you think that made the rest of us feel, the ones who had to keep practicing just because our mothers were alive? In one of his more quoted lines, he said that "all coaches like their players. The difference is, I let mine know it now, instead of when they finish playing." How can you respect a coach like that?

Bum had strange ways. He always was giving guys second chances. Where are they now, Duane Thomas, Hollywood Henderson, Tim Rossovich, Jack Tatum, and Ken Stabler, guys who would last a week or a year and then sort of disappear? For a while there the Oilers were the Bermuda Triangle of pro football.

So now you bleeding hearts know why the Oilers didn't win the Super Bowl in 1980.

As for Eddie Biles, we really believe he can take us there. He's tough and smart and we like him fine, although we reserve the right to change our mind if he gets fired.

THE HARD WORK COMES FIRST

NOVEMBER 14, 1985

NEW ORLEANS—When Bum Phillips met with his football squad the night before the game against Seattle, he gave the players some fatherly advice about life and the work ethic.

He said there were players on the Saints who were cheating their families out of four to six years of big money. They were the ones whose careers would not last ten years because they were unwilling to pay the price—the price, in this case, being hard work and self-discipline.

Bum mentioned two or three of their former teammates who were already out of the league. And he told them about Bob Young, who lasted sixteen years as an offensive lineman, who put in the kind of hours that would embarrass a Cambodian rice farmer, and who was still playing for the Oilers with a back so bad they almost needed a winch to help him sit down. "That guy," Bum said, "was stronger than mustard gas."

The talk was personal, uplifting, and only slightly out of tune with the fact that the Saints would suffer their seventh loss in ten games the next day. But Bum truly cares about his players, the way some worry about the lost and unfortunate children of the world. Such an interest can be a burden in the age of drugs and megabucks.

He ended his talk with a kind of locker-room homily: "Hard work and good times go together. But the hard work comes first." Regrettably, it is in the good-times department that the New Orleans Saints have come up short.

After Bum met with his special teams and looked at game films, I joined him in his hotel suite. It is his custom the night before a home game to cloister his players at the Hyatt Regency Hotel, connected by a walkway to the Superdome.

There was a separate dining area, and the hotel's management had sent up large bowls filled with pretzels, chips, and dips. The bar was fully stocked. Except for two half-empty diet Pepsis, nothing had been touched. Bum breezed past the spread and into the living room. Between the two of us, it took only ten minutes to figure out how to turn on the TV set.

He plopped his boots on the coffee table and settled back. Five years of not winning haven't aged or changed him in any obvious way. There is no sense of sympathy or gloom about him, only frustration. It wasn't the pressure to win that wore him down, just the not winning.

Taking on a team that had lost fifteen games, and never had won more games than it lost in any season, Bum made the Saints respectable in two years. In three he had them at .500. And midway through the fifth, he has had his fill of coaching. Where in Houston he once vowed to kick in a door, he is closing this one behind him, at sixty-two.

The Saints, under Phillips, were the victims of high expectations. It is an old malady. Give the fans an inch and they'll want a first down. His detractors will say that Bum did not draft well, his quarterbacks were either too young or too old, and he let sentiment cloud his judgment, collecting too many ex-Oilers. His friends think he had too much bad luck.

There will be time to look back later, after Bum has retired to his ten acres at Quail Valley, south of Houston. For now he says, "Luck? Let me tell you about luck. I'm lucky just to have gotten here." He rattles off his odyssey through the high-school ranks, with intermediate stops as an assistant at four colleges. How he took the head coaching job at Texas-El Paso, produced an instant winner, and quit after the school broke a promise to him. When Bill Yeoman tried to hire him for the Cougars, Bum didn't want to go, until he got his first look at the Astrodome. "That got me fired up," he says, "so I went."

Pro scouts were always coming through Houston, and dropping by the campus to visit. For the first time, Bum began to think about the NFL. Just before the 1967 season, the line coach at San Diego dropped dead. Sid Gillman began to call around the country, looking for "the best defensive coach I can find." Among those he asked for recommendations were Bear Bryant, Darrell Royal, and Frank Broyles. They gave him the same name: Bum Phillips.

When he got off the plane in San Diego, he realized he didn't know what Gillman looked like. He waited at the gate, then wandered through the terminal and back to the gate. Finally, there were just two of them left. "Are you Bum Phillips?" the other man asked. Bum said, "Yep, you must be Sid Gillman."

In one of those small miracles not uncommon to football, the following happened: Four years later, Gillman quit when the owner tried to tell him which quarterback to start. Knowing how proud his assistants were, Sid quit for them, too.

Bum went back to the colleges, where in 1974 he received another call from Gillman, summoning him to the Oilers. The next year, Gillman stepped down and handpicked Phillips to succeed him. At fifty-one, he was a rookie coach in the NFL. His last three teams would win thirty-three games and twice reach the conference finals. He had Houston thinking Super-Bowl-or-bust, not .500.

His ability as a coach often seemed to be overshadowed by his popularity as a cowboy cult figure. Long before he won a national following with the Oilers, Royal had referred to him as "an innovator whose ideas have spread across the country."

Not many know what those innovations were, and Phillips has never advertised them. One was the triple option. Not the veer that Yeoman introduced at Houston or the wishbone that Royal and Emory Bellard made famous at Texas. This was the basic triple option—the belly option. A quarterback slapped the ball against the fullback's tummy, then slid along the line a yard or two before letting go or pulling the ball back. If he kept, he had the choice of cutting upfield or throwing a pass. They were using that offense at Nederland High School in 1953.

"Actually," says honest Bum Phillips, "I didn't develop it. Our quarterback did. D. D. Perkins. He was five-feet-two and weighed 129. One day in practice he asked me, 'Do I have to give it to him if I see the tackle is going to take him?'

"I said, 'Can you *tell* if he's going to take him?' He said, 'Sure, every time.' So I said, 'Hell, no. If you can tell, just keep the ball.' And that's how it started."

One of Bum Phillips's great gifts to the science of football was that he made it seem so simple. "I never worried about getting the credit or the blame," he says. "I just wanted to make the decisions."

He has made them, big and small, without apology. When I left, Bum was alone in his room, with the pretzels and chips that would go uneaten, the wine that would go unopened, and the party that would not take place in the best party town in America.

ALOHA, OILERS!!!

AUGUST 1, 1982

On the flight home from Hawaii in that summer of 1961, Lou Rymkus, then head coach of the Houston Oilers, grabbed the intercom and spoke the words that became part of the team's legend: "Let's have no more pinching of the hostesses. If there is any pinching to be done, from now on, the coaches will do it."

It is safe to say that nothing endeared the Oilers to Honolulu quite so much as their leaving it. Why they had traveled there was never fully understood. But what they did there won't be forgotten.

When the Oilers' owner, Bud Adams, decided to send them across the blue Pacific to train for the 1961 season, the team made football history. No pro team, before or since, ever conducted its summer exercises away from the U.S. mainland. The trip was a near-disaster for the Oilers, may have cost the head coach his job, and, in truth, left Honolulu a bit frayed around the edges. But it was a public-relations triumph of sorts, considering that the adventure is still talked and written about twenty-one years later.

To put the story in perspective, you must first know a few basic truths about pro-football training camps. Coaches prefer to place them at sites away from trees, water, and neon, ideally near a monastery or next door to a Marine Corps recruit depot. There, the players are exposed to a conditioning program designed by mad scientists and Roman emperors.

When Woody Hayes was at the crest of his powers as head coach at Ohio State, he once delivered his team to California three weeks early for the Rose Bowl. Why? "When you fight in the North Atlantic, you train in the North Atlantic," he said.

Now, Woody was not suggesting that California is in the North

FOOTBALL FOLLIES AND THE CIRCUS MAXIMUS

Atlantic. He was merely reflecting a mind-set among coaches: If your team is to face Green Bay on a Sunday in December, you practice feeling cold all week.

In retrospect, Houston's decision to move its camp to Hawaii, lock, stock, and whirlpool is even more remarkable than it seemed then. The Oilers that year would play their home games at Rice Stadium, outdoors, where the late-autumn heat causes many a coach to repent his sins.

The Oilers were coming off a championship year in the maiden season of the new American Football League. Their previous training camps had been an air base outside Houston and a high-school field across the street from the stockyards. Team owner Adams meant well. What better reward than two weeks in that Pacific paradise, where at night the natives roast a pig in the sand, little flowers float in your cocktail, and they bury old quarterbacks at sea?

When Rymkus heard the news, he asked, "When a tropical moon is out, and the palm trees are swaying, and you can hear the surf crashing against the beach, and it's 10:30 and you know the bars are full of lonely schoolteachers from Iowa, how am I going to convince the players they ought to go to bed?"

It was quite simply the zaniest, zingiest summer training camp any sports team ever experienced. No example we can think of even comes in second. Old Oilers still get a twinge whenever *From Here to Eternity* pops up on the late movie. The players saw themselves as Burt Lancaster, bodysurfing on the beach with Deborah Kerr. But the coaches wanted them to look and act like Ernest Borgnine.

The expedition got off to an uneasy start when the Oilers stopped off in San Diego and lost to the Chargers, 28-14. The teams would compete again a week later in Honolulu.

It's a home game for the Oilers, and the whole scene is frantic: Rymkus is boiling—he hates to lose to Sid Gillman, the San Diego coach. A rookie has to start at left tackle because Al Jamison, a tough character, is hurt, and the Oilers are facing a problem.

The problem was named Ernie Ladd, six-feet-eight and 300 pounds, an off-season wrestler regarded around the league as a kind of mutation. Houston's quarterback, George Blanda, roomed with a center named George Belotti, a sensitive type who genuinely was worried about what Ladd was going to do to Blanda. Belotti kept saying things like: "Jeez, George, he's going to kill you. No rookie is going to stop Ladd. I mean, you're gonna get kilt."

Such words did little to build up the quarterback's confidence. "Hey," recalled Blanda, "after a while some of that stuff gets to you. Every time Ladd got near me, I unloaded the ball." He threw five interceptions and, at halftime, the Oilers trailed 39-0. Leaving the field, Hogan Wharton, a veteran guard, whispered to Blanda, "Let's sprint to the dressing room and lock the door, so Lou can't get us."

But Rymkus won the race to the locker, and, with his eyes like vulture slits, he wheeled around the room and roared, "If you sons of bleeps want to tell your grandchildren you were members of the first pro team ever to get beat 100 to nothing, you go out and play the second half just the same way you played the first half!"

The Oilers rallied to lose respectably, 45-28. Rymkus gave the lads two days off. Armed with aloha shirts, porkpie hats, and a thirst and lust that surpasseth understanding, they hit the beach. One lineman injured an ankle jumping out of a second-story hotel window—one leap ahead of the husband of the woman whose room he was sharing. Three rookies drove a rented car into a canal.

The busiest fellow in Honolulu at that time was Bobby Brown, the team trainer, whose job it was to keep the Oilers together, body and soul. It was a losing battle, but Brown tried. He is writing a book about his experiences in sports, *Two Yellows and a Blue*, and he may give the Hawaii caper an entire chapter. Brown worked for football teams in four leagues and trained the Houston Aeros in the World Hockey League. His eyes have seen the glory, and the goofiness.

The coaches and players were quartered at Hickam Field, out at Pearl Harbor, while Adams, his guests, the front-office staff, and the press stayed at a luxury hotel on the beach. Rymkus avenged himself by running up a tab at the hotel bar and signing the name of the team's general manager, Don Suman. He might have gotten away with it had he not misspelled Suman.

"Curfew was at 11 P.M.," recalls Brown, "and the players were on the streets at 11:05. The morning workouts were wild. The players looked like they had all been rode hard and put up wet. A man could get high just smelling the breath of the players in the huddle. One morning, I tried to sober up one of our tackles. He was sitting on the floor in his room with a coat hanger in his hand. He said he was trying to call his home in Houston."

The Oilers pulled themselves together to defeat Oakland, 35-17, before leaving that enchanted island. Last to board the plane was Brown, who, according to Rymkus, looked worse than the players. Big Lou shrugged his great Ukrainian shoulders and yelled toward the cockpit, "Paint a red cross on this thing, and let's find Houston!"

Rymkus did not view his team as having been caressed by lovely hula hands. The Oilers lost three and tied one of their first five games, and Rymkus, the AFL's first Coach of the Year, was fired. Quiet Wally Lemm took over. The Oilers shook the sand from their toes and won their next eleven games and a second championship.

That was the last experiment with transpacific training camps for Houston—or anyone else. Adams did toy with the idea of taking his team to Spain or Mexico City the next year.

Last month, as they have since 1978, the Oilers trained in West Texas, at San Angelo, the home of Fort Concho—John Wayne country. It is a pleasant college town, and at night, when 10:30 rolls around, you do not hear the palms swaying or the surf crashing.

THE RETURN OF THE SNAKE

AUGUST 30, 1981

Through the years, you note with pride, no team in pro football has enjoyed a more exotic history with quarterbacks than the Houston Oilers.

A week ago, new coach Eddie Biles seemed less in need of an offensive coordinator than an air traffic controller. In effect, he had three starting quarterbacks—one hurt, one retired, and one who had been fetched out of a Florida real estate office. His backup man also was listed as a wide receiver and kick returner, meaning he had yet to play a game in the NFL at three positions.

The accident that removed Gifford Nielsen from the picture caused some observers to sit down and reflect on the Meaning of Life. Here was a young artist who had waited without a whimper for three years to show he could do the job. His heart was pure, his habits impeccable. He did not smoke, drink, swear, bar-hop, or run out of the pocket. Finally, he gets his chance, and in the first five minutes of a practice game he bangs up his shoulder and is lost for a month or more.

The injustice of it all strikes you as profound. If a straight arrow like Nielsen can't get a break, what chance do the rest of us have? If you are going to wind up in a sling anyway, one might as well live like Dan Pastorini.

Houston fans tearfully blew a farewell kiss to the 1981 season. Then, as abruptly as he disappeared, the white knight rushed to their rescue. Ken Stabler gave up his promising new career as a professional tannist and left the sun-kissed shores of lower Alabama to answer his team's distress signal.

The return of the Snake pretty much reunites the cast of a year ago. Eight days before the season opener, life with the Oilers is as close to normal as life with the Oilers ever gets.

The list of quarterbacks who have carried the torch in Houston is not a long one, but it has style and balance. The line began in 1960 with the irascible George Blanda and continues now, again, with the elusive Stabler. The Oilers have not always treated their quarterbacks like royalty, but by and large they have treated them better than their coaches. Blanda held the job for seven years and Dan Pastorini for nine.

Pastorini entertained us around the clock, with his splendid arm and his daredevil lifestyle. He remains a candidate for the *Guinness Book of World Records,* having injured himself in three forms of transportation—cars, boats, and bicycles.

Pete Beathard and Charley Johnson bridged the gap between the Blanda era and an Oiler youth movement that lasted approximately ten years. The Oilers went to the play-offs once and finished .500 twice behind Beathard—numbers that began to look mighty good to them after Pete was gone.

Everyone respected Johnson, a veteran and a scholar, who earned a doctorate in chemical engineering. The Oilers didn't win with him, but they made him appreciate a good education.

Then there were the prince consorts, Jacky Lee, Don Trull, Bob Davis, and Lynn Dickey, who for one reason or another never really got a chance to establish themselves.

Still, what could be more fitting, more round or fully packed, than a tradition that stretches from Blanda to Stabler? They are out of the same bloodline, having played under Bear Bryant nineteen years apart, Blanda at Kentucky and the Snake at Alabama. In 1970, they wound up as teammates with the Oakland Raiders.

More than teammates, actually. Benchmates and soulmates. They would play golf together, and they shared space on the sideline while Daryle Lamonica started at quarterback for the Raiders. That was the year Blanda thrilled the Geritol generation, coming off the bench to win three games and tie another with his passing and kicking.

Stabler was a rookie that year, a third-stringer, a kid not much older than George's own son, and it was an effort for him not to call Blanda "Sir." Can you imagine Stabler ever being that young? With his flowing gray hair and beard, and his eyes avoiding the glare of the television lights, he looks like a biblical prophet about to accept the Ten Commandments.

Of course, appearances can be deceiving.

So far, the most impressive thing about Stabler's comeback

FOOTBALL FOLLIES AND THE CIRCUS MAXIMUS

is the fact that he didn't phone it in. When he retired, the Oilers got the news through a call from his agent. None of his teammates were contacted, and the press felt stiffed because there was no press conference, with free coffee and meatballs and other party favors. Some thought a more personal approach would have been nice. Stabler defended himself by citing the example of his old mentor. "When Blanda decided to retire," the Snake said, "he didn't tell me about it."

The fact is, Blanda never retired. In his own mind he was fired, and he went kicking and screaming into the night. The Raiders released him, at forty-nine, the third and last team to do so after the Bears and the Oilers. Blanda swore he could still play, and probably still thinks so, even though this summer he was stuffed and mounted and enshrined in the Pro Football Hall of Fame.

Several weeks before the Oilers went to camp, before it became known that he would not be there, Stabler met Lou Rymkus, the first Oiler head coach, at a charity golf tournament. Lou greeted him diplomatically. "If you were playing for me," he said, "you'd have to beat out Gifford Nielsen."

Stabler gave the old coach a long, unblinking look. "Yeah," he said, "I heard all about you from Blanda."

There was no way for certain to know the spirit in which Stabler spoke those words, but Rymkus took them as a compliment.

A QUIET GOOD-BYE FOR JOHNNY U.

JULY 28, 1974

Johnny Unitas knew he had arrived, knew he had it made, when he returned to New York two weeks after quarterbacking Baltimore to a monumental victory over the Giants in the title game of 1958. The Colts had won in sudden death, in what was to become The Greatest Game Ever Told.

He and his wife wandered one night into a swank eatery, the Harwyn Club, and the headwaiter recognized him, the hot new celebrity in town. "Right this way, Mr. Unitas," he sang out. They were led to a corner table, the most prominent in the joint. It was at that very table, the headwaiter confided, proudly, that Eddie Fisher and Liz Taylor had their rendezvous, the night before Eddie flew home to Hollywood to tell Debbie Reynolds he wanted a divorce.

It was not your ordinary table. It wasn't your ordinary decade, either. But Johnny Unitas was right for the times, and for pro football, which had begun to take off.

The trail that ended the other day with the retirement of Johnny U., at forty-one, had begun nineteen years ago. The year was 1955 and the times were promising. The Cold War had eased, yielding to something called the "Geneva Spirit." Ike was just what the country needed, a president who didn't meddle in the affairs of government. A new sound called rock 'n'roll had triumphed over pop music: The nation's #1 song was Bill Haley's "Rock Around the Clock," followed by—you may not believe this—"The Ballad of Davy Crockett." Book buyers were gabbing about Herman Wouk's new novel, *Marjorie Morningstar,* the plot of which we wish we had time to explain.

And in Montgomery, Alabama, a weary Negro seamstress defied a local ordinance and refused to give up her bus seat to a white

FOOTBALL FOLLIES AND THE CIRCUS MAXIMUS

man, casually touching off a social and civil revolution that was to change the country forever.

That year Johnny Unitas was fresh out of college, married, soon to have a family, living with his in-laws. He was a rookie quarterback drafted by the Pittsburgh Steelers, signed to a contract that would have paid him the sum of $5,500 if he had made the team, which he didn't. The coach, Walt Kieseling, gave no real indication that he ever knew Unitas was in camp. If anyone else did, it was possibly the result of the one puff of publicity that fell his way. A photographer, needing a player who wasn't busy, grabbed the rookie to pose with a Chinese nun, to whom he demonstrated the correct passing grip.

Now, it is a scientific fact that no deskman worthy of the name can resist a photograph of a Chinese nun looking at a football. And so the picture of Johnny Unitas appeared the next day in newspapers all over America. That was nearly the high point of a very brief career. A few days later, the Steelers cut him. He put their bus fare in his pocket and hitchhiked home.

That winter he took a job on a construction gang, as a pile driver, and on Thursday nights he played quarterback for a local semipro team called the Bloomfield Rams, in the Greater Pittsburgh League. It was not exactly the NFL. It was not even the University of Louisville, where Unitas had spent his college time, often hurt, always outmanned, but making a losing team better than it was.

The Rams performed on a field with no grass. The players had to get out and sprinkle it with oil before every game to keep the dust down. They never played before crowds larger than a few hundred, but Unitas was paid his salary, $6 a game, empty stands or no. After each game Johnny collected his six bucks, in cash, in the basement of a dairy on Liberty Avenue. He would take the payday home and hand it over to his wife.

In the light of later and historic events, that experience seems the height of irony. But it was never a fit subject for humor to John Unitas, and it pained him whenever someone failed to understand what the money represented. "I was making $125 a week on my construction job," he said, "so we weren't starving. But what I needed was the chance to prove that I could play football. The $6 that I gave to Dorothy every week was important, not because I had earned it but because I had earned it playing football."

FOOTBALL FOLLIES AND THE CIRCUS MAXIMUS

The rest is the stuff of legend. An anonymous letter from a fan—his coach, Weeb Ewbank, always accused Unitas of writing it himself—led to a trial with the Colts. He would carry them to two championships, and go on to become the classic quarterback of the 1960s. He could do what the great ones always did: race the clock, and bring his team from behind.

But he was much more than that. He may have been pro football's Last Hero. We have plenty of superstars, of course. Television and big money make them easy to find. But there are not many heroes left, and that is what is poignant about the leavetaking of Johnny U.

SUPER MEMORIES FROM SUPER BOWLS

JANUARY 25, 1981

Super Bowl moments to remember, while pondering this question: If Dan Pastorini is Oakland's forgotten man, why is he getting more publicity than Jim Plunkett?

Best Performance by a Player With a Hangover. Max McGee, of the Green Bay Packers, who did not expect to play and did his celebrating the night *before* the first Super Bowl. Whereupon McGee came off the bench to catch seven passes from Bart Starr, including two for touchdowns, as the Pack wrecked Kansas City 35-10. (Of the members of this year's cast, the inheritor of the McGee tradition seems to be Oakland's John Matuszak, another graduate of the Errol Flynn School of Social Development and the only player on either side known to have been fined for breaking curfew.)

Best Reprisal. Against Fred Williamson, the Kansas City cornerback and a self-described karate expert, who had boasted all week that he had a secret weapon, a blow he called "The Hammer." In the fourth quarter, the Packers ran a sweep to Williamson's side, and when the play ended, poor Fred was carried off the field.

Best Putdown after a Reprisal. Asked why it took his team so long to take care of Williamson, Green Bay Coach Vince Lombardi replied, "He was never close enough to a play until then."

Biggest Upset and Most Meaningful Game. What else? The New York Jets' ambush of Baltimore in 1969, giving the outlaw

FOOTBALL FOLLIES AND THE CIRCUS MAXIMUS

AFL a respectability it had never had, and fulfilling the prophecy of Broadway Joe Namath. The Jets were a nineteen-point underdog but never believed it. As Coach Weeb Ewbank ran the film of the Colts' 34-0 slaughter of a good Cleveland team, Pete Lammons cried out, "Stop showing us those movies, Weeb. We're getting overconfident." There was an eerie silence among NFL loyalists, as the Colts blew early scoring chances and the Jets hacked out a 16-0 lead.

Best Answer to a Hypothetical Question. Asked if the game might have turned out differently if the Colts' Earl Morrall had not overlooked a wide-open Jimmy Orr in the end zone in the first half, Joe Namath replied, "If a frog had wings, it wouldn't bump its ass."

Most Touching Reminiscence. Colt kicker Lou Michaels, on picture day in 1969, talking about facing his brother Walt, then the defensive coach of the Jets. Tears trickled down Lou's cheeks as he recalled their home in Swoyersville, Pennsylvania, and their early life. Explained his teammate, Jimmy Orr, "If you were out drinking vodka until 6 A.M. and there was a stiff wind blowing across your face, you'd be crying, too."

Most Poignant Moment. When Ewbank, watching his Jets upset his former team, the Colts, looked across the field in the fading seconds and yelled, absentmindedly, at the quarterback he had not coached in five years, Johnny Unitas: "No interceptions now, John."

Weakest Psychological Ploy by a Coach. Minnesota's Bud Grant complained that his team's practice facilities were so poor in Houston that the Vikings had to hang their clothes on a nail, and pigeons were nesting in the showers. In view of Minnesota's one-sided loss to Miami that year, the pigeons deserved a separate locker room.

Funniest Interview With a Coach. Portly Weeb Ewbank, explaining how he kept his New York Jets loose by telling them dirty jokes, then stopping in the middle of one to ask the waitresses to leave the room.

Funniest Unintentional Line by a Coach. Tom Landry, telling reporters why he broke with the usual practice and allowed the players' wives to share their husbands' rooms the week of Super Bowl X: "Everyone likes a change now and then."

Weirdest Interview With a Player. Duane Thomas of Dallas, in 1971, his rookie year, when he was still talking, sort of, to the press. He was discovered one morning sitting on the beach at Fort Lauderdale, his playbook in his lap. "I'm thinking about what's over there," he answered a question, nodding toward the Atlantic Ocean. "I was thinking about New Zealand." Now, New Zealand is not exactly on the other side of the Atlantic, but never mind. Added Thomas, "Steve Kiner [then his roommate] said it was a good place to retire." The press did a double take. Retire? But you're just a rookie. "That's the best time to think about it," said Thomas.

Worst Play Suggestion from a U.S. President. Richard Nixon revealed that he had called Miami Coach Don Shula after the play-offs and advised him to throw the down-and-in pass to Paul Warfield against Dallas in Super Bowl VI. "That gave the Cowboys two weeks to prepare for that pass," said Warfield after Miami had lost 24-3. "They made sure that under no circumstances could we complete it."

Most Comic Play. With the Dolphins leading Washington 14-0 in the final two minutes of Super Bowl VII, Garo Yepremian had the misfortune to get a field-goal attempt blocked. Even worse, the ball bounced back to him. He cocked his arm to pass and, oops, the ball slipped off his fingers. Then he swung at it as if he were playing badminton, batting it into the arms of Mike Bass, who raced forty-nine yards for the only Washington touchdown. After the game, Shula ordered his son to quit playing catch with Garo on the sidelines at practice.

Most Exciting Finish. Baltimore 16, Dallas 13, on rookie Jim O'Brien's thirty-two-yard field goal with five seconds on the clock. O'Brien later revealed that he had dreamed the week before about making the winning kick. Labeled the "Blunder Bowl," the game featured four lost fumbles, six interceptions, and a blocked extra point. Had that 1971 struggle gone into overtime, said one wit, the extra period would have been called "Lingering Death."

Wildest Halftime Show. The 1970 classic at New Orleans. The wind blew two guys in a hot-air balloon into the stands, scattering a girls' drill team. A steamboat float got stuck in the mud. While a cast of hundreds reenacted the Battle of New Orleans, a cannon went off and a horse carrying Andrew Jackson bolted out of the stadium. They have not been seen since.

Dullest Game. Any of the four lost by Minnesota.

Most Interesting Private Conversation During a Game. Before

FOOTBALL FOLLIES AND THE CIRCUS MAXIMUS

Super Bowl I, before it was even known as the Super Bowl, Jerry Mays, the Kansas City defensive end, admitted to a certain admiration for Forrest Gregg, the veteran Green Bay tackle, and, like Mays, a graduate of SMU. At one point in the game, the Packers reached the Chiefs' two-yard line. As the Packer linemen settled into their stance, Jerry Kramer looked across the scrimmage and turned to Gregg. "I'll get Number 58," said Kramer, "and you take care of the guy whose hero you are." And they did.

And that, as Oakland and Philadelphia ought to know, is what the Super Bowl is all about.

SUPER BOWL SHOWTIME

JANUARY 29, 1984

Hi. Thank you for being here. Aren't you nice. We have a great lineup, beginning with our postgame show, featuring a follow-up, recap, and review of however many exciting Super Bowl stories your heart can stand. Let's get right to it.

Speaking for myself and each viewer, those involved in the Super Bowl coverage were an inspiration to all of us and especially to each other. These are just a few of the stories coming your way: an interview with the author of a new book based on a fatty-acids diet; a preview of what you can expect for Super Bowl XIX, a TV headset that plugs right into your eyes; and a selection of swear words from Lyle Alzado, a giant among Goliaths. He paid his dues. He did it until he got it right. He can hit any ball this town can throw. Don't touch that dial.

Coming up next: Jimmy the Greek's sportcoat was made possible by a grant from Exxon. A twenty-year dream came true for Milo Stooksberry when, while watching a pregame pep rally in the lobby of the Hyatt Regency, he spotted a fan who owed him money. On "Full Figured Gals," Jane Russell interviews the Dallas Cowboy cheerleaders. We'll be right back as soon as we return.

What's hot, what's not. Would you like to have as much sex as you could get? One woman did when she accidentally walked into the locker room of the Tampa Bay Bandits. She's here to tell her story after this word, and a few more. It's 10 o'clock. Do you know where you are?

Stay tuned for "Wide World of Whatever is Going On," which will include segments on a man who juggles midgets; how to lift weights with your earlobes; and a group of women who like to dress up like Dwight D. Eisenhower. Irv Cross will moderate a panel discussion with eight writers who can recite from memory the entire menu for the halftime lunch at the Super Bowl, but can't remember the score of the game. Watch the monitor.

FOOTBALL FOLLIES AND THE CIRCUS MAXIMUS

Don't miss "Firing Line," "Nightline," "Sportsline," "Dateline," and "Lineline." Later in the show, Brent will interview a washed-up baseball chicken, and Charlsie files a think piece on four Los Angeles couples who spend their entire lives in a Jacuzzi, bathing for love and watching pro football on TV.

John Madden does a guest shot on "Fantasy Island" and realizes his lifelong fantasy—to be Gilligan. Coming up: an instant analysis, an answer to it, and a rerun.

Our viewer-response poll indicates that everyone in the country can identify the Smurfs, the Hogs, the Fun Bunch, and the Pearl Harbor crew, but nobody can name two leading American physicists. Kids today can't memorize two lines of poetry, but most of them know by heart the words to 200 commercials. Does it matter to you that Barry Manilow decided to lip-synch the national anthem, which is the musical equivalent of signaling for a fair catch?

A tip on next year's Super Bowl: Never watch the game in a bar where they show the picture on the back of the bartender's neck. Also, the Raiders will star in a new television show that combines the best elements of psychology and soap opera. The show will be called "The Jung and the Restless." Roll the tape.

Well, let's face it, we live in a torn and divided and befuddled country. Half the people are suffering from pro-football burnout, tired and depressed and praying that they never see another wide receiver split at the top of the screen. They would like to leave a wake-up call with the operator for whenever the United States Football League season ends. The other half are those with a chill in their hearts, wondering how they can possibly fill the gap of nearly a month that still exists between the Super Bowl and the first USFL game.

Someday we must deal with these serious questions: Is there a shortage of football in this country? Does television devote too little time to this activity? If China had discovered football before us, would Fu Manchu have bothered to invent the opium den?

We now resume our regular programming schedule, already in progress. The Super Bowl post-postgame show has been brought to you with a lot of money and promotional considerations, which we prefer to a sharp stick in the eye. More than ever the one to watch, when you're watching only one.

BIGGEST OF THE BIG

JANUARY 26, 1986

NEW ORLEANS—Bigness is what the Super Bowl is all about. Bigness, as in William Perry, a dainty, elephantine fellow at 308 pounds.

Bigness, as in a half-ton of shrimp, chicken, and spareribs to feed a party of 2,000 media and officials.

Bigness, as in the game that has so much, NBC had to donate a vacant minute of television time to the nation's health, sixty seconds of silence in a Niagara of noise and dazzle.

And bigness, as in: If you have to ask how much a ticket costs, you can't afford one. It is somewhere between ordering a yacht and getting your car repaired. You no longer simply buy a ticket. You ask for an estimate. (Face value is $75. The street price is out there where the meter doesn't register.)

A stockbroker who flew in from New York needed four tickets for an important client. A friend ran across a scalper willing to part with a set for $2,000, or $500 apiece. The friend phoned the broker to see if he wanted to take advantage of this bargain. Possibly he could sell his IBM shares to meet the tab. The call went unanswered, but when the friend turned around, the tickets were sold.

No ticket in memory has been hotter than the one featuring the Chicago Bears and the New England Patriots, in this game to decide all earthly matters. The crowds are so hyper, the teams so attractive, that even this most jaded and seductive of cities has pulled out all the stops.

One of the pregame parties was held at Antoine's, in the French Quarter, in a salon called The Japanese Room. And therein lies a story. Business has been so good that the room was recently restored to its original decor and reopened, after having been closed for forty-four years. The owners had shut it down on December 7, 1941, the day the Japanese attacked Pearl Harbor.

In New Orleans, they know how to hold a grudge.

FOOTBALL FOLLIES AND THE CIRCUS MAXIMUS

Nothing quite this dramatic or promising has grown out of the early taunts and threats between the Bears and the Patriots. And the smart money is overwhelmingly on the side of a Chicago victory, in a breeze if not a shuffle.

It may come as a surprise to many of those attending Super Bowl XX, but the Chicago Bears are not a solo act. It only seems that way. The Bears have a quarterback, Jim McMahon, who is taking acupuncture treatments in an area where some people think his brains are. They have a defensive tackle, Perry, who has run for two touchdowns and caught a pass for another. They have Walter Payton, tradition, and their own music video.

In the face of this array, the Patriots are supported by members of the immediate family, their neighbors, and those who by instinct root for the underdog, the oppressed, the child abandoned.

Both are teams new to the Super Bowl, with young and refreshing coaches. Chicago's Mike Ditka is so emotional that by the end of a game he looks as though he is trying to strangle himself with his own necktie. Raymond Berry is that rare animal, the taciturn Texan.

If the Bears were not here, people would be celebrating the greatness of John Hannah and asking Mosi Tatupu what they do for fun in Samoa. But the Bears are here.

The tactical side of the game has drawn only scant attention, mainly because it seems to offer little hope for those who favor the underdog. The Patriots lead with their chin. They are a running team, featuring Craig James and Tony Collins. Trying to run on the Bears is like trying to sneak a sunrise past a rooster. The Bears didn't allow a touchdown to seven opponents and shut out two more in the play-offs. Tony Eason is not a picture passer, but the Patriots must give him time to throw, or the Bears will feed their remains to the alligators in the nearest bayou. If you like the Patriots, you can get ten points and a limo will meet you at the airport.

Like every other Super Bowl, this has been a week of wretched excess, of gluttony and goony humor. Next to buying a ticket or catching a taxi, the biggest topic among tourists was The Great Slut Controversy. The writers kept wondering what McMahon would do next. If he wasn't getting a needle in his aching bottom, or leading a parade through the French Quarter, or lowering his drawers at the drop of a helicopter, what was left?

The answer turned out to be nothing, and to fill the void a local TV sportscaster aired a report, unchecked and untrue, that McMahon had referred to the natives as "stupid" and the women as "sluts." Outrage was high, until the station apologized and the announcer was suspended and the innocence of McMahon was established. The virtue of their women isn't taken lightly in New Orleans, and the effect of this kind of loose talk on Bourbon Street was hard to calculate. Business might have doubled.

No one can be quite sure at what point the machinery leaves the control of the writers and broadcasters and takes on a life of its own. It is as if Rod Serling were the host, and the knobs and dials on the TV set no longer respond to your touch.

No matter what antics or color or conflict writers imagine, Jim McMahon and the Bears have imagined it better. Chicago won fifteen out of sixteen games, including a 20-7 victory over New England. As the Patriots straggled into the locker room, their quarterback coach, Les Steckel, told reporters, "We just got beat by the best defense in the history of the NFL."

Says Steckel now, "There were some snickers in the room when I said that, but no one is laughing now."

And this would appear to be New England's problem: How do you beat what may be the best defense the game has known? For openers, the Patriots are counting on the fact that their lineup that day did not include the injured John Hannah, Irving Fryar, and Stanley Morgan. Beyond that, they are letting the Bears do the talking . . . which may be their best hope of all.

"The Bears have had a lot to say," noted Gil Brandt, the Dallas Cowboys' personnel director. "When you have everything going your way, that can come back to haunt you."

The Bears are so confident, so full of themselves, that they do not think of the outcome in terms of winning or losing. They think about the Patriots not scoring on them. In truth, they act as if the game has been played.

"They can say what they want," noted Ronnie Lippett, the New England cornerback. "There's going to be a lot of hitting and the team that hits best will win. A good hit will shut up a big mouth."

And there is the point. Enough has been said. Let the hitting begin.

NEW ORLEANS IDEAL FOR RAIDERS

JANUARY 18, 1981

A survivor's guide to the cosmic bowl.

This is the week we find out how strong America really is. If we can survive in the same week a presidential inauguration and the fifteenth (XVth) Super Bowl, we will have nothing to fear but inflation, unemployment, high interest rates, an oil embargo, and holding calls in crucial situations.

Let us say straight out that Oakland will conquer Philadelphia, mainly because New Orleans is Al Davis's kind of town. It is a great town to get spooked in, what with all those cemeteries above ground, and exotic shops featuring voodoo masks and vials of dragon's blood, incense, stuffed bats, tarantulas and toads, and hex-removing sprays (which come in aerosol cans).

Breathlessly, the 2,000 or so newspeople on hand wait for the big story to break, as it did eleven years ago when Len Dawson, accused falsely of consorting with gamblers, led Kansas City to a jolting upset of the Minnesota Vikings. For dramatic content, that story has not been matched in Super Bowl legend. What passes for a big story now is when one of the players drives his moped up a utility-pole guy wire on his way home from the big pregame party at Shorty's Barbecue.

The Raiders, that rowdy gang of renegades, coached by the stoic Tom Flores but masterminded by the sinister Davis, are expected to observe a strict curfew this week. To quote an old French saying, you can't soar with the Eagles if you howl with the Owls.

Otherwise, the usual Super Bowl hoopla has already begun. The local gendarmes have warned tourists against an influx of shady ladies, confidence men, pigeon-drop artists, and NFL owners trying to scalp their tickets for five times the going rate.

FOOTBALL FOLLIES AND THE CIRCUS MAXIMUS

There appears to be no truth to the rumor that the commissioner was victimized by a family of gypsies, who blacktopped his hotel room with inferior materials.

All fans are urged to get off the streets around sunset, which is easy to do in New Orleans, if you allow yourself to be shoved by the milling throngs into the nearest topless and bottomless bar.

Insider notes: Jimmy the Greek has established Philadelphia as a three-point favorite, but privately likes Oakland to win on the basis of execution, persecution, and five intangible factors. Nobody knows what that means, which is how Jimmy stays in business.

Society note: The pregame ceremonies will open with the whistling of the national anthem by a graduate of the Ted Weems School for Famous Whistlers. Compulsory prayer will follow.

The Super Bowl has so completely captured the public consciousness, has become such an institution, that you almost expect to see signs posted saying that all federal regulations have been suspended and, for this one day only, fans inside the stadium can purchase beer, Wild Turkey, and legal drugs.

New Orleans is a town that clings to its traditions like cobwebs. Somehow it doesn't seem quite fitting for the Raiders and the Eagles to be playing in the enormous and futuristic Superdome. They are tough and street-smart teams, and a better location would be the waterfront. One grows nostalgic for the now-vanished Tulane Stadium, which in its later years was often compared favorably to the Black Hole of Calcutta. At Super Bowl IX, fans of the female persuasion complained that the washroom floors were submerged under three inches of water, making them wish on every NFL owner broken pipes at midnight, when the tab is double.

Nevertheless, those who plan on attending the Super Bowl cannot fail to enjoy themselves, unless they hibernate in their rooms and only go to the game. New Orleans is a party town, a blend of French and Spanish colonial, and magnolia and mint juleps.

It is the home of the best black and white music in America, from riverboat to rock. It is where the blues were born, the home of Al Hirt and Pete Fountain and Preservation Hall, where the white-haired survivors of the funeral marching bands still play the music the way it was.

FOOTBALL FOLLIES AND THE CIRCUS MAXIMUS

You should know that Bourbon Street slows down around four in the morning; after that, there are only the sad-eyed and solitary drinkers and some of the fun has drained away. This is the hour for Morning Call, the famous old coffee-and-cruller house down at the French Market.

Comes daytime, and Bourbon Street and the French Quarter are transformed. When the lights go out and the sun comes up, you can appreciate the graceful lines of an ageless architecture—if you can get your eyelids to open. The balconies provide high, open spaces to catch the breeze from the Mississippi; the streets are made narrow for shade. The history begins to come through, too. Every street and almost every building in the ten-square-block area of the Quarter has its own history. The Custom House was once a Confederate prison. The names of the buildings and streets have their own appeal: Madam John's Legacy; the Fencing Masters' Homes; Congo Square, where slaves once did voodoo dances; and the house on Royal Street where Antoine Peychaud invented that priceless gift to humanity, the cocktail.

In the light of day you can see clearly the Old Absinthe House, once a tavern where Andrew Jackson is said to have planned the defense of New Orleans in 1815. Before that it was supposedly the haunt of the pirate brothers, Pierre and Jean Lafitte.

So doesn't it figure? In a town that once celebrated and entertained the notorious buccaneers of another time, a football team in black and silver, known as the Raiders, ought to feel very much at home.

Off the Field

DIAGNOSING SICKER AND SICKER SWC

MARCH 24, 1987

Doctor, Doctor, help me, please, with this problem I have. I am becoming a Southwest Conference scandal junkie. To each day's bulletin, I look forward with the same helpless amazement as people awaiting Marvin Zindler's rat, roach, and slime report.

What are we to think, Doctor, of the newest allegations at SMU, that other students took exams for football players and some coeds were paid to "entertain" high-school recruits? I mean, is this a case for Dr. Ruth, or what?

Of course, we both know that there is no such person. Dr. Ruth is actually Robert Blake, the actor who played Baretta, wearing a blonde wig.

Now, where was I? Just love your couch, Doctor. Is there room here for the entire Southwest Conference, not including Rice and possibly Arkansas? Heaven only knows what goes on in those hills.

You asked about my childhood. Yes, I remember when coeds were asked to entertain football players, it meant baking fudge brownies and playing the piano in the lobby of the sorority house. Then everybody fell in love and got married.

Anyway, Doc, I was still trying to feed all the charges against SMU into our computer—we have only a 750,000-word memory, Doc—and had just gotten through the part about cash payments, cars, free apartments, bonuses, monthly allowances, surrogate exam-takers, complimentary sexual favors, and putting on airs . . . when guess what?

Out of the blue, or a little to the left of there, the NCAA announced it was investigating the University of Texas for sixty-

OFF THE FIELD

two rules violations in nineteen categories. Now we do not wish to suggest that this news touched off a wave of howling and celebrating in outposts around the state, or that other schools would revel in another's discomfort.

That's all right, Doc, let me help you off the floor. Went to SMU, did you? Well, sir, it would be like walking into Oral Roberts' prayer tower and catching him glued to the Playboy Channel.

If any program was considered untouchable over the years, it has been Texas. And, in many ways, the Longhorns have been above the usual trespasses of their neighbors. For one thing, Texas did not have to cheat. As the largest and most prestigious university in the state, Texas usually had its pick of the bluest chippers. If a Texas ex gave a kid a suit or a hundred-dollar bill or anything larger than a breadbox, it was for the sheer joy of giving.

At least, this has been an article of faith within the conference. True, there was a bit of a flap a few years ago when it turned out that dozens of Texas players had been paid for jobs that did not exist at the state capital. At the time, the Texas faculty rep was the president of the NCAA, and the matter was written off as a bookkeeping error.

It was impossible to figure out how much money actually went to the players. Some were paid for not working two days a week, and some were paid for not working five days a week. But the Longhorns wound up with a reprimand, which is as serious a penalty as the school ever suffered.

Now SMU, Doctor, is more like your hardened repeat offender. The Mustangs were out on parole when they got busted the last time, which resulted in the Ponies getting strung up by the tail. They have been banned from football in 1987, and will compete—if at all—on a limited basis in 1988 and 1989.

So what a lot of us fans are asking, Doc, is whether there is any hope that this torture will ever end. My mother wants to ship chicken soup to all the athletic departments.

Seriously, Texas stood for the best and the cleanest in the conference, and now we have almost no illusions left. We are told the monies involved are "minor." But virtually every charge listed against Texas has gotten another school placed on probation in the past.

Oh, maybe not scalping tickets. That never caused a jury to do much more than giggle. But the complaints range from cash to free rent, wheels, and airfare, all of which sounds vaguely familiar. And it remains to be seen whether the Longhorns were getting free brownies from the girls in the band.

Tell us the truth, Doctor, we can take it. Or could you at least give us a Latin name to describe whatever condition the Southwest Conference is in?

THE GREEK'S COMEBACK ODDS

JANUARY 31, 1988

SAN DIEGO—The most talked-about figure at the Super Bowl, after Doug Williams, John Elway, and Dexter Manley, is watching this one from the fringe.

Jimmy ("The Greek") Snyder isn't in hiding, but he isn't throwing any parties, either. Nor is he elaborating on his recent social theories or how the thigh bone connects to the the backbone.

Arriving quietly late in the week, The Greek checked into a hotel a few blocks from the Marriott, where the media armies are headquartered. In other years, this would have been a week of fun and high profile for him—mingling with the NFL brass, entertaining friends, picking a winner, offering an opinion to anyone who asked and to some who did not.

This week, and for an undetermined time to come, Snyder is simply trying to live down the unfortunate remarks that led to his firing as a TV analyst for CBS.

His friends describe him as bewildered by the swiftness of events and stricken to find himself at the center of another debate on racism in America.

"I never tried to hurt anyone in my life," he said. "I've gotten into jams before and come back from them, but this is different."

The plaintive note in Snyder's voice leaves a great deal unsaid. When he was ten, his mother and an aunt were murdered by his uncle, a war hero who went berserk.

Two of his children died of cystic fibrosis, a disease he has helped raise millions of dollars to fight.

Gangsters once rolled him inside a carpet, threatened to shoot him and drop his body in the river. Snyder talked his way out of it.

He was convicted in 1963 of transmitting betting information across a state line and pardoned eleven years later by President Ford. He had quoted odds over the telephone to a gambler in Salt Lake City and learned later that the FBI was tapping the gambler's line. He paid a fine, was on probation for a year or two, and lost the legal bookmaking parlor he ran in Las Vegas.

Snyder doesn't talk about those things, but he included them once in a book I helped him write. He would rather tell the colorful, less serious stories he collected along the way, such as the last time he ever placed a bet with a bookie, an old-timer in Vegas named Doc Connick.

Four horses came through for him, and he asked Doc to hold his winnings, $13,000, until he returned from a trip. A few days later, a friend reached him in Chicago. "Greek," he said, "I got good news and bad news. Which do you want first?"

"Give me the good news first," he said.

"It wasn't you."

"What the hell is the bad news?"

"Doc Connick just dropped dead."

Jimmy Snyder traveled in circles where a man made his own luck. He retired from gambling, more or less, in the 1960s. But with his sports connections around the country, he promoted himself into a mystique and became America's best-known oddsmaker, the Wizard of Odds.

Eventually he landed on network television, not a position even his well-wishers would have forecast for him. He had found a way to make his opinions pay off—until he expressed a couple that were out in left field.

He tried to explain the success of blacks in sports by saying they were bred for size and strength in the days of slavery. You didn't know whether to laugh or cry at his statement that blacks have "large thighs that run up into their backs." One black athlete asked, "Where did Jimmy the Greek take his anatomy class?"

No one laughed when Snyder said that if pro football teams start hiring blacks as head coaches, "There's not going to be anything left for white people."

There was no way to defend his words. And Snyder didn't try. Those who know him wondered, How could a fellow who has been on television for twelve years get himself in such a dumb fix? It was his need to be the oracle, and not out of bigotry. In the 1950s, when a lot of teams were still all-white, Jimmy helped send twenty or more black football players to college.

Now he is the object of jokes on the Carson and Letterman shows.

Adversity? Snyder has known some. But he is seventy now, with a couple of clogged arteries that landed him in a hospital last week. CBS walked around him as though he were a swamp.

Can he come back? This is one time not even Jimmy the Greek can quote the odds.

WAIST-DEEP IN DISHONESTY

JUNE 30, 1987

One of President Reagan's favorite stories is about twin brothers whose personalities were totally opposite.

One was an optimist, the other a pessimist. A psychologist decided to test them, and filling a barn with manure, he announced there was a present inside for each.

The pessimist went in first and moments later came flying out in tears. Then the optimist entered—and stayed. A half hour later, the doctor threw open the door to find the little boy shoveling his way through the mound of manure. Not even pausing from his efforts, he looked up and vowed, "I know there must be a pony in here somewhere."

Whatever you imagine is piled almost to the ceiling in the athletic offices at SMU or even into the governor's mansion in Austin, this much is beyond argument: You know there is a Pony in there somewhere.

If a forty-eight-page report issued by the Methodist bishops is to be believed, Bill Clements allowed, approved, helped to maintain, covered up, and lied about systematic cash payments to SMU athletes. He did so in his capacity as chairman of the Board of Regents while campaigning for the highest office in the state.

You recall the firing of Bobby Collins, the SMU coach, and the retirement of Houston's Bill Yeoman after months of public debate, bordering on a tug-of-war for his soul. Elsewhere across the country, coaches whose programs ran afoul of the rules were tossed out like dishwater.

The question that confronts us now is this: Should the governor of a state be held to standards at least as high as those of a football coach? Should we be as outraged if our political leaders fail or disappoint us as we are when an admired coach is accused of going beyond the going rate for a halfback?

OFF THE FIELD

And the answer, obviously, is naahhh. It is not that we expect so much of a moral example from our coaches but that we expect so little from our governor.

A motion has been made in the state legislature to have Clements impeached, whereupon the people of Texas yawned, buffed their nails and turned to the comics. The news media was pretty much unable to rouse the passion, the sense of betrayal, that greeted the reports that Bill Yeoman had slipped a kid 300 bucks to get his teeth fixed.

The bishops' report has been largely ignored. The numbers are what grabbed us: $400,000 a year in a slush fund that covered payments to players; $800,000 in severance pay to ensure the silence of three former athletic-department members.

Behind the numbers, there are incredible glimpses of a program gone amok. It is part *Back to School* with Rodney Dangerfield and part *The Untouchables* with Robert De Niro. Here is Sherwood Blount, fingered as the most serious offender among the SMU boosters, telling the bishops that the NCAA investigators "are a bunch of Communists."

And this is what happens when arrogance meets ignorance: Two players broke into the desk of an assistant athletic director and stole the monthly payroll for the team. The players refused to return the money, judging correctly that no one would expose them. One rip-off begets another. Quietly, a booster replaced the missing funds.

Confusion rules in sports today. We must conserve our anger, our piety, knowing that today's headline may be obliterated by tomorrow's.

Billy Martin helped underscore the problem when he took a shot at Jesse Jackson, who had urged the lords of baseball to move more swiftly on hiring black managers and executives. Billy, who has never known prejudice, declared hotly that the reverend was wrong. "He ought to stick to religion," Martin said, "and keep politics out of sports."

Of course, he could as easily have meant that Jackson should stick to politics and keep religion out of sports. Or he might have advised Bill Clements to stick with politics and keep business out of football.

It is all mighty confusing. We only know for sure that there must be a pony in there somewhere.

SYMPATHY BECOMES SCARCE

MARCH 16, 1986

You try to get a fix—no pun intended—on the career of John Lucas, past, present, future. It is like trying to lift a bale of hay. No handles. It comes apart in your hands.

Simply put, the tragedy of John Lucas is this: There was nothing in his life—not his family, his profession, his teammates, his reputation, not even money—that he held so dear he could not give them up for the moment of pleasure he enjoyed from drugs.

Now he is finished forever as a member of the Houston Rockets and possibly as a big-league basketball player, although the latter is far from certain. There are always teams so desperate to win they will take another chance on a confessed or convicted drug addict.

There may be a market for a player, like Lucas, who is capable of giving them right at sixteen points and nine assists a game.

In time, we lose track of the chances... the Warriors, the Bullets, the Rockets twice. Is there really any reason to keep score? The truth is, no matter what happens to him in that clinic in California, we know now that Lucas can't be saved—by anyone or anything but John Lucas.

And no matter how saddened you feel, or how angry, or how hard we draw the line, punishment won't work, either. You can ban the John Lucases—or all the other drug offenders in all the other sports—for life, and what you will get is a broke junkie instead of a rich junkie.

But the point now is not to save John Lucas. The point is to keep the next one from getting started, from picking up the cocaine habit, from shoving tomorrow up their noses.

Every day, with each pathetic new disclosure, people wonder

OFF THE FIELD

where it will end. Micheal Ray Richardson is in seclusion, Lucas is in rehab, Mercury Morris is in prison, and Big Daddy Lipscomb is still dead. Yeah. What if it *doesn't* end?

If a bright, attractive, talented, savvy fellow like John Lucas can't figure it out, what does it take? Did any athlete ever hit Houston with a bigger future than the one we quickly dubbed "Cool Hand Luke?" He was no reject, no dropout, but the product of a stable home, the son of two educators, good enough at tennis to play the game for a living. There was nothing to dislike about John Lucas.

There still wasn't, even after he turned to drugs. The only change was in the pattern of his behavior. He became less reliable. In the Bay Area and in Washington, he missed buses and planes and games. In Houston, the second time around, it only took a missed practice to set off the alarms. His drug test was positive and he was gone.

But no one knew, from the way Lucas performed, that he had slipped. He was the leader of the team, playing some of the best basketball of his career. Until the minute the procedures were put in motion that ended his season here, Lucas was as much a role model for kids as anyone else on the team.

If you could make it illegal for athletes to be role models, it might be possible to overlook the drug crisis that exists in sports today—except for one thing. The use of drugs is a crime. We should not be confused about this point, simply because most athletes do not go to jail or lose their freedom, and only rarely their jobs.

The indictment of Tulane basketball players for fixing games was the result of their involvement in drugs. And this is where it gets hairy. Drug deals start with people who are criminals. When a jock has a chemical dependence, the risk of a game being rigged is increased because you are doing business with that element of society.

Remember this when Don Fehr, the head of the baseball players' union, and some of his members, speak so forcefully about individual rights. No one who believes in a system of law wants to see those rights trampled. But recently Fehr claimed that drugs are less important than the issue of the owners trying to roll back salaries. This is more than stupidity and arrogance. It is, under the circumstances, an obscenity.

There is still sympathy for those, like John Lucas, who lack the will or the strength to avoid their own destruction. But that sympathy is in limited supply, and it is running out faster than the players want to believe. It flies in the face of the visible evidence to think the problem is declining, or that the players can provide their own enforcement. Drug testing may indeed violate the idea of a presumption of innocence. For that matter, so may a blood test when you get married or an eye test when you take the driver's exam.

Drug abuse is a plague, and it corrupts our sports because the fans want to believe their heroes are clean and their teams are trying. If the players don't understand even this simple truth, they will lose it all.

MASTERS OF THE MEANINGLESS GESTURE

JULY 22, 1984

To all the coaches I've shoved before; Who traveled in and out my door,
To all the coaches who shared my losses; Who now are under other bosses,
I'm glad you came along, I dedicate this song ... To all the coaches I've shoved before.
—*with apologies to Willie and Julio*

This was a big week for coaches, coming and going. The Houston Oilers assembled in San Angelo under Hugh Campbell, their thirteenth head coach in twenty-five years. And the Houston Gamblers said a graceful good-bye to Mouse Davis, all but throwing themselves in front of the moving van.

First, the Gamblers should be commended for doing in one season what many franchises fail to do in twenty-five. They have mastered the art of the Meaningless Gesture.

They went to court to obtain the services of halfback Billy Sims, and when they lost the suit, they said it didn't matter—they would have traded him to Oklahoma, anyway. When they discovered that the Astrodome doesn't give discounts no matter how much money a team loses, they threatened to move to Rice Stadium, which didn't want them. Then they withdrew their offer of a promotion and pay raise to Davis, after learning he had accepted the head coaching job with the Denver Gold.

In their eagerness to create a mystique, and to give the impression that they had something no other team could duplicate, the Gamblers raised Mouse Davis to the level of a media hero. They did this, in part, at the expense of Jack Pardee, who had done a solid job of putting together a winning staff and team under conditions less than ideal.

Patting their little pointed heads, the management of the Gamblers let it be known that "five or six" teams were after Davis. "No way" they were going to lose the Mouse, they said. He was the only one who knew how to operate the offense, which they had spent "millions of dollars" to install. Millions for offense, but not one cent for defense? They could not survive without the Mouse. If not the heart of their USFL franchise, he was at least the left ventricle.

Having painted themselves into this corner, the Gamblers stood there with egg on their chin, watching Davis disappear over the horizon. Whereupon they knocked him down as an ingrate, whose disloyalty and lack of candor and inattention to duty had led to the team's loss to Arizona in the play-offs. "No man can serve two masters," wisely observed part-owner Jerry Argovitz.

Davis had worked for them a long time, nearly a year. They had made him a star, and now he wanted to leave merely to become a head coach and make lots of money. The Gamblers tried to bluff Denver out of hiring Davis by threatening—and then filing—a tampering charge. And when another coach, June Jones, expressed a wish to join Davis, his friend and mentor, the ownership reacted in the usual way. They said they would sue him. You can afford to sue lots of people if you don't pay your lawyers, as the Gamblers have been accused of doing, or not doing.

If anyone deserves our tolerance, if not our sympathy, it is that breed of vagabonds known as assistant coaches. These are people who virtually need a hiring hall where they can report daily to see if work is available. It is sort of like being a longshoreman; you show up with your hook and hope for the best.

So when an assistant gets promoted to a top job, the proper response is to applaud and wish him happy trails, not to toss grenades in his path. If you want to know what kind of security these people have, you need look only as far as the Houston Oiler record book.

As for the Gamblers, mere words cannot console them. They should, indeed, remember the old saying: The quiet mouse gets the cheese.

The Write Stuff

APRIL BROUGHT YOU ROCKETS, EL TORO

MAY 3, 1981

Fernando Valenzuela is the best argument we have heard yet in favor of bilingual education. At the rate the rookie Dodger southpaw is going, every baseball fan in America soon will be able to speak Spanish.

He looks like a combination of Cantinflas and the Pillsbury doughboy. They love the way he looks in Los Angeles, the way he walks, the way he sits there, patiently waiting for the translation of a question he has already heard many times.

The discovery of a new player, a new hero in the spring of a baseball season is a gift from heaven. Valenzuela has appeared on the scene like a nova, like no one since Mark ("The Bird") Fidrych at Detroit, and before him your old friend Robert Boris ("Bo") Belinsky.

Fidrych enchanted the fans by talking to the ball and other curious habits. Belinsky waltzed out of a pool hall in New Jersey twenty years ago to win five in a row for the Angels, including a no-hitter. He dated an array of Hollywood starlets, became a pet of Walter Winchell, bought a pink Cadillac on credit, and then stopped winning. It is unclear whether Bo pitched or talked himself out of the big leagues, but at least the latter isn't likely to happen to Valenzuela.

What a parlay you would have had, what a ticket you would have cashed, if you had bet the farm in April on Fernando and the Houston Rockets—the Man of the Month, the Team of the Month.

We associate the two in our minds because all the Rockets really need to complete their storybook season is a left-handed Mexican who speaks no English. Without a doubt, the Rockets are the strangest, gutsiest team ever to play for the championship of the NBA.

THE WRITE STUFF

As one of the lads in the office was saying, decrying the fact that the Rockets seemed to lack a certain championship style, "They look like Baby Huey and the Munchkins."

The Baby Huey reference can only apply, one guesses, to Billy Paultz, also known as "The Whopper." Not to be unkind, but Paultz looks a little klutzy. Which is exactly the point. This year the klutzy look is in. Fernando Valenzuela will never be mistaken for a ballet dancer, either.

Although the twenty-year-old Dodger sensation is, at five feet eleven inches, a foot shorter than Paultz, both have thick necks and sturdy bodies. They both give the impression they would not be dazed if a safe fell on them from the top of a twelve-story building.

Formerly known as the Not-Ready-for-Prime-Time-Players, the Rockets are the first team in fourteen years to reach the NBA finals with a regular-season record under .500. (Consult your local listings to see if CBS, out of the goodness of its eye, has consented to show the weeknight games live. Watching on taped delay is like getting a letter from someone who, in the meantime, has died.)

Coach Del Harris traces the turnaround of the Rockets to his decision in January to install Paultz in the starting lineup. We would not argue with Coach Harris. He has been calling the shots in the play-offs, and he has called them pretty well. Paultz has been terrific, helping Moses Malone on the boards, dishing off to Robert Reid, setting picks for Calvin Murphy, knocking home a few hooks and soft two-handers, even blocking shots. When he leaps as high as he can go, one arm clawing at the sky, Paultz can get as much as five or six inches off the floor. And the Rocket crowds love him for it.

The team from the wrong side of the tracks must wait now to find out what Sunday will bring: Boston or Philadelphia. As if it matters. Does any sane, informed basketball fan really believe that either team stands a chance against the combat-hardened Rockets? It is to laugh. Compared to what Houston has endured, the Celtics and 76ers have been sipping tea in the Ivy League.

The Rockets had to win five of their last six just to make the play-offs. Then they swiped two out of three from the Lakers, four out of seven from San Antonio, and steamrollered poor Kansas City in five.

Remember the TV commercial in which Kareem Abdul-Jabbar

says he is glad he won't have to face Atari in the play-offs? The rules are clear: You don't face Atari, or anyone else, if you lose in the first round.

So there they are, the April destroyers, the revived Rockets and a burly immigrant who throws an almost-untouchable screwball. The numbers of Fernando are staggering: five starts, five victories, five complete games, four shutouts—two against the Astros—an earned-run average of 0.20, a batting average of .438.

He has captivated the city of Los Angeles as no Latin has done since Rudolph Valentino. A newspaper held a contest to give him a nickname, and from more than 3,000 entries selected "El Toro." The losing suggestions included "The Big Enchilada," "El Pauncho," and "Tortilla Fats."

Another newspaper dispatched a reporter to visit the shrine of his birth, a small village in the state of Sonora, where seventeen members of his family live in one four-room house. Fernando, when he slept there, shared a space with six brothers.

Suddenly, the Spanish-language reporters are the most popular media guys around. One of them asked Fernando if he thought he could win the prized Cy Young Award in his rookie year. The other newsmen, the gringos, leaned closer and waited.

He considered the question and replied, modestly, *"Que es eso?"* ("What is that?")

Fame has not yet disturbed the placid nature of El Toro, possibly because he doesn't know it is out there. Fame hasn't bothered the Rockets, either. Up to now, it hasn't known where to find them.

THE TEXAS SPECIAL

NOVEMBER 25, 1984

Until Saturday, the Texas Aggies had reinvented the Bermuda Triangle. Coaches, players, teams, entire seasons vanished into thin air, leaving no trace except for an occasional oil slick at the 40-yard line.

So if Jackie Sherrill and his Lost Patrol need more inspiration, they might note that this is the twentieth anniversary of the most theatrical play in the Aggie scrapbook. It was called The Texas Special, and it almost earned them a colossal upset.

Now, *almost* isn't exactly the secure word coaches crave. But in the spirit of the season, one can only offer hope; happy endings aren't guaranteed.

In 1965, Texas was struggling, but had returned most of the team that won ten games a year earlier. The Horns were a big favorite to trash the Aggies, rebuilding under a new coach, Gene Stallings.

In the middle of the week, Stallings asked a writer to join him for a drive. Said he had some thinking to do. He whipped his maroon school car through the campus and suddenly pulled under the stands at the baseball field. He folded his arms across the steering wheel and dropped his head against them. It looked like a case for Crisis Hotline. All sorts of wild thoughts rushed to mind, none so shocking as the words Stallings spoke when he raised his head: "I've got a play that's guaranteed to score a touchdown against Texas, if I got the guts to call it."

As it happened, the Aggies had been shut out four times, including three in a row. In two other games they had scored once. They had nearly wrecked one of the school's most cherished traditions, in which the Cadets kiss their dates after each Aggie touchdown. Every mother in the state felt safe, knowing her daughter was attending an Aggie game.

Logic tells you that if a team can score, it has a chance to win. But the way Stallings described the play, it sounded like something out of burlesque: "The quarterback bounces the ball to a flanker. Everybody acts like it was just a bad pass. They turn around as if to go to the huddle. Then the flanker straightens up and throws the ball as far as he can. Our wide receiver runs under it. Touchdown."

The trick was this: The play had to look like a forward pass, when in fact it was a lateral, with the ball still alive. If you threw it a certain way, Gene insisted, it would hop right into the receiver's hands.

Of course, they had not worked out all the wrinkles. Eleven backs tried out and only one could throw the ball far enough: Jim Kaufman, a defensive back, left-handed, a junior who'd played no offense in college.

They had practiced the play all week. They had not yet completed it.

Stallings wanted to make the call at midfield, so if it misfired they might contain the damage. But the Aggies never got to midfield. They spent the entire first quarter turning back Texas near their own goal line.

Early in the second period, with the ball at the nine, Jim Kaufman trotted onto the field. The Aggie quarterback, Harry Ledbetter, took the snap and threw a long lateral that reached Kaufman on one bounce. Even the Aggie linemen kicked the dirt in disgust and turned their backs to the field.

Downfield, end Dude McLean stopped his pass pattern, but only for an instant. Suddenly he took off, past relaxed Texas defenders, gathered in Kaufman's pass near midfield, and sped ninety-one yards for a touchdown.

The Texas Special so unsettled the Longhorns that the Aggies scored again on a seventy-one-yard drive and added a field goal just before the half to lead, 17-0. After the game, Darrell Royal was asked what he thought when he saw the ball in the air. "I knew we'd been had," he said. "McLean was so wide open it looked like he had come out early for practice."

At the half, Royal went to the blackboard and wrote in chalk, 21-17. A trick play and adrenalin could carry the Aggies only so far. Texas's power wore them down and UT won by the very score Royal projected.

There were several odd aftermaths to the game. Kaufman did not return for his senior year, and the only pass he ever threw is still the record for a touchdown pass in a Southwest Conference game. The Aggies who played as sophomores that day went to the Cotton Bowl in 1967 and beat Alabama, coached by Stallings' old mentor, Bear Bryant. Three years later, Stallings was fired.

Exactly what the moral of the story is, Sherrill and the 1984 Aggies can decide for themselves. There is no point in getting sentimental about nearly winning, or the merit of losing creatively. As Gene Stallings said that night, "I'd rather have had a sorry old play and won the game."

THE FIRST LADY OF SPORTSCASTING

JANUARY 16, 1983

When Phyllis George was just breaking into television, a male colleague refused to answer her questions, or share any information with her, pointing out that "you'll be taking airtime from me."

At that moment, a little red warning light went on, and it wasn't the one that tells you which camera to face. "From then on," she recalls, "I needed no reminder that I was in a male-dominated arena. I didn't exactly put on my boxing gloves, but I kept them nearby." She paused and added, "I've never had to put them on."

If the rumors are true about her "feud" with Jimmy ("The Greek") Snyder, her CBS teammate, this latter statement may be open to question. The Greek is a colorful figure who has the ability to amuse and infuriate at the same time. He is lovable, like the bears you find wandering around Yellowstone Park. One moment you want to pet them, the next you are trying to remove them from your windshield.

Phyllis says they are on pleasant terms again, possibly because she sees him as a terrific candidate for her *I Love America Diet Book*, a current hot seller. "Jimmy is Jimmy," she says. "The other day he was quoted as saying that CBS gave him a $70,000 raise so he would get along with Phyllis George." She laughed, a throaty, unaffected laugh, but at the same time her hands tightened the way they do when you are thinking about strangling someone. "I'm going to ignore the fact that he said that. I'm going to kill him with kindness."

Phyllis George is a master, or mistress, of the glancing blow. There is a gift to getting people to reveal themselves. Phyllis

THE WRITE STUFF

has the gift. Her subjects look into that face, those eyes, that smile, and they seem to feel an obligation not to send her away empty-handed.

In her first network interview, Dave Cowens, of the Boston Celtics, revealed that he rented a room with a middle-class family in the suburbs, and sometimes liked to rent a taxi and drive around all night picking up fares. It was his way of staying in touch with the real world. A baby-faced halfback out of Pittsburgh, Tony Dorsett (*DOR-sit*), told Phyllis on television that he planned to change his name to *dor-SETT* because he liked the sound of it. And then there was the day Roger Staubach defended his image as a square, telling Phyllis, in front of God and everybody, "I probably enjoy sex more than Joe Namath. The difference is I enjoy it with one woman, my wife."

That quote was picked up by the wire services and translated into thirty-six languages and piped to the armed forces overseas. Suddenly, Staubach was seen as a Real Person. And Phyllis was seen as a bona-fide interviewer, if not quite a hard-hitting newshawk.

Phyllis George may not have been the first to prove that there is life after the Miss America contest, but she has been the most visible. Once, the stereotypical Miss America contestant baked brownies on the day of the big game, played the piano, and wanted to help little kids or else go to Hollywood. Not Phyllis. When she won the crown in 1971, out of North Texas State, she looked a national television audience right in the eyeball and said that her goal was to go into broadcasting.

She was co-hosting the Miss America pageant when Bob Wussler, then overhauling the CBS sports department, caught her act. "I was doing a silly song-and-dance number titled 'Call Me Mizz,' " she remembers. "This was right when the women's liberation movement was coming on strong. Later, I met Bob with my agent at the Dorset Hotel in New York." She interrupted herself to say, "We now refer to it as the *Dor-SETT* Hotel," and then went on: "He told me, 'I think you've got something that can work on television. You speak well. But I don't want you to be cute about it. I want you to be a woman. You're going to be putting your neck on the line.' "

Her neck is still there. More correctly, it is back again, after a two-year recess during which Phyllis became the wife of the governor of Kentucky, John Y. Brown, and the mother of a son,

Lincoln, now two and a half. She loves politics and loves Kentucky, and she had doubts about returning to television. "I worried about getting the images confused," she says. "I thought it might hurt John. But he was the one who talked me into doing it. He said, 'That's part of what I fell in love with.'"

She works at being the governor's wife, just as she worked at refining her role on "The NFL Today," the show that won an Emmy for Brent, Irv, Phyllis, and Jimmy.

Ex-Miss America, governor's lady, working mother, sportscaster, and author, Phyllis George flew into Houston this week for a whirlwind tour to plug her *I Love America Diet* book, written with Bill Adler. Actually, the whirlwind was Phyllis. In seven hours she gave four television and two newspaper interviews and caught a plane to New York.

Between stops, she sat in a coffee shop and talked about her career. "In 1978," she recalled, *"People* magazine ran a cover story titled, 'Miss America Becomes the First Lady of the Locker Room.' I never was and never want to be in a locker room. A lot of women reporters have told me they need that access to cover their beats. I understand that. Luckily, I never had to fight that battle. I'd rather talk to him when he looks good and smells clean."

While she talked, her secretary brought over a hamburger and gave us each a half, dividing the french fries equally. Phyllis laughed. "That's on the diet," she assured us. "If you follow it, you'll lose weight."

Her thoughts drifted back to her television role. In her early years, a lot of people wondered what she was doing there. Was she the token woman? Art Deco? Television's answer to the Cowboy cheerleaders? She made it a point to quit reading the papers. "I feel at home there [on TV]," she says now. "I think, finally, I'm accepted. For years it was, oh, Phyllis, how does she look today? What's she wearing? The producer would come up and suggest that I would look better in red. Now they care more about what I say than what I wear." For the record, she likes the Jets and the Cowboys in the Super Bowl.

As the waitress removed my plate, Phyllis George casually, and with great self-assurance, reached over and picked off one last French fry.

STILL WANDERING AFTER FORTY YEARS

APRIL 14, 1987

There were no black generals or senators or Supreme Court justices, and no black children in white Southern schools when the Brooklyn Dodgers brought Jackie Robinson to the big leagues in 1947.

Ten years later, when Jackie retired from the sport whose complexion he had changed forever, the columnist Red Smith wrote, "His arrival in Brooklyn was a turning point in the history and character of the game; it may not be stretching things to say it was a turning point in the history of the country."

Now it is forty years later. In celebrating the unique contribution of Jackie Roosevelt Robinson, baseball finds itself embroiled again in a sad and timeless debate. Al Campanis, an aging and muddled man, unprepared and uneasy on television, a last-minute replacement on a show honoring Robinson, raised a storm by suggesting that blacks might not be qualified to hold positions as managers or general managers.

Ironies abound. Forty years after Jackie crossed the line, the issue of black representation other than on the playing field is with us still. And as penance for the insensitivity of his remarks, Campanis, seventy, was forced to resign as vice president of the Dodgers. They had been teammates in the minors in 1946—Al at short, Jackie at second base.

A few months before he died, in 1972, I collaborated with Robinson on a magazine story under his byline. I do not pretend that this assignment gave me any special insights or any claim on his friendship. He was wound tight and had an edge of anger in his voice and manner. He didn't go out of his way to charm you or exchange banter.

I asked him what he thought when he drove past the apartment complex where Ebbets Field once stood. "Nothing," he replied.

"No tingle?"

"Nothing," he repeated. "I figure they need those apartments more than they need a monument to the memory of baseball. Besides, I've had my thrills."

Indeed he had. He established himself as a superb hitter, infielder, and base runner, but those skills are not his legacy. No man in the history of professional sports ever endured more abuse, performed under closer scrutiny, withstood heavier pressures.

But, always, there was a towering sense of dignity. Jackie never let anyone, not his teammates or his opponents, forget that he was a man. All he really asked was to be treated as one.

He told me that he made a lot of speeches, often to troubled young people. Many of them, he said, had only the faintest notion that he once played baseball for a living.

I am looking at the notes I kept from our interviews. He has been dead for fourteen years, and it is almost as if time had stood still. In a way, it has. Jackie was responding that week to statements by two former stars, pitcher Bob Feller and Alvin Dark. The printed quotes were not too far removed from those of Al Campanis.

"Bob Feller is just a stupid ass," Robinson said, "but Alvin was talking out of ignorance. He had been brought up to believe that God made the white man superior, and put him on earth to take care of the black man.

"It isn't necessary for whites today to carry the burdens of their grandfathers. All any of us should do is take a good look at ourselves and ask, 'Am I doing all I can to make America the kind of place it should be?' "

Jackie Robinson, who blazed his own trail, made it clear that baseball rated no higher than third on society's list of needed improvements. "The greatest need," he said, "is for better housing. What good does it do a kid to come home from school, or a ballfield, if he has no decent place to sleep?"

We were together two days, hours at a time. At one point he laughed, and said, "The whole mystique of managing is a joke.

The best example I can think of is Casey Stengel. I like Casey. But he was a clown when he managed the Boston Braves. He was a genius with the Yankees. He went out as he came in, a clown and a loser, with the Mets.

"The day of the black manager is coming," he was saying, across the years. "The game is what it always was, a great game, operated at the whim of wealthy men who like to manipulate people."

THE CHALLENGE STILL MATTERS

FEBRUARY 1, 1987

Does anyone out there remember the seventies? I know. It is almost as though someone erased a tape of the entire decade. But perhaps these clues will help:

Roots. Digital watches. The Fonz. Patty Hearst. The Pet Rock. *Rocky.* The whole enchilada. Petrodollars. Racing stripes. Pong. Live via satellite. Macho. Watching Johnny Carson's hair turn white. Ten-four, rubber duck.

And Billie Jean King.

Yeah, sure, it is all coming back to you now. The seventies. Tennis became a truly national sport, with the cash purses to prove it. And Billie Jean made certain we knew it was woman's work, as well as man's.

More than a symbol of the seventies, like it or not—and Billie Jean never really said she didn't like it—she became a symbol of the women's lob movement. Part tennis, part social liberation.

The show was advertised as "The Battle of the Sexes." In September of 1973, before a glittering crowd of 40,000 in the Astrodome, Ms. King wiped out a fifty-five-year-old hustler named Bobby Riggs, and removed from the sport the last of the chauvinist pigs.

The match was no contest. She womanhandled him, winning in straight sets. And now, thirteen years and four months later, she cannot visit the city, as she will this week, without reliving one of the truly Bizarre Moments in Sports Biz. It was the classic confrontation, a geezer approaching his dotage playing junk shots against a girl who wore glasses, and in thirty-six countries millions tuned in via satellite TV.

When you consider the achievements of Billie Jean King—the twenty years of world-class competition, the women's pro tour and Team Tennis, the thirty-five major titles including six singles titles at Wimbledon—you ask if this is her legacy, a match not much more than a carnival stunt?

"The ones most likely to bring it up," she says, "are the nontennis people. The hard-core fans want to talk about Wimbledon and Team Tennis and the championships I won.

"But it's funny. Bobby and I were on *The Odd Couple.* The show is in syndication and it still runs every night in New York. They have a little cult up there. And every time one of our segments runs, people stop me on the street and tell me about it."

In whatever Billie Jean says, there is no trace of a complaint. She does not give the impression of someone who suffered for her art, and is casting a sideways glance to see if the world has noticed. The fact is, she bounces around pretty good for someone who has undergone five knee surgeries (and one on her foot).

The pain that moves Billie Jean is not her own. The goal, not the glory, is what always drove her and drives her still. She is still a missionary bringing light to the natives.

"The championships are minor," she says, "because those things are temporary. What matters is what we have been able to change, what opportunities we helped create.

"When I met Bobby Riggs, we helped raise the awareness that tennis was a sport. Eighty million people saw that match. In 1973, tennis was still a small sport.... It may have been a gimmick, but it was a gimmick that worked. It helped put us on the map.

"What I didn't expect was how it helped women in general to gain a little courage. Their self-esteem went up a little bit. I walked into a newspaper in Philadelphia a few days later, and the people in the newsroom stood up and applauded. The women gathered around and said they had felt underpaid for a long time. They deserved a raise, but didn't have the guts to ask for it. They said, 'The day after you played Bobby, we went in to see the boss and asked for a raise.' "

"I said, 'The important thing is, did you get it?' And they said yes.

"People draw strength from odd places. If my winning encouraged someone to take a little more control of their destiny, if it gave them the guts to take a chance, even if they failed, then that makes me happy."

Causes have always drawn Billie Jean, like a moth to the flame.

One of them brought her Saturday to Houston, where she will appear at The Challenger Cup women's doubles tournament. Billie Jean will play an exhibition match at 10 A.M. today against members of the news media. Whether she will take them on one at a time or as a group isn't clear, but whatever the arrangement, she is a heavy favorite.

Few public figures, and fewer athletes, have been more generous with their time, or as tireless in their effort to advance a cause. The Challenger Cup—in memory of the two women, astronaut Judith Resnik and teacher Christa McAuliffe, who died aboard the space shuttle—will raise funds for scholarships at the University of Houston.

"They called," King says, "and I wanted to do it. Sally Ride [the first U.S. woman astronaut, who played college tennis at Stanford] has been a friend of mine. She showed me around NASA about a year and a half ago, and I have tried to keep up with the program. This is a chance to honor those two women, and help raise money for the scholarships."

In the prime of her playing career, Billie Jean circled the earth many times. She still travels most of the year, still conducts clinics and organizes community leagues, still endorses a few products and plugs a few companies, and gives up to four or five interviews a day.

The victory over Riggs was, in a sense, her coronation as the Queen of Tennis. You can have your Chrissies and your Martinas, but for those who came of age in the 1970s, she still is . . . the King who would be queen.

Billie Jean has no illusions about the Riggs promotion. But she has another memory of Houston: as the place where a revolution was born.

In 1970, at the Racquet Club, Billie Jean was one of nine women who declared their independence from Jack Kramer's pro tennis tour. They formed the USLTA and announced their first tournament, sponsored by the manufacturer of Virginia Slims. "What people forget is that we were kicked out," she says. "We didn't break away. We were fortunate because Gladys Heldman [a magazine publisher and tennis enthusiast] promised us a sponsor, and she delivered."

The tour prospered, and in 1974 King was one of the founders of another radical movement: Team Tennis. This grand social experiment met with mixed results. Operating the franchise in

THE WRITE STUFF

Philly, Billie Jean encouraged the crowds to boo, hiss, jeer, and stomp their feet—a form of anarchy in a sport where spectators generally behave like patrons at a British art gallery.

But B. J. hasn't quit. She never does. Even her retirement as a tournament player, first disclosed five years ago, has been less than airtight. "I play in four or five matches a year for Rosie Casals," she says. "I've started to play more lately because I need to lose weight. As an executive"—and she says this with a smile in her voice—"I am getting a little pudge-o. I have to do the weights like crazy. The knees are gone, and the more weightlifting I do, the less pain I feel. But it's *borrrring.*"

On balance, there is nothing else about Billie Jean's life that is. Nothing in her private story, the social slings and arrows she has endured, seems to have dimmed the public affection for this high-voltage lady.

She has a five-year contract as a TV analyst at Wimbledon, and she is the president of her own production company, called GFI. It does not take a naval decoding expert to decipher those initials. Anyone who has ever met or read about Billie Jean King knows her slogan is "Go For It."

And so she has. "I might try to play in the Open next year," she confides, "as a wild card, if they would let me. I can't imagine getting very far, but that doesn't matter. I just do better when I have goals, and my goal right now is to get in shape, and to make the Team Tennis concept work.

"We have started recreational leagues in 200 cities. We want to quadruple the number of kids playing tennis. We want the kids in intramurals, the kids on military bases . . . . It's a lifetime sport once they get into it. We're not trying to replace anything. We just want more tennis."

Once, she was little Billie Jean Moffitt, who grew up in Southern California rooting for the Lakers and the Dodgers, a girl as gifted as the boys but without a team to play on.

Now she creates teams, leagues, entire sports. A lot of men felt that civilization as we knew it ended on a September night in 1973 at the Astrodome. Bobby Riggs did everything but wear a sandwich board that night onto the court. But it was Billie Jean King who emerged as the queen of mixed singles in tennis.

WORDS OF WISDOM FROM WILL

OCTOBER 6, 1985

Whenever confusion reaches a peak in sports, one is permitted to call on a time-honored tradition known as the Guest Columnist. The guest of choice is often a British journalist named William Shakespeare, who has the unselfish attitude and deft touch typical of sports scribes the world over.

Here's Bill:

Q: The hot topic at the moment is the widening recruiting scandal in the Southwest Conference, which has found SMU slapped in the pokey for three years, seven TCU players off the squad, and other teams waiting for the second shoe to drop. Is there a lesson in all this?

A: You pay a great deal too dear for what's given freely. (*The Winter's Tale*, Act I)

Q: Two weeks after losing his title to young Michael Spinks, in what he said was his last fight, Larry Holmes is talking about ending his retirement. Is this a good idea?

A: An old man, broken with the storms of state, is come to lay his weary bones among ye; give him a little earth for charity. (*Henry VIII*, Act III)

Q: The Houston Oilers have lost three in a row since defeating Miami in their opener. Can the defense continue to carry the team until the offense gets untracked?

A: Beggars mounted run their horse to death. (*Henry VI*, Act IV)

Q: Your old friend Howard Cosell has a new book out. What is your impression of what Howard has to say?

A: He draweth out the thread of verbosity finer than the staple of his argument. (*Love's Labour Lost*, Act IV)

THE WRITE STUFF

Q: Is Hugh Campbell, the Oilers coach, as quiet and serious a fellow as he seems in his postgame interviews?

A: They laugh that win. (*Othello*, Act IV)

Q: For the fourth year in a row, the attendance of the Houston Astros showed a decline. Does this mean the fans are losing faith?

A: The miserable have no medicine, but only hope. (*Measure for Measure*, Act II)

Q: Can you compare the misfortunes of the Oilers and the Astros?

A: We have kissed away kingdoms and provinces. (*Antony and Cleopatra*, Act III)

Q: A parade of major-league baseball players, including Keith Hernandez, Dale Berra, and Enos Cabell, took the stand recently in a federal court trial in Pittsburgh and testified to their dealings in cocaine. Each named other teammates as users and each received immunity. Some observers found it hard to decide which was more unpleasant, the disclosures or the way they were stage-managed. What was your reaction?

A: If this were played upon a stage now, I would condemn it as improbable fiction. (*Twelfth Night*, Act III)

Q: At the age of twenty, Dwight Gooden of the Mets has dazzled all of baseball, winning twenty-four games and leading the majors in strikeouts. How would you describe Gooden?

A: Young in limbs, in judgment old. (*The Merchant of Venice*, Act II)

Q: Warren Moon was sacked twelve times by the Cowboys. The feeling is that the Oilers must establish a ground attack to have a chance against Denver. How would you advise them to run the ball?

A: Wisely and slow; they stumble that run too fast. (*Romeo and Juliet*, Act II)

Q: In the biggest baseball story of the year, many years, Pete Rose at the age of forty-four broke Ty Cobb's record for most career hits. Would you classify Rose as a self-made player?

A: Some are born great, some achieve greatness, and some have greatness thrust upon them. (*Twelfth Night*, Act II)

Q: The Oilers have an offensive line said to be loaded with potential, and a quarterback who can run and throw, when someone isn't sitting on him. In rookie Glenn Davis, the Astros discovered the home-run hitter they have lacked for most of their twenty-four seasons. The Rockets, led by Ralph Sampson and Akeem Olajuwon, are legitimate contenders in the NBA. Do you think Houston may soon be calling itself "The City of Champions"?

A: It would be argument for a week, laughter for a month, and a good jest forever. (*Henry IV,* Act II)

Thanks, Bill. Drop in again. The next time we need some straight answers.

The View From the Press Box

THE UBIQUITOUS ONE

FALL 1975

In the spring of 1972, I strolled into a nightclub in New York a few blocks off Broadway, just in time to be startled by a familiar voice. On the stage, a comic was doing his impression of Howard Cosell broadcasting the Crucifixion.

What forces brought me to that place, at that time, I cannot guess. (For all I know, Brigham Young felt the same way about Utah.) But the fact is—and there is no clever way to say this—I was trying to get *away* from Howard Cosell, with whom I had worked the past few months *unrelievedly*. His word, not mine.

I became convinced that night that you cannot get away from Howard Cosell. He is harder to escape than the Eyes of Texas. After a while, I am not sure that you would if you could.

All that spring, Howard had told me the story of his life, later to become his record-selling autobiography. In theory, I was hired to help him prepare it. Actually, I served as an audience of one as Howard relived himself. When people learned that I had actually spent weeks at a time as his houseguest, they would look at me with respect, as though I had seen the tiger cages of Saigon.

Our workdays always began with the same ritual. Howard would awaken at 5:30 to do his first of three radio shows. Shortly thereafter, a whiff of cigar smoke would indicate an alien presence in my bedroom. Then, tentatively, the way it is with people whose hearts don't start beating until noon, I would open one eye. Howard would be leaning over me. "Just checking," he'd say, "to see what time you want to get up."

I enjoyed Howard, marveled at his capacity for work, and learned from him. It is not possible to be unmoved, in one direction or another, by his stories, his heartfelt opinions, his

THE VIEW FROM THE PRESS BOX

account of the battles he has fought with the dragons of television-land, his ups, his downs.

A month after I returned to my home in Houston, my friends claimed that I was still walking around the house talking in Howard's voice.

These small reminiscences were prompted, in part, by a wire-service story that appeared not too long ago in newspapers across the land. The headline that caught my eye read, "New Orleans Rips Cosell."

In his own warm and tactful way, Howard had assured a group of television columnists that ABC was "getting rid of the clinkers from this year's [Monday night] schedule. And that definitely means the Saints. They were simply dreadful."

The citizens of New Orleans could hardly have been more outraged if he had attacked the virtue of the girls on Bourbon Street. Howard had struck again. And the world struck back. Fair is fair.

But it is worth taking stock as Monday Night Football—"an American cultural institution," Howard called it—begins its sixth season. We are prepared to say that it has stood the test of time, although the cast of characters has changed a couple of times. Through it all, one factor remained constant: Cosell.

He is one of the most imitated men in America. You can hardly turn on the tube or pick up a comic book without encountering another Cosell parody, which would go something like this:

"Bronko, your left knee is crushed . . . a gruesome mass of shattered bones and nerves and cartilage that can never be repaired . . . the excruciating pain is still etched in your face . . . you'll never play another game of football.

"Tell me, Bronk, how does it feel to be a quitter?"

Cosell doesn't mind such send-ups. He understands the inherent flattery of the well-drawn caricature. The put-on is his shtick, too.

It is astonishing how many people have the time, and the curiosity, to want Howard explained to them. One wishes one could. He has a mind that's out there where the meter doesn't register. I have heard him, catching just the first echo of a song in the piano bar, instantly recite: (1) the Broadway musical in which it was introduced; (2) in what year; and (3) the names of the singer, the composer, and the supporting cast.

There is no point in describing his pace, or his workload,

except to say that he has no patience for those who can't keep up. I know I disappointed him along the way. Once, while the book was nearing completion, it was necessary to visit Houston on personal business. I promised to be back in five days. Unfortunately, while playing basketball with one of my sons, I broke a thumb—my doctor said it was a death wish—and had to stay the rest of the week. When I returned to New York, Howard told me I wasn't a persevering fellow. He did not say it unkindly. When your best friends won't tell you, Howard will.

So what can one say? I believe he has been good for sports, and good for most of us. As he himself might put it, he has transcended the world of petulant outfielders, Neanderthal linebackers, and unprincipled owners.

BIG DADDY OF THE WISHBONE-T

JANUARY 1974

A legend has grown up about a motel room in Austin—it's probably not what you're thinking—and an autumn night in 1968.

The legend is best brought into focus by an incident that took place this past season. A drummer was looking for his leader, Tom T. Hall, the country-and-western singer who had been Darrell Royal's guest at that night's Texas game. (If Royal marches to a different drummer, you can be sure he plays in a country-and-western band.)

The drummer stopped at the front desk of the Villa Capri, across from the Texas campus, for directions. "Where's the Texas party?" he asked the clerk.

"The what?"

"The room where the Texas coach has his party."

"Oh. You must mean the press conference." The clerk's eyes brightened, and in his voice was the sound of trumpets. "That's Room 2001—where the Wishbone-T was born!"

It may be stretching the truth some to say that Room 2001 has become a kind of shrine. But it has assumed an importance far beyond what God and Jones Ramsey intended for it: a place to feed, water, and entertain the press, a place where Darrell Royal played back his victories and explained those rare, unexplainable Texas losses.

What ghosts roam that room. The acres of fried chicken we ate there . . . the witty lines we tossed off . . . the laughs we shared . . . the booze we drank . . . the brilliant writers we carried out.

And that couch. See that couch over there? The orange one, twelve feet long. Right there is where the Wishbone-T was first spoken.

There are witnesses who will swear to it, who can recall every detail, every nuance of the scene. And it's a darned good thing because I—from whose innocent lips the name sprang—remember almost nothing about that night.

It never occurred to me, not in my wildest flights of imagination, that I would achieve a certain underground fame for having named the Wishbone-T. I mean, if one had only known, one might have taken notes, or something.

Some men invent vaccines to cure dreaded diseases, such as acne. Others pose in the nude for magazines catering to liberated women. Still others achieve immortality by getting kidnapped by little men with metallic skin and hands like lobster claws.

I named the Wishbone-T.

Revisiting the scene of this deathless moment on a night in 1971, the historian Jack Gallagher was startled to find an argument in progress about the seating arrangement in 2001. Gallagher described it as follows:

"He was sittin' right over there," Blackie Sherrod, the Dallas author, pointed to a spot on the couch. "No, he was sittin' over here," corrected Bill Little, UT's assistant sports information director.

Darrell Royal refused to be drawn into the controversy over where Herskowitz's 5-foot-5, 130-pound frame was located at the time, but did add, "I just remember he said, 'Gee, coach, that isn't a very original name, just calling it the Y formation. How about' "—and at this point you can hear the muffled drumbeats of history—" 'the Wishbone-T?' "

Well. To begin with, I suspect that Darrell's recollection is quite reliable. I have never known him to misquote a sportswriter. Also, 'Gee, coach,' sounds like something I am quite capable of saying.

It would seem appropriate to pause here, and acknowledge the contribution of Emory Bellard, then the Texas backfield coach, who designed the new alignment. And James Street, Steve Worster, Ted Koy and Chris Gilbert, who ran it. I could not have done it without them.

The formation actually had no name as Texas opened its season on September 21, 1968, against the University of Houston (whose coach, Bill Yeoman, had popularized the triple option). The Longhorns had returned to the laboratory after three straight 6-and-4 seasons, years of disaster according to the Darrell Royal standard.

Great pains had been taken that fall to keep the formation a surprise. They did everything but post signs reading LOOSE

THE VIEW FROM THE PRESS BOX

LIPS SINK SHIPS. Royal was therefore somewhat aggrieved when Harry Kalas, one of the University of Houston broadcasters asked him in an interview before the game, "Coach, I understand you're lining your fullback up a yard behind the quarterback." Royal's cheeks took on the hues of a Tahitian sunset.

The Longhorns and the Cougars fought to a 20-20 tie that night, and the Wishbone-T was on its way to becoming a part of the football language.

Curiously, the actual christening did not occur until the night of the season's fifth game, a 39-29 knockout of Arkansas.

Though what was to become the offense of the seventies was introduced against Houston, the scene described by Gallagher didn't take place until after the Arkansas game. Some of the finest minds in the state—Royal, Gallagher, Lou Maysel, Bill Little, my own—assumed it had all transpired on the same fateful night, and in the first draft of this essay, that's how it was written.

One man dissented, steadfastly. Jones Ramsey insisted it was after the Arkansas victory. "I remember we were having a good time," argued Jones, who is a purist, "and there was no reason for us to have a good time after a tie."

Also, that week, Ramsey clearly remembered Royal approaching him before practice and demanding, "Hey, when are you guys going to come up with a name?"

I learned long ago, or thought I had, that there are things you simply do not do: You don't tug on the Lone Ranger's mask, you don't pull on Superman's cape, and you don't argue with Jones Ramsey's memory.

Ramsey is the kind of chap who, when they call, will entertain his sportswriter friends by reciting passages from stories they wrote ten years ago. The way Ronald Coleman recited poetry, is Ramsey quoting the opening paragraph of a Texas football victory no one else remembers.

Of course, this often happens with moments of historical import. Facts tend to blur and become intertwined. I mean, if we can't remember which Thursday Thanksgiving falls on, or which way to move our clocks for daylight savings time, how can we expect to recall the exact night the Wishbone was named?

Ramsey might not have been vindicated had it not been for an accident of timing. I had been forced to beg off from a party, and I apologized to my host by explaining that I was working on a story about how I became the godfather of the Wishbone-T.

"Oh, yeah," he said, cheerfully. "I was there with you that night."

"You were there?" I gasped.

"Yeah, we went in my car."

A light flashed. He was absolutely right. We did drive to Austin together, and back. Hesitantly, I said, "It was the Houston game, right?"

"No," he said. "Arkansas. There was this orange couch, and you were sitting . . . . "

Today it is no longer clear how many were actually in the room, although it seems fairly certain that the number is less than those who claim they were there. (It's kind of like Bobby Thomson's home run.)

Within a year, word was drifting back to me that in his travels around the country, Darrell Royal was making a point of telling interviewers how the Wishbone got its name. It was characteristic of Royal to feel that the credit was worth giving.

What really surprised me was the reaction of people who, unanimously, seemed to think that naming the Wishbone-T was a good thing to have done. Those who were there that night have a tendency to remember it with a sense of history, the way people remember where they were when the bombs fell on Pearl Harbor.

Whatever the timing, or the circumstances, or by whatever name, the success of the Wishbone has been astounding. Since exposing it to the Cougars, the Longhorns have won fifty-five and lost nine, captured six straight Southwest Conference titles, and made six trips to the Cotton Bowl.

Of course, some cynics will claim that players, not labels, win football games. But such an attitude ignores the fact that we live in a marketing-oriented society. Today no one knows or cares how the tobacco is picked, cut, dried, processed, or rolled. But all of us honor the genius who thought up the name "Lucky Strike."

One day my then-fifteen-year-old son came home from football practice in a state of high excitement. A classmate had read Lou Maysel's fine book, *Here Come the Longhorns,* and had run across the name of Steve's father. As often happens with teenage boys, in matters not related to teenage girls, one of them got his facts slightly confused.

"Dad, dad," cried Steve, "a friend of mine saw your name in a book. Is it true? Did you really invent the Wishbone-T?"

THE VIEW FROM THE PRESS BOX

Before he could ask me to visit his school and lecture the team, I confessed that I had not. When I explained that I had only given the offense a name, he shrugged and said, "Well, I guess that's something."

In retrospect, perhaps it is. Looking back over our great years together, I can only add that it is a pleasure to donate a name to a Texas team that wears it so well.

COSELL TACKLES THE CINEMA

JUNE 23, 1971

In the windmill of his mind, the dedicated movie buff pauses to review the great moments in cinema history.

There was Rhett Butler telling off Scarlett O'Hara with Southern-fried scorn: "Frankly, my dear, I don't give a damn." We wondered if our ears would ever be clean again.

Then came Jane Russell, her blouse barely holding its own, crawling under the blankets to cure Billy the Kid's cold chills. You won't find *that* in your first-aid book, boy. (That scene ended the age of innocence, as a lonely nation turned its eyes to hers.)

And there was Lauren Bacall reminding Bogey: "You know how to whistle, don't you? Just put your lips together and blow." On cue, the entire male population of America puckered.

Finally, who among us will ever forget King Kong dangling from the side of the Empire State Building and holding Fay Wray in his hand as though she were some kind of hot-dog bun.

To this rare list of famous scenes, one more must now be added: Howard Cosell, appearing as a sportscaster named Howard Cosell, in the opening scene of Woody Allen's new film, *Bananas*, a deep and poignant story about social reform in Latin America.

When the dictator of San Marcos gets himself assassinated, Howard is there to cover it for ABC's "Wide World of Sports." We see him interviewing the dying *el presidente* on the steps of the Capitol.

After one question, only a gurgling noise rises in the poor fellow's throat. Howard leans closer to the body. "You're upset," he says, sympathetically. "It's understandable."

Cosell doesn't bat an eye as the old boy, clutching the bullet

THE VIEW FROM THE PRESS BOX

wound in his chest, kicks off. "Good luck to you, sir," sings out Howard, cheerily, and signs off.

It is possible, at this very moment, that Howard is trying to decide if, in good conscience, he can accept the Academy Award for best actor. Or should he follow the lead of George C. Scott, who declined on the grounds that it was purely a popularity contest, and did not honor the actor's skill? We know Howard, and he would not want to win simply because he is so popular.

It is pleasant to be able to report to you that his new acclaim, his success in an alien field, hasn't changed Cosell. He is the same lovable, low-keyed, self-effacing guy you see on your television screen.

There is no pretense about Howard. He accepts praise in the same unquestioning spirit in which a sultan collects taxes. He has raised the fine old art of name-dropping to a level where, in one sentence, he can drop names, countries, important dates, and great events.

Fondly, he recalls his first meeting with Woody Allen: "I was in a gambling joint in London back in May of 1966. I went over to join the cast of *Dirty Dozen*—Lee Marvin, Jimmy Brown, and Telly Savalas—in a poker game. Woody was in London making another movie and he was in the game. He kept me out of it. I hated him for that.

"The next time I saw him was in Earthquake McGoon's in San Francisco, a Dixieland place where a guy named Turk Murphy was playing the horn. I went there one night while I was out to do the Ellis-Quarry fight, and in walked Woody. He went right up to the bandstand and began playing the clarinet. I had no idea he was a fine clarinetist.

"When he stepped down, I got up to leave. He said hello. I reminded him that he wouldn't let me in the poker game in London. He explained that he had been losing, and he felt the game was overcrowded. I understood.

"I wound up taking Woody, John Forsythe, Herman Franks, and Willie Mays to the fight. We were very friendly that night, but I didn't hear from him again until suddenly I got a call from his manager, asking me if I would fly to Puerto Rico and do the opening scene in his new movie."

To say that Howard enjoyed his role is on the order of saying that Pete Maravich has hair. Howard was pleased to be able to give the film crew, accustomed as it was to the likes of Elliott

THE VIEW FROM THE PRESS BOX

Gould and Paul Newman, a chance to see him work. "Naturally, they flipped," he confides. "They cheered and applauded and yelled, 'Attaway to go, Howie. Tell it like it is.' "

Actually, it isn't Howard's style to talk about himself, if there is a chance that someone else will. He suggested I should seek a more objective view of his performance.

"To get the totality of the picture," he cried, "you should talk to Woody."

Actor, comedian, writer, and noted amateur stickball player, Woody Allen was reached at his New York apartment, where he was between phone calls, as he usually is.

Woody is clearly a Cosell fan. "Cosell was crazy about being in the movie. He's a tremendous ham, a cartoonlike character. He comes across that way on television, too. He's the same way if you're eating dinner with him—he broadcasts the meal."

Having written a sportscaster into his script, his choice was inevitable. "To me," said Woody, "he represents everything a kid dreams of in a sportscaster. It's the urgency in his voice, the tone, the cadence of his sentences."

He was most impressed by Howard's easy control of the situation. "In the opening scene," recalls Allen, "we used hundreds and hundreds of Puerto Rican extras, as peasants and revolutionaries. Howard, with his self-confidence, his enormous ego, gets off the plane and he shows up at the set and here are these hundreds of extras, none of them can speak English, and Howard takes one look and says, 'Well, they're . . . all . . . here . . . to . . . see . . . Co-sell.' "

In keeping with the loose, flexible touch that Allen brings to all his films, Howard improvised his way through both of his scenes. The film ended with a kind of bedside, wedding night, postgame interview, with Howard intoning the deathless words: "Whatever the action is, wherever it takes place, ABC's 'Wide World of Sports' will be there to bring it to you."

I asked him if he had ever acted before. Instantly, I knew the question was a pointless one.

Over the long-distance line, you could hear Howard Cosell chuckling softly.

SWEPT OFF HIS FEET

AUGUST 26, 1979

The best recent account I have heard of The Thrill of Victory and The Agony of Defeat comes from a young fellow who for years has eaten my food, worn my clothes, and borrowed my car. So if I can get a free column out of the kid, well, it seems a small enough repayment.

Steve, as he is known, returned last week from the high country, from Colorado Springs, where America's best amateur athletes took part in a grand idea called the National Sports Festival. He was one of five middle lightweights competing in judo, the last "new" sport accepted at the Olympic Games (in 1964).

Steve qualified for the U.S. team, which will tour Hawaii, Japan, and South Africa, and he came within a minute or so of winning a gold medal. Meanwhile, his younger brother, Brian, entered as a lightweight, injured a foot in his first match, had to settle for a bronze, and missed the traveling squad. But each coached and cheered the other, and that has to be a warm fuzzy for a parent who remembers the brotherly fights of years ago; the cries of "He bit me," and "He bit me first," while The Patriarch applied his iron discipline: "Stop it. You know the rules. No biting."

Steve almost missed the whole show, twice. But, as they say in Japan, where there is a yen there is a way. Weeks after he had been passed over, he was invited to Colorado Springs when a vacancy occurred in his division at virtually the last minute. "I had a sore knee and couldn't run," he remembers. "Between Monday and the world team trials on Saturday, I had to lose eight pounds (down to 143). So I wasn't in shape. And I had to starve myself. I figured my chances of doing well were not very high."

The morning of the weigh-in, Steve and two of his teammates overslept. He went racing through a coed dormitory, barefooted and wrapped in a bath towel, and was disqualified for being ten minutes late. Then a committee went into special session to consider reinstating Steve and the other delinquents. He waited for an hour, in his towel, shifting his feet, his heart pounding, until the committee relented. Only in America.

So there he was: entered on a pass, unable to train, a week without solid food, scared out of his wits even before he stepped on the mat. Whereupon he swept three straight opponents and was the only unbeaten contestant going into the finals, against Jimmy Martin, a Californian who now trains out of Chicago, a three-time national champion. Martin is four years older and four inches taller than Steve, who at five-feet-five is built like a Volvo. Halfway through the match, Steve was dominating it. The crowd was on his side and he knew he was winning. "I looked up," he recalls, "and I saw Brian, and his face was on fire."

Then something happened. Martin caught him with what amounted to a foot sweep, the basic technique in judo. Steve flopped on his back and before he could react, he was pinned. It was over. Although both finished with 3-and-1 records, in the total scoring system, Steve had lost the gold by one point.

"I was stunned," he said later. "I got to my knees and just stayed there with my hands over my eyes. Then I bowed and backed off the mat. I still had my head down when I realized a guy from a local TV station was following me with a camera."

Steve gave him a look that would exterminate head lice. At that moment, his grief was so real and so proud he did not feel like sharing it. "You better not be pointing that thing at me," he hissed.

The cameraman turned to no one in particular, shrugged, and said, "I'm not going to argue with him."

Later, Steve had regrets. "I felt bad about being rude," he said. "Also, I was kind of curious to know what the expression on my face looked like."

There were 5,000 athletes at Colorado Springs, all with the same goal. They want to get to Moscow and the 1980 Olympics so much they can almost smell the caviar. One out of five will make it. The festival, a two-year success, represents America's best chance of staying even with those European countries that train and support their athletes year-round.

The competition, the coaching, the science, the scenery, everything at the Air Force Academy complex was first class—

THE VIEW FROM THE PRESS BOX

with the possible exception of the food. "It was inedible," said Steve. "They served the same food they give the cadets and just added portions for 5,000 more plates."

In any such environment, track-and-field has the golden boys and girls, and rates the most attention. But the off-Broadway sports—such as judo and archery and gymnastics—figure to benefit in a dramatic way from the exposure. "In the past," said Steve, "we thought only about beating each other. Now we're thinking about the rest of the world."

Although Brian's Olympic hopes were set back, but not dashed, by his injury, he consoled himself in the traditional way. He dated one of the prettiest girls in the camp, a marksman—marksperson?—on the rifle team. It is one of the ancient rules of romance that a fellow should avoid girls who shoot straight. But Brian is young and has time to learn.

"Every time she walked into the dining room," said Steve of the blonde gunner, "the place would get quiet. Brian kept saying, 'I'm going to get a date with her,' and we'd laugh. Well, one day she walked in and he was right beside her, grinning from ear to ear. Without any signals, or anything, our table broke into applause. The girl handled it real well. But Brian turned red and looked as if he wanted to fall through a crack in the floor."

The agony of defeat, indeed.

BEST STORIES ALSO RAREST

JANUARY 1, 1984

Herewith the best sports stories for 1983:

A rookie halfback realized his life's dream by being drafted in the first round by a team in the National Football League. Because he was strong of back and could outrun a puma, the team agreed to his agent's demand for the usual contract: a million a year and a stock-option plan that would enable him to retire at twenty-five.

The rookie halfback refused to sign.

"I'm not worth it," he cried, while all around him strong men fainted and a few borderline cases gasped. "Pay me a reasonable salary—whatever is fair—and give the rest to the clerks and secretaries in the front office. They've earned it."

The rookie worked very hard and was beloved by the fans as well as his teammates. His heart was pure and his habits clean. He did not smoke or drink and always ate grits for breakfast. He had taste and did not dress like a Tiffany lamp. He went to church, but accepted the fact that God was probably too busy to follow the pro football standings.

His fame grew, and his team won, but he refused to profit unduly from the success he achieved at a sport he loved. He would not endorse mouthwashes, antiperspirants, popcorn poppers, foot powders, enchiladas, or hair-control spray. "I could never endorse a product," he declared, spurning their offers of gold, "in which I did not believe."

His greatness assured, he retired from the game and wrote his memoirs. It was a clean book in which no mention was made of sex, drugs, gambling, or the brutality of football.

The book sold thirty-seven copies.

The coach and his staff sat in an office with high windows, through which shafts of light failed to reach all the corners.

THE VIEW FROM THE PRESS BOX

The room was furnished with arm-desks, a movie projector, and a coffeepot with half-washed cups.

"Man, what a bore this is," said one of the younger coaches, rubbing his eyes.

"It does seem kind of silly," said the Old Coach, pushing away his projector. "Why don't we all go down to the Erstwhile Bar and Grill and get drunk instead? We're going to get our tails whipped this week anyway."

And they did. But no matter what the films showed, the Old Coach refused to blame his players. "We've made a lot of mistakes this season," he said, "and most of them were mine."

Nor did he rage against the news media. "I know how hard it makes your job when we lose," he said. The news media agreed, and suggested that he exercise more self-control on the sidelines. He tended to pace back and forth, his arms flapping like a seagull. He thanked them and said he would try to do better.

After each game, the Old Coach reminded his players that winning was fun, but giving your best, abiding by the rules, and never second-guessing the officials were the values that last forever.

At midseason the coach was fired.

"I'm not surprised," he said. "I had it coming. I did a rotten job."

Asked if he would come out to the games and root for his former team, the Old Coach replied, with great sincerity, "Of course not." And he never did.

The new owner of the pro football franchise announced that he knew nothing about sports, but he wanted to give something back to his city. He realized, he said, that a football team belonged to all the people, rich and poor, young and old, Republicans and Democrats.

He promised the fans that he would never interfere with the men he had hired to run the team. And no matter how badly the team performed, he kept his word. Through the lean years, the green years, and all the in-between years, he avoided the spotlight. He got no closer to the action than the field box seats, where he smiled bravely whenever the team lost, which was nearly every week.

He seldom posed for photographs. All questions were referred to his general manager. He had no suggestions to offer, even when it came time to design a new logo for the team. When a public-relations type came to his office and proposed a halftime show in which the fans would dive for silver dollars in a large vat of maple syrup, the owner ignored him.

This season, after all those years of building, of hardship and heartache, the team went undefeated and won the Super Bowl. When the coach and the general manager dropped by his office to thank the owner for keeping his promises, they found to their surprise that he had been dead for three years.

They buried the owner. He would have wanted it that way.

Auld lang syne, y'all.

GENDER-GAP HEROES

DECEMBER 30, 1984

It is traditional at this time to extend a list of holiday wishes, or to offer a variety of awards in the fun-and-games category.

The object is to avoid any thinking that might be heavier than a soufflé. What is the end of a year for, if not to look back in (pick one) anger, relief, joy, or indigestion?

Time is growing short. The toll of holiday freakish accidents already includes a man who was gored by a water buffalo and a man in Denver who shot a snowplow, claiming it had pulled a knife on him.

For weeks now you have been reminded of the highs and lows of 1984, the greats and the ingrates, the broken records and unkept promises, who won, who lost, and how many piggies stayed home.

So if there are any awards still ungiven, they must be for those who did the most to prove that in sports the gender gap is mostly in the mind. And that may be the best place for it. The envelopes, please:

The Phil Donahue Sensitivity Award. To Iowa Coach Hayden Fry, recalling life as a college undergraduate at Baylor in the 1940s, when an athlete survived on $15 a month for laundry money: "It wasn't that big a deal . . . you could find a little dumplin' to do the wash and then take her out to eat."

Fry was swamped with mail and phone calls from women's groups in Iowa and elsewhere, offering to run him through the presoak and rinse cycles.

The Vanessa Williams Memorial Award. To golfer Jan Stephenson, for declining a $50,000 offer from *Playboy* magazine to pose in the altogether. "I wouldn't expose myself completely for any amount of money," she said. "I could never face my parents again, for one thing." Jan is content to remain the LPGA's queen of cheesecake—a quaint word from the past.

THE VIEW FROM THE PRESS BOX

The Pete Rose Trophy for Persistence. To Morganna Roberts, the kissing bandit, who has favored with her kisses fourteen players and the San Diego Chicken in her thirteen-year career. One conquest was California outfielder Fred Lynn, after which the Anaheim police flung her into the clink, setting up a classic exchange: "What are you in for?" her cellmate asked Morganna, who replied, "Kissing Fred Lynn."

Morganna is not to be confused with Chesty Morgan, a onetime exotic dancer who married and divorced Dick Stello, the National League umpire. When Chesty met Stello and told him her bust measured seventy-two inches, he said, "My God, that's six feet." And they almost lived happily ever after.

The Short-People-Got-No-Reason-to-Live Plaque. With apologies to Doug Flutie, this one goes to songwriter Paul Williams, whose hits include "We've Only Just Begun" and "Evergreen." A frustrated race-car driver, the five-foot-two Williams appears in a commercial for a sports car and is a regular in the Long Beach Grand Prix celebrity pro-am races. "The first year," says his friend, Parnelli Jones, "they almost waved him off the track because they thought it was a driverless car."

Williams is well liked by the pros but takes a ribbing in Gasoline Alley. "Hey, Parnelli," someone will say, pointing at pudgy Paul, "the hood ornament just fell off your car."

The Love-Hath-No-Fury Cup. To Lee Trevino, mystified as ever by his ex-wife Claudia: "All the time we were married, I wanted to buy a ranch. She was always against it and wanted to live in town. Then when we split, guess what's the first thing she bought?"

Trevino is evidently not a superstitious fellow—his young bride is also named Claudia. "We didn't even have to change the name on the bath towels," he said, proudly.

The What-is-Tennis-Without-Loving Cup. To Chris Evert, whose marriage is said to be rocky because her husband, John Lloyd, refused to get serious about the game. Says one pro, "He's so lazy. John practices an hour a day with Chris and thinks that's enough to keep him sharp. She goes crazy when he loses a final set 6-0 or 6-1, with no guts or determination." Adds a woman pro, "It may be a rare case of a guy losing his marriage on the tennis court instead of in bed."

The Conan the Barbarian High-Fashion Award. To retired Baltimore pitcher Jim Palmer, who collects about $125,000 a year

THE VIEW FROM THE PRESS BOX

for posing in his Jockey shorts. The company has spent $7 million on the Palmer ads to date. Among his teammates, Palmer's nickname was "Cakes." No, not as in beef, but from his routine of eating pancakes on the day he pitched. About the ads, Palmer says, "People consider me a sex symbol. Obviously, I'm in that category. But it doesn't change you as a person." Sure, Jim. Bo Derek said the same thing.

The One-is-the-Loneliest-Number Award. To none other than Ronald Reagan, who usually is gifted with a jersey bearing the numeral 1 when visiting athletic teams call at the White House. The president has at least six of those, including souvenirs of the Redskins, Dodgers, and 76ers. An exception was a Dallas Cowboy tunic bearing the number 12, presented by Roger Staubach, the former owner.

For those who have wondered what number Reagan wore in his movie role as George Gipp of Notre Dame, the answer is . . . none. In the early 1920s, college football jerseys had no numbers, so neither did Reagan's in the film.

And that seems as good a way as any to end the year. May you always beat the point spread in 1985, and may all your takeoffs and landings come out even.

LOCKER-ROOM QUOTABLES

OCTOBER 15, 1978

I don't feel it is appropriate for the president to use locker-room humor on any issue.
—Judith Chavez (close companion of ex-Russian spy)

What Jimmy Carter said was: "If the woman's figures are correct, which they aren't, it would be highly inflationary." Not a bad line, really, when you consider that the typical presidential press conference is about as funny as the reading of a will.

But there is a larger question being begged, one that goes beyond the lifestyle of an ex-Russian spy, or the president's good taste, or even the war on inflation, in which we are all foot soldiers (join up now; throw a hand grenade at a beggar).

No, the question that lingers is this: Is someone out there giving locker-room humor a bad name? Frankly, the reaction of the Russian spy's Rent-a-Friend reflects the popular misconception that a locker room is some kind of stag party without the booze and popcorn.

Having spent most of a lifetime going in and out of assorted locker rooms, I can assure you that the humor one finds there is: (1) infrequent, and (2) not very funny. If any lady sportswriters feel they must gain admission to the locker room to do their jobs, then I say let them pass. There is not much more nudity there than one would find in your average city morgue, and sometimes the conversation is just as interesting.

Lissen. They can have my ticket if they want. I have been in the Cotton Bowl dressing room after a Texas-Oklahoma game when the plumbing didn't work and the pipes froze and no one could shower, and the players just milled around sending up fumes and occasionally fainting. Firemen stood at the door trying to hold back the bravest of the newsboys, shouting, "Don't go in there . . . you'll never make it."

THE VIEW FROM THE PRESS BOX

Once in a great while, maybe every twenty years, the real story of a game can be found in the locker room, meaning that the quotes are better than those the writer can invent.

There was the time Bear Bryant lost a football game and said he didn't go for a tie because "a tie is like kissing your sister." That line had a kind of wild poetry about it. Eventually it made every sports column in the land and was translated into several foreign languages.

And what locker-room fan can forget the night Gene Mauch had his tantrum in old Colt Stadium, sweeping all the barbecue chicken and ribs and fresh fruit off the buffet table after his Phillies had blown a game to a hapless Houston team in the last of the ninth. Barbecue sauce splattered the $200 suit of outfielder Wes Covington, who looked around at the walls and the floor and observed, "Boy, the food sure goes fast around here."

Locker-room humor? How about the time Bill Peterson, then the coach of the Houston Oilers, asked his players to kneel so he could lead them in the Lord's Prayer, and in the thick, reverent silence he began, "Now I lay me down to sleep . . . ."

I wonder if anyone has asked Earl Lawson, the Cincinnati baseball writer, how he feels about admitting women to the locker room. Lawson is probably the greatest authority in America on locker-room humor. He was punched out twice by Redleg players, first Johnny Temple and then a few years later by Vada Pinson. Asked to compare the two, Lawson replied, "Temple punches harder."

Where the tradition began isn't clear, but one suspects that television was largely responsible for writers having to make a ritual of visiting the players' boudoir. TV brought the game into our living rooms, assuming the living room is where you keep your set, and reporters had to keep digging to get a story the viewers had not already seen.

But the arrangement has never been a happy one. The story has been told before of how a writer sat unnoticed in the private quarters of the New York Giants as one of the coaches described in fine detail the weaknesses of their opponent, the Philadelphia Eagles. The comments made great reading in the next day's sports page, and even better reading when the Philadelphia papers picked them up.

At a team meeting, the coach of the Giants sought to turn

the situation around. "They're going to come in here Sunday," he snarled, "with fire in their eyes, spoiling for blood . . . *our* blood. So—what are *we* going to do about it?"

Up jumped Rosey Grier, the gentle giant of a lineman. "Maybe it ain't too late, " he shouted. "We could send them a telegram and apologize."

A locker room is a place where the steam will take the wave right out of your hair, and the fragrance will clear your sinuses, and the language will put a bloom on your cheeks. It is a place where a hitter will say that his home run came on a fastball, low and away, and people will take notes as though it really mattered. And coaches will offer such profound thoughts as, "They wanted it more than we did," and "The officials didn't beat us, but . . . . "

The conscientious reporter tries not to ask a question that will get him (or her) punched, because we know we are on company time. Finally, the ladies can be sure they are receiving equal treatment *not* when they get admitted to a locker room, but when they get thrown out of one.

The Tyler Rose, the Ryan Express, and The Bear

WELL WORTH THE WAIT

NOVEMBER 26, 1978

Many years ago, when the world was young, a writer described what it was like the day Willie Mays hit his first home run for the New York Giants.

"The crowd," he wrote, "leaped up and roared and cheered as though Willie had just won the World Series. It was a strange, tingly thing to be a part of, because all that the crowd was saying, really, was, 'Welcome, Willie, we've been waiting all our lives for you.'"

Anyone who has been inside the Astrodome this season, who has seen Earl Campbell run and heard the angels sing, knows the feeling. Oiler fans have been waiting nineteen years for Earl. Softly, they ask, "What took you so long, Earl?"

I am sorry now that I did not save the letters that arrived before the season began, the letters that objected to the publicity Campbell had received even before he had played a single down as a pro; letters protesting that Campbell was another fraud being peddled by the local press as a convenience to the Oilers; and, finally, those letters denouncing any attempt to compare Earl to Tony Dorsett, the previous year's Heisman Trophy winner, now the temperamental darling of the Dallas Cowboys.

True, most high Oiler draft picks of the past have fallen on their hairstyles, their press notices proving as welcome as a kiss from the Mafia. But those who questioned whether Earl Campbell was genuine or not are to be treated today with compassion; they would not know a diamond from a dental filling.

It is a matter of record now that Houston ran the ball forty-two times against Miami, and on twenty-eight of those, the carrier was Campbell. Out of every three rushing plays, Earl had the ball twice.

In the brute game the pros play today, when a back has had

THE TYLER ROSE, THE RYAN EXPRESS, AND THE BEAR

his number called twenty-eight times, you inspect him later for small signs of wear, such as how many ribs are missing, or how much remains of his kidney.

Yet on his twenty-eighth carry, Earl turned the corner of the Miami line and whirled eighty-one yards to the touchdown that claimed a 35-30 victory for the Oilers, in what is turning out to be their most euphoric year.

And did you notice Earl as he hugged the sideline, looking back over his shoulder to check out the pursuing Miami linebacker, Steve Towle? He actually measured him, and paced his step, the way a mailman does when he wants to leave a mean dog behind quickly, but without appearing desperate.

It is a Campbell trademark not to waste motion. After he scores, as he did four times Monday night, he merely drops the ball, he does not spike it, fondle it, or act as though he had never seen one before. When he is down, he rises slowly and catches a quick rest, as Jimmy Brown, the great Cleveland back to whom he is so often compared, always did.

Whether Campbell carries the ball too little or too much—and he has done both this year—it is a fact that any objection has to come from someone other than himself. Earl's dedication is total and his ambition is uncomplicated. No one has heard him complain about anything.

The Oilers are no one-man team and so far there has been no tendency to treat them as such. But Campbell is having an astonishing year, pointing him toward a record for rushing as a rookie, and almost certain recognition as Freshman of the Year. He leads the league in touchdowns and running yardage.

But the most remarkable feature of all this industry is the modesty with which Earl has handled it. He has a fine skill for getting along with people, a skill that many athletes in his position have found quite unnecessary. The Oilers, right now, seem not only content but delighted to put Earl forward as their showcase, reducing themselves to the role of supporting actors. It takes a pretty special fellow to keep his teamates in this frame of mind.

Greg Sampson, the veteran out of Stanford who is having an All-Pro season at tackle, says it for the entire offensive line: "Blocking for Earl is a whole lot of fun. You know that if you get a good fit on your man, there is a chance Earl will break the play for a touchdown. In addition, he is very complimentary.

He thanks us if we've opened a hole. And he keeps quiet if we haven't."

For just a brief, fleeting moment, Greg Sampson had a chance against Buffalo to walk in Earl's moccasins. On a flukish deflection of an Oiler pass, he suddenly found the ball in his arms.

"I have a statistic now," he says, proudly. "One reception for minus one yard. I remember Dan Pastorini stepped up in the pocket. The guy I was blocking went past him, and I turned to see where Dan was, and here came the ball. I'm surprised I caught it. It was a screwball thing.

"All of a sudden, instead of having people trying to get away from you, they were all converging. I saw a little daylight to the left and suddenly it was gone. Now I know how Earl feels. When you have the ball, people are drawn to you like a magnet. You appreciate any block you can get."

Earl doesn't always need an opening. But being an honest young man, if you ask him whether he prefers to run over people or around them, he will tell you he would rather not have them there at all.

SIMPLY DOIN' WHAT'S RIGHT

JANUARY 15, 1984

Earl Campbell once described how, at the age of five, he would rise before dawn to help his papa tend his rose plants in the fields outside Tyler.

Our conversation must have sounded like an old Abbott-and-Costello routine. I asked him, "How much could a five-year-old do?"

"I did the doin'," replied Earl.

I thought he was jiving me. "What did you do when you did the doin'?"

"That's when you take a twig," said Earl, "and brush the dew off the roses so the sun won't burn 'em."

"Oh. *Oh.* The *dewin'*," I said. "You did the *dewin'*!"

It hasn't been easy to understand Earl Campbell. He did not always wish to be understood. But this much is certain: In six years with the Houston Oilers, he has done a man's work, and more, and he deserves something other than the harsh judgment he has suffered since November.

One senses a rising sentiment among Oiler patrons to deport Earl, warning him not to darken our door again. Still others want him traded for his mental health, and a chance to finish his career with a winner.

Whatever his fate, many will feel he brought it on himself. As a tactical move, he scored no points when he complained that he would not treat a dog as he had been treated, having been benched late in a game his team was losing by forty-one points.

No doubt Earl had in mind his own dog, a middle-aged boxer named Pam, who might resent being treated like a football player. Pam has a lot of pride.

Soon it dawned on Earl that his remarks cheapened his trade value and reflected unfairly on Chuck Studley, who had tried to spare him for a better day. Earl responded in a way that was right in character. He spent the rest of the season overcompensating, praising Studley for the good job he was doing in leading the team to two wins in its last ten games.

For most of his career, Campbell tried hard to please everyone. Only in the last three years has he discovered it can't be done. As John Wilson concluded in the *Houston Sports Journal,* "Campbell always said the right things, so far as God and mother and football and country and team were concerned. But he never said more than was necessary and often said less than interviewers wanted . . . . "

Which may explain why his demand to be traded—a code for wanting his salary adjusted, so routine in today's sports commerce—has been treated in Houston like a kind of scandal.

His complaint about being taken out of the Cincinnati game was wrong. But he deserved credit, or at least understanding, for wanting not to be protected, even for wanting to pursue his personal goals. If an Oiler had no personal goals in 1983, he had no reason to play.

Management was wrong, too. While legally correct, holding a document valid for two more years, the Oilers have an obligation to be open, even generous, to one who has performed as Campbell has. No runner endured more punishment with less protest. He led the NFL in rushing his first three years, and became the most admired athlete this town had ever known. He got involved in community service in a way that few do. He did the doin'.

Funny, how often we have been reminded in recent years that the Oilers were so dull under Bum Phillips: Earl left, Earl right, Earl up the middle. The team hugged that great green bathmat like a garden snake. Yet those who saw it still cherish a Monday night in 1978, when the Oilers upset Miami 35-30. Earl rushed for 199 yards and four touchdowns.

Earl is believed to earn $350,000 a year, plus incentives, what in normal times would be viewed as the Rockefeller Trust. These are not normal times. When you pay higher wages to two rookie linemen, and are prepared to pay a million or more to land a quarterback named Warren Moon, you can't expect squeals of joy from your best athlete.

Earl came into the league quite untraveled, and his agent struck a quick deal with the Oilers that deferred much of his money to the end of the century. Ladd Herzeg recognized the unfairness of the original deal and renegotiated the terms in 1980. The Oilers no longer renegotiate.

One who disagrees is Al Davis, who routinely tears up the contracts of players who, for one reason or another, are seen as underpaid. This isn't to say that Davis's approach is right. But the Raiders are the ones playing in the Super Bowl, and the Oilers are the team with an unhappy halfback.

NO TEARS, NO FEARS, NO REGRETS

AUGUST 20, 1986

Earl Campbell can recall the precise instant when he decided to end his football career. He was standing on the sideline Saturday night in the fourth period of the New Orleans Saints' preseason loss to New England. He raised his eyes and glanced at the huge video screen hanging from the ceiling of the Superdome.

"They were running a replay of my last carry," he said. "I noticed how quick the hole opened, and how quickly I accelerated and got to the hole. And it wasn't good.

"The next day I saw it again when the team reviewed the game film. I waited until nearly everyone else had left the room, and then I walked over to Coach Mora and I told him, 'In the morning, I'm going to announce my retirement.'"

Jim Mora, the new coach of the Saints, did not exactly faint dead. But he did suggest that Earl take a couple of weeks and think about it.

"I told him two weeks wouldn't make any difference," Earl said. "Physically, I was fine. My weight is down. I don't have any hurts. But my body won't do what it used to do. I wasn't getting that jump. I only know one way, north and south. I don't know east and west. It was like looking at yourself in the mirror and seeing the way you really are. It was time to go."

So Earl Campbell came home to Houston Tuesday to see his family and meet his future. He is beyond argument the most honored football hero this city has ever known, and nothing in the way his career ended can dull the legend of how it began. As if to emphasize that point, he wanted to make a trade in his first hours of retirement. He hopes to find the fan to whom he gave his first football shoes at the Dome.

"If they will get in touch with your paper," he said, "I'll give them the last pair I wore in return."

Those shoes were made for roughly five yards a carry, with gusts up to fifty.

Fans will compare Earl's runs like bathing beauties on a beach. There were his 200-yard games, and the four touchdowns against Miami the night the Oilers fans waved their "Luv Ya Blue" pom-poms at a national TV audience.

Earl was the symbol of all that, but anyone who expects him to single out a play or a game as his favorite moment is doomed to be disappointed. His biggest thrill in football was his first helicopter ride.

"We came in from Intercontinental and landed on the practice field. What I remember is the way the veterans looked at me, and talked to me, and took care of me. Conway Hayman and Tim Wilson. Later, Carl Mauck called me aside and said, 'Earl, I won't lie to you. You're going to be a big hit in this league. An agent can't do anything for you. What you need is a banker and a lawyer.'

"That was the start of an unbelievable year. Three years. We had something special going. I was fortunate in being with the people who were on that team, and having a coach, Bum Phillips, who cared about us."

The years were 1978 through 1980, and Earl led the league in rushing each season. He was Rookie of the Year and Player of the Year and the legislature named him an official state hero. And he did not even have to die at the Alamo.

Those were the early days, glory days, and we thought they would never end. But then the locusts came: Phillips was fired, Campbell suffered some leg and occasional back miseries, the offensive line slipped, and Earl finished his career in New Orleans, hitting the hole a step too late. No one planned it this way, but in a way Bum and Earl went out together, before the 1986 season could roll around.

No one so far has asked Earl to post a bond guaranteeing he won't change his mind. But when he drove across the Louisiana line, he didn't look back.

"This decision was mine," he said, "and I made it cold turkey. I didn't ask my wife, my mom, the bank, or my accountant. It was all Earl. This morning my accountant, Gardner Parker, started saying, 'What about this, what about that?' I told him there was no point in asking *what if*. I don't play football anymore. I'm not 20 or 34 or 35. I'm not a number. I'm just Earl. It's time to do something different.

"It's like that Merle Haggard song, the only thing I got to worry about now is, 'What am I gonna do with the rest of my life?'

"But I won't worry about it very long. I'm not afraid of life. Like Willie Nelson says, 'Cowboys are special with their own brand of miseries.' "

Anyone remotely in touch with the world of Earl Campbell knows he can carry on an entire conversation just by quoting lyrics to country-and-western ballads. It's part of his charm and a tribute to his memory.

But Earl can dazzle you sometimes with his clarity. "If I ever had to be honest with myself," he said, "yesterday was the day. This was an honest retirement. I could have hung around a year and drawn a salary. But my pride wouldn't let me. Whatever I do, I believe I will be successful. I would have liked to play long enough to reach 10,000 yards, but I wouldn't put that ahead of spending the rest of my life walking on a leg that was shorter than the other. I'm getting out while I'm healthy. I can get on the floor and play with my son, Christian. A year ago, I couldn't."

Campbell says he has no regrets about finishing his career in the land of the blue bayou, where the losses were thicker than gumbo.

"That was part of my manhood," he said. "For me, the best years were the ones I spent at the University of Texas. Everything after that, the good and the bad, made me appreciate what I learned at Texas.

"I got a wife, and soon we'll have a second child, and I'll find an honest way to support them. And I know it will be a big adjustment. It's like that George Jones song, 'We always wanted a two-story house, and now we live in a little old cabin.' "

Earl may be taking a bit of dramatic license here. He has done well financially. He owns an expensive home in Houston and other property, including a ranch in Tyler. His father once worked on that land as a sharecropper, and Earl helped with the chores.

I asked him how he felt on this, his first full day out of captivity. There was a long pause. "I'm not happy," he said, "and I'm not sad. I'm not bitter. It's hard to know when you've had enough.

THE TYLER ROSE, THE RYAN EXPRESS, AND THE BEAR

It's easy to go chasing rainbows. I probably could have gotten away with it for another year. But you have to weigh what you gain against the boos, and the second-guesses.

"I will miss it. But every day I practiced, I got paid. The two-a-days and the minicamps and the games, I got paid. And I hope the Oilers and the Saints feel that I earned whatever I got. You know something? If they came to me today and told me they didn't think so, I'd give it back to them."

We are not prepared to put Earl Campbell, or any athlete, to that particular test. But we believe him, as we believed what our eyes told us in the best of his years. He was one of pro football's great running backs, the best the Oilers ever had.

"Do me a favor," he said. "Thank the fans of Houston for all the cheers. They were appreciated. And if they booed, that was appreciated, too. It made me a better person."

OF NO-HITTERS AND HOMERS

OCTOBER 4, 1981

After Nolan Ryan had separated himself from all the other mortals who have thrown a baseball in the last 100 years, he autographed for a friend a souvenir of the fifth no-hitter of his career.

On one of the baseballs the Los Angeles Dodgers waved at so unsuccessfully, and so historically, Nolan wrote, "I'm glad you were able to see this game." Underneath that line, in parentheses, appeared the word *(over)*, and on the other side of the ball he added, proudly: "I can hit, too."

Only Nolan Ryan would be so considerate, so decent, to alert the reader of a baseball that the message was continued on the other side. Sure, how many people go around reading baseballs? But what we have here is the prospect of a fertile and revolutionary new field for literature. Players could write entire stories, or at least opinions, in this manner, and at the bottom they could make the notation, "Continued on ball two."

The reference to Ryan's hitting was not simply a piece of whimsy, or a display of macho, although pitchers talk about their hitting with the kind of love in their voice that bankers use when talking about money. It was one thing to become the first pitcher in the recorded history of civilization to throw a fifth no-hit game. But Ryan, pleased though he must have been, did not want that achievement to brand him as a one-dimensional fellow, able to play only on defense.

The fact is, Ryan is haunted, even tormented, by the memory of the first game he ever pitched in a Houston uniform, in front of the home folk, on April 12, 1980. The day is remembered not because he pitched well—he lasted six innings against the Dodgers and had no decision—but because he batted well. In fact, Nolan hit the first and only home run of his major-league career, a three-run smash off an unfortunate fellow named Don

THE TYLER ROSE, THE RYAN EXPRESS, AND THE BEAR

Sutton, whose spirit and confidence were so shattered that he left Los Angeles and moved to Houston to be near Ryan, hoping to learn from him the meaning of life.

Ever since, Ryan has been desperate to hit another home run. The no-hitter, of course, was unplanned, the last thing he had in mind. It may even have hurt his concentration at bat.

So obsessed is he with getting that second homer, he actually has bet money on it. The wager is with the same friend who received the souvenir ball, which explains what would seem to be an uncharacteristic boast by Nolan about his hitting. The money involved is not thought to be large, although Ryan, a cautious investor, has brought in Sutton, Terry Puhl, Alan Ashby, and Joe Niekro to help cover his action. According to Nolan, he wanted to let a few close friends in on "a good thing."

The friend does not wish to be identified, making the point that he is in this for the money, not the publicity. The terms of the bet are somewhat loose. The only time limit is whenever Nolan retires, meaning he will play until he homers or his arm falls off. His friend has told him flat out that ketchup has a better chance of becoming a vegetable than Nolan has of hitting another homer.

Ryan actually did not miss by much as the Astros strolled past the Redlegs 8-1 Thursday in his first start after the no-hitter. He had a bunt single and a double off the wall in right center, 380 feet from home, a terrific wallop when you consider that he was bailing out—as described by Larry Dierker—and hitting to the opposite field.

That blow, and his two-straight pitching performances, confirm the deceptive strength of the Alvin farm boy. He has to be one of the strongest people alive just to throw as many pitches as he does—129 in each of his last two games—at the speed he throws them. You conclude he must have lifted cows, or something, when he was a boy. When you think of the players who represented power and strength, you think of Boog Powell and Frank Howard and J. R. Richard, who looked like they could charge people just to let them live. Nolan looks like he should be shaking a tambourine and singing with the New Christy Minstrels.

It really isn't just an image, of course, the clean-cut looks and the All-America label. The Dodgers made a point of it when they saluted Nolan and what he stands for after he blew them away 5-0 at the Astrodome. "He has done it without intimidating people," Reggie Smith said, "without knocking them down. He's done it on sheer determination and a fastball, and now he has learned how to pitch. You can't sit on his fastball any more because he can get his curve over."

He is thirty-four years old and still learning, and if you are trying to measure the enormity of what he has achieved, consider this: There have been 4,000 pitchers in the big leagues, and five of them in their careers held more than two teams hitless. The others were Sandy Koufax (four), and Bob Feller, Cy Young, and Larry Corcoran (three each).

Young retired in 1908, his greatness so established that the award given each season to the best pitcher is given in his name. You may have forgotten Corcoran. His biggest year was 1880, when he started sixty games, completed fifty-seven, and won forty-three. Nice numbers.

Ryan's numbers will assure him of a place in the Hall of Fame. He has won 179 games and lost nearly as many, but in five of them no one on the other team hit safely, and because of that, he belongs to the ages. At the business of striking out people there was none better, except possibly Walter Johnson, known in his prime as "The Big Train." Johnson would be known as "The Big Amtrak" today.

Very little of this is what I had planned to write today. I had intended to write about a pleasant coincidence involving Ruth Ryan, who a few weeks before her husband pitched the game of his life rediscovered a newspaper account of his first big-league victory. The date was Easter Sunday, 1968, and Ryan, then with the Mets, beat Houston and Larry Dierker 4-0 in the Astrodome, while most of Ryan's family watched. Both pitchers were twenty-one and handsome. The writer, a clever fellow, described it as a "teenybopper's dream match."

Ryan struck out seven of the first ten hitters and allowed just three singles, leaving in the seventh because of a blood blister. There is nothing else space will allow, except to report that Nolan went hitless in three times at bat.

RYAN BACK WITH CINDERELLA

OCTOBER 7, 1986

And now the Pest of the West meets the Beast from the East. This is what we have waited twenty-five years to see, the Astros and the Mets going head to head for the National League championship in this, their sterling-silver seasons.

One player has something more at stake than all the others. This is Nolan Ryan, who has a chance to do what no one else can ever claim: that he pitched in the first World Series for both the New York Mets and the Houston Astros.

Seventeen years apart.

As fans of pain and suffering are aware, the New York and Houston teams were once expansion twins, created in 1962, separate but equally awful. Ryan joined the Mets as a rookie in 1968, and a year later became a part of the daffiest, happiest, wildest Cinderella story baseball has ever known.

(Until this year.)

In a pensive mood, Ryan recalled how fortunate he was to be a Met that season, "a part of all the things that happened." The Mets had been baseball's answer to Pinky Lee, existing largely for the purpose of taking a pie in the face. They were the most lovable losers the game had seen, a team that finished last or next to last every year until it won Manhattan and ruled the planet.

Ryan remembers the 1969 World Series as the Broadway musical it really was. The Mets, a kind of freak of nature, rated no chance against a great Baltimore team, the pride of the American League.

"Rod Gaspar joined our club late in the season," Ryan said. "After we beat Atlanta in the play-offs, he was quoted in the paper saying, 'Bring on the Orioles.' A couple of days before the Series opened, Frank Robinson was on "The Tonight Show," and he said to Johnny Carson, 'Who is Rod Gaspar?'

"The truth is, we really didn't know what we were doing there. Most people thought it was a joke and we kept thinking we would wake up and find out they were right. We had a meeting the day before the opener to go over the hitters. The Orioles had guys like Frank Robinson, Brooks Robinson, Boog Powell, Don Buford. Our scouts kept saying, 'Don't throw this and don't throw that.' It went on like that with each hitter. Finally, Jerry Koosman said, 'Well, what the hell do we throw these guys?' We never did get an answer."

A few minutes before the first game in Baltimore, Ryan was sunning himself in the Mets bull pen when some of the boys noticed a stir in the bleachers. A group of the Mets' wives were parading through the stands, the Baltimore stands, carrying a huge bedsheet emblazoned with the stirring words, GO, METS, GO.

Ryan laughed. "The fans were throwing hot dogs and popcorn boxes and pouring beer on them. I said, 'Man, it's a good thing I told Ruth not to leave her seat. Then somebody said, 'You better take another look, Nolan. She's right in the middle of them.'

"I said, 'Gimme those binoculars.' Sure enough, there she was. I had a fit. I don't know what I said to her later, but I let her know how I felt about it."

Ruth Ryan, listening sheepishly to her husband's recital, smiled and said, "I was young and impulsive then. I wouldn't do it now."

Nolan Ryan grinned and said, "I'm older and less emotional. It wouldn't bother me now."

The Astros, the team of his golden age, would seem to have more in common with the team of his flaming youth than the 1986 Mets do. Managed by Dave Johnson—who played second base on the 1969 Orioles—these Mets won 108 games, a wipeout number. They washed over the field like a tidal wave.

The 1969 edition had a dazzling young pitching staff, one genuine .300 hitter in Cleon Jones, and people named Al Weis, J. C. Martin, Tommy Agee, and Art Shamsky. The third baseman, Ed Charles, wrote poetry in his spare time. "His nickname was 'The Glider,' " Ryan said. "Once he hit a home run, ducked into the dugout, and yelled, 'You never throw a slider to the

Glider.' All during the series, we were laughing and having a good time, and the Orioles were getting tighter and tighter."

And now we have a confession to make. If these stories seem familiar, they are. We wrote them in 1980, the last time the Astros played for the National League pennant and a ticket to the World Series. It just seemed like a good time to recycle them, and Ryan, to wish him well in his quest for a twice-in-a-lifetime feeling.

A MAN OF STYLE AND POWER

JULY 14, 1985

You study the eyes of Nolan Ryan. They are brown and soft and there is no meanness in them. Gads, imagine the hours they have spent staring at the discolored leather of a catcher's mitt. When you consider the hitters he has seen, you are left with an image that is Kiplingesque: Hitters to the left of him, hitters to the right of him, volleyed and thundered.

If the eyes show no fatigue, you wonder about the arm. In amassing 4,000 strikeouts, Ryan has averaged one an inning, in a career that began nearly twenty years ago. This is power. This is consistency. This is the essence of the game: the will of the solitary man to take on another.

Nobody has done it better than Nolan Ryan. Two scenes linger from Nolan's historic performance against the New York Mets.

There was the moment when umpire Dave Pallone missed a third strike in the fourth inning. The pitch, a curve ball, broke so much that it seemed to have parachuted over the outside corner. It was so clearly a strike that Sid Fernandez, who was at bat, started to walk away from the plate. Ryan stood on the mound and grinned and gave a slight, philosophical shrug. He had fooled the hitter and he had fooled the umpire and one canceled out the other. What was a guy to do? Nothing except come back with another third strike, which is what Nolan did. A fastball, belt high.

Then came the sixth inning. On three pitches, Ryan struck out Danny Heep, and Ryan had his magic number. The crowd stood, the better to scream. Nolan doffed his cap. Now we waited to see what his reaction would be when he walked off the field to another grand ovation, having achieved something no other pitcher had done.

THE TYLER ROSE, THE RYAN EXPRESS, AND THE BEAR

He got real emotional. I think he snapped his chewing gum. He didn't spike the ball or high-five the world. The game, you see, wasn't over.

This was vintage Nolan Ryan. And vintage Houston Astros. They dropped a fly ball and blew a rundown that Ryan started, and let in the two cheap runs that tied the score. Ryan was out of the game for a pinch hitter, and long gone when the Astros won it in the twelfth, 4-3, for someone else (Dave Smith).

So all Nolan had to show for his heroics was just another piece of immortality. As far as the won-lost record is concerned, he didn't work that night.

The fact is, Nolan Ryan is the exception to the oldest rule in sports. He has made an honest man out of Grantland Rice, who tried to tell us that it didn't matter whether you won or lost, but how you played the game. This sentiment was so contrary to the American sporting ethic that Rice was denounced as some kind of Bolshevik (or should have been).

Then along comes Lynn Nolan Ryan, the squire of Alvin, Texas, to prove the point. That's right. Don't try to tell us that he has lost almost as many as he has won. That dog won't hunt anymore. If you bring it up, I am going to ask my friend Rambo to stop by and spray your house with 10,000 bullets.

The greatness of Ryan is no longer open to argument, if it ever was. He stands as the most dramatic pitcher of his time, the proof of which is this: They have been playing baseball for 110 years and he is the only pitcher ever to strike out 4,000 batters in his career. No other pitcher, dead or alive, has thrown five no-hitters or fanned 300 or more in each of five seasons. At thirty-eight, he throws a fastball that was clocked against the Mets at 97 mph. Do you know what this means? He has defied time and physiology. When most fastball pitchers near forty, they are throwing knucklers, if they are not playing first base.

Ryan's achievements have been so epic, his manner so modest, that he has left behind a trail of disbelievers. When a correspondent wrote that Ryan, in his first year in the minors, had 313 strikeouts in 205 innings, an editor decided the figures were a typing error, and he turned them around.

If the game's critics and accountants have not always given him his full due, Ryan has rarely complained. He is far from a showman, but he possesses a star quality entirely his own. He also has a sense of the moment. When he really needs something, wants it, just has to have it, Nolan pumps up like Arnold Schwarzenegger and blows people away. He had ended the fifth inning by getting Darryl Strawberry on a called strike, for #3,999. That brought up Heep, a former Astro, to lead off the sixth. Didn't you see it coming? Couldn't you feel it? Three pitches. Ryan just exterminated him.

He finished his service with a season high of eleven strikeouts, and a career total of 4,004. It was the 158th time he had whiffed ten or more in a game. He is hanging the targets high for young Dwight Gooden, the inheritor of his flame, sitting in the opposing dugout. The fact that Nolan reached this altitude against his original team, the Mets, added a certain fullness to the night.

An unusual footnote to the game was the fact that two of the announcers, Houston's Milo Hamilton and Bob Murphy of the Mets, had been present when Ryan recorded his first big-league strikeout: Pat Jarvis, of the Atlanta Braves, on September 11, 1966.

Over the years, Ryan has changed hardly at all. He never has tried to conceal the enjoyment he gets from what he does. He is an artist without temperament, more relaxed than, say, a Sandy Koufax or a Steve Carlton, who enjoyed their fame but not at ground level. A friend who once visited Koufax, and needed to use the phone, found that he had shoved it in his oven.

A lot of athletes seize on a modest amount of success to flaunt their temperament. Not Ryan. He has been a splendid role model, not only for kids, but for other players.

With remarkable patience, Ryan has mapped his campaign over the years. He is his agent, his coach, his chaperon. He has built his monument one brick at a time. Have you ever read where Nolan Ryan knocked a manager, a teammate, anyone?

Indeed, Nolan feels a debt to the early Mets, the Angels, and the Astros—teams that had to scratch for runs and lost more than they won. If they had provided him with such luxuries as a three-run lead and errorless defense, he might be less than the competitor he is today. Misery made him strong.

ONE MAN: BRYANT

AUGUST 1981

One man brushes many lives. The bigger the man, the broader the brush. And that is why I am sitting here now, trying to decide which would be the best way to begin telling you about the Bear Bryant I know: with George Blanda, or Frank Broyles, or Amos Alonzo Stagg, or the Junction boys, or Johnny Musso, or one of my sons.

In a lifetime of coaching, Bryant has shaped, changed, or touched the futures of, let's risk a guess, three thousand young men. Forty-three of them, former players and assistants, went into business for themselves as coaches, among them Bum Phillips and Paul Dietzel and Jack Pardee and Steve Sloan and Charlie McClendon. Most of them preached the gospel according to Bryant.

Big man. Big brush. Big Bear.

This is the year of the countdown in college football. Alabama's Crimson Tide needs to win nine games this season to give Bryant a career total of 315 victories, breaking the record held by A. A. Stagg. It is a wondrous and exciting and staggering achievement when— not if—it falls to the onetime farm boy from Fordyce, Arkansas.

To get a sense of what is involved, consider Amos Alonzo Stagg and his times. He was born in 1862, three years before Abraham Lincoln was murdered. The schools where Stagg gained his fame, Chicago and College of the Pacific, dropped football twenty or thirty years ago. He was in his prime in those lilac days before World War I, a time of candy-striped shirts, gaslights, and horse-drawn streetcars.

Stagg's teams were the first to huddle, to quick kick, to placekick, to use a man in motion. He was a head coach for fifty-seven years, retiring at ninety-one. He died in 1965 at 103.

Bryant may feel as old on certain days, but he will have beaten Stagg's mark in two-thirds the time. That he has lasted as long in today's meat-grinder game is a small miracle in itself. The planet has changed since the heyday of Stagg. Radio and teletype and TV carry the news instantly to every corner of the map. With each passing week, Bryant will see more cameras, more tape recorders, more people bearing pads and pencils. When Stagg won his 314th game, he was not chasing a goal; his record was probably of great interest only to Pop Warner, who would finish with 313.

Many of the coaches who were riding high when Bryant began his career—Frank Leahy, Earl Blaik, General Bob Neyland—are no longer living. The championship coaches who came along at about the same time—Bud Wilkinson, Duffy Daugherty, Bobby Dodd, and Woody Hayes, and even the young Turks who came along years later, Darrell Royal, Frank Broyles, and Ara Parseghian—have been out of coaching since the mid-1970s.

It was Broyles who said, "I think it is paramount to the future of college football that Coach Bryant set the record. His doing so would be a tremendous boost to the sport. He is the only one who can . . . . He has been more willing to give of himself and his talents than, maybe, the rest of us. Then I'll say this: After he sets the new record, his will never be broken. The man was made to coach. We will not see one like him again."

Bryant was in his twelfth year, on his third job, when he sent his Texas A&M team against Missouri in 1957. Frank Broyles was making his debut as head coach of the Tigers. The Aggies won a shutout.

By the time their teams met again in the Sugar Bowl, both had moved on—Bryant to Alabama and Broyles to Arkansas. At a New Year's Eve party the night before the game, Broyles was paid a flowery tribute by the president of the school.

Then came Bryant's turn at the microphone. He turned to his younger colleague: "I just want to say one thing, Frank. About this business of loving you just as much if you lose. Don't you believe a damned word of it."

Bryant was not often on the wrong end of a scoreboard. He played at Alabama on teams that lost three games in three years. He played and coached under Frank Thomas through most of the 1930s, then assisted Red Sanders for two years at Vanderbilt. He was on his way to see the governor of Arkansas about the head coaching job at the University of Arkansas when he heard the news of Pearl Harbor on his car radio.

So his pursuit of Amos Alonzo Stagg did not begin until 1945, a few weeks after his discharge from the Navy. His Maryland team—salted with tough ex-sailors he had thoughtfully brought with him—wiped out poor Guilford College, 60-6.

I am not sure at what point he actually became a legend, but he was already one to many of us long before the national media discovered him.

A fellow named George Blanda, the oldest human ever to get paid for throwing passes, remembers his sophomore year at Kentucky, when the team's new coach walked into a meeting room for the first time. Paul William Bryant was starting his second salvage job. Said Blanda, "I thought to myself, 'This is what God must look like.'"

You begin with that face, that bold, cracked-stone, made-for-Mount Rushmore face. You can read his entire career in that face, all 306 victories, and seventy-nine losses, and sixteen ties. It is a glorious face, the lines so deep that the jaw appears to be hinged, like that of a puppet.

In retrospect, I think I know what George Blanda meant, how he felt. Forgive me if this gets a little personal. My relationship to Coach Bryant is, after all, unique. I am the only writer in America who covered every game of the only losing season he has suffered in thirty-six years of head coaching.

The last twenty-three have been at Alabama, where his roots were, and where his teams have won or shared six national championships. But I know him best from the years and the teams I covered, and those were at Texas A&M. He was still restless and hungry then, as another admirer put it, "with the fear of plowing cheap bottom land in his soul."

I was in his office the day that a reporter from *Time* magazine asked why it meant so much for him to win. Bryant gestured idly with his hands, then made two or three false starts, and finally thundered, "Hell, I don't know. All I know is if you have on a different-colored jersey than me, I want to beat your butt."

His first Aggie team, in 1954, lost nine games. Its only win came over Georgia by a score of 6-0, a victory so precious that after the game Bryant danced a jig in the locker room with his trainer, Smokey Harper, who was white-haired and wore a hearing aid.

The impression the Bear made on Texas A&M, and vice versa, is oddly out of proportion to the years he spent there, four out of thirty-six. Part of the answer lies in the nature of Bryant, who went there as a coach still young, and left there knowing he would never have to give that much again. When he arrived,

A&M was a cold, drab, womanless world, perhaps the toughest recruiting challenge in college football. Trying to prove it wasn't, Bryant landed on probation.

The 1954 Aggies were the smallest and weakest team Bryant would ever have, and yet one of the closest to his heart. To whip that team into shape, to teach them the joys of sacrifice and self-discipline, Bryant hauled them off to a desolate patch of sand in the Texas Hill Country called Junction. There they held the last off-campus fall practice the NCAA ever allowed, working out on a field with no grass, sleeping in quonset huts.

Eight sophomores survived that torture to go unbeaten as seniors and win the Southwest Conference championship. One of them, Gene Stallings, was asked years later if Junction was as rugged as the stories suggested. "All I know," he replied, "is that we went out there in two buses and came back in one."

Around Bryant, even sportswriters dropped some of their sissy habits. One day we sat in his office, both nursing winter colds, both armed with bottles of cough syrup. The Bear twisted the cap off his and guzzled it like soda pop. He stared at me while I fumbled with a spoon and slipped it back into my pocket. I think of that as the day Bear Bryant taught me to drink cough medicine from the bottle.

Once, he interrupted a practice when he spotted me throwing a football to a student manager. He walked off the field, shaded his eyes, squinted, and said, "Oh, excuse me. I mistook you for Sid Luckman." Then he blew his whistle and went back to work.

I was the same age as his players then, and I feared him just as much. But he was enormous fun to write about: stern, warm, profane, sentimental, gruff, a man of color and strength. I learned from him.

Of course, the Bryant you see today is Father Flanagan compared to the one who coached at A&M. The Aggies had a tendency to appreciate him much more after they no longer had to play for him. So did some of the earlier Alabama players—Joe Namath and Ken Stabler, to name two. Both were bounced from the team for bending the rules. Both would have hesitated to say, at the time, as linebacker Barry Krauss did, "I love him. The biggest thrill is that I can walk in and talk to him, and he knows and cares about me."

Bryant has always known and cared about his players, but he didn't always show it. There is no mystery to why he has kept on coaching and kept on winning. He is a superb motivator who once convinced a group of freshmen that they would have to work harder than the players before them because they were war babies. He did not invent the art of poor-mouthing , but he did advance it, saying of one opponent, "They're big and mean and have blood in their eyes, while we're Peaceful Valley." To my knowledge, he was the first coach to credit victories to his players having "good mamas and papas."

Above all, he has been willing to change, as the country has changed, the game changed, and the kids changed. He relented on the hair issue as far back as 1971, when Johnny Musso, his star running back, was given an audience on behalf of the squad.

"Why in God's name do you want hair hanging out of your helmet?" asked Bryant. Musso replied, "It's important to us."

Bear sat silent a moment, then answered, "If it's important to you—and damned if I know why—let me think about it."

After he left A&M, we saw each other, except by accident, when Alabama played a team from the Southwest Conference, or when I was assigned to one of his bowl games. But we talked on the phone and exchanged letters. I am looking at one now, dated November of 1970. The Tide was headed for a subpar year, 6-5-1. Bryant wrote, "I could really use Smokey now to tell me what a great coach I am." His faithful trainer, Smokey Harper, had died two months earlier, at seventy-three.

I named my younger son after him, but it was the older one, Steve, who went out for football in the eighth grade and made the team at linebacker. Bryant dropped him a note: "Dear Steve. It is refreshing to hear that some young men still like to play defense. The ones I meet all want to play quarterback."

Three years passed. I saw Coach Bryant at the Sugar Bowl, and he asked how Steve was doing. I said, "Well, I wasn't going to brag, but he made all-conference at linebacker in the Texas Prep School League, and he's only a junior."

There was a flicker of interest in Bryant's eyes. "All-conference," he repeated. "Only a junior. How big is he?"

Proudly, I answered, "He's five-feet-five and weighs 145."

The light went right out of the Bear's eyes. He walked away, chuckling.

I yelled after him, "Boy, you sure have gotten picky at Alabama. He could have played for you at A&M."

THE RECORD AT LAST

NOVEMBER 29, 1981

BIRMINGHAM, Alabama—After thirty-five years, all those Saturdays in all those stadiums, it hardly seemed fair to expect that grand, imposing old gentleman in the houndstooth hat to stand out there in the gathering chill of a darkening night and wait until the fourth quarter to learn if The Record was to be his.

But he did and it was. Paul William ("Bear") Bryant reached his magic number Saturday as Alabama gave him the 315th victory of his fabled career. The Crimson Tide was fit to be tied, twice, and fell behind once by a field goal, before subduing archrival Auburn. The win came late and tough and hard, exactly the way the Bear says he likes them.

"Lordy, we had eighty yards in fumbled punts, or something like that," he said, an exaggeration, but not by much. Even as he talked, the celebration spilled off the surface of Legion Field and onto the parking lots and out to downtown Birmingham and across the state of Alabama. Bryant squinted into the television lights and said, "To turn around and come back and win, well, if I could have charted it, I'd have wanted to come from behind and win it. That shows our kids have some character and class."

Alabama did not exactly deliver up a work of art to lift Bryant past Amos Alonzo Stagg and into that special place in heaven reserved for the coach with the most wins. The Crimson Tide lost four fumbles, two on dropped fair catches. Auburn retaliated by blowing three field goals and throwing three interceptions.

"Our mistakes killed us," Auburn Coach Pat Dye said, "and their mistakes kept us in it."

Dye, like nearly everyone else in the crowd of 78,000 fans, and in a press box filled with newsmen from around the land, has a previous relationship with the Bear. Dye coached under

Bryant at Alabama, and Bear's recommendation helped Dye land his present job.

Bryant's former players gathered from various points on the map to be near him for the historic moment. John David Crow, his Heisman Trophy winner at Texas A&M, was on the field before the game. Joe Willie Namath was in the television booth. They came as if in response to some silent whistle that only former players can hear. Out of his Alabama past came Dan Ford, now the coach at Clemson, and Bud Moore, one-time coach at Kansas. Don Watson flew up to help represent the Aggies, and Leon Fuller, a linebacker on one of Bryant's early Alabama teams, was scouting on behalf of the Texas Longhorns, who engage the Tide in the Cotton Bowl on New Year's Day.

With the game tied at halftime, Fuller shook his head and prayed softly. "Man, I hope Auburn doesn't leave the record for us."

President Reagan and former President Carter called, and Bryant was properly touched.

"President Reagan reminded me that he stopped by our practice early this fall in a tuxedo, which he did," said the Bear, not bothering to explain if the president was on his way to a function, or if formal wear is required at Alabama practices. "And I reminded him that when we played in the Rose Bowl [in 1935] and he was out there as a cub reporter or sportscaster or whatever he was, he came out to watch us practice every day.

"I appreciated his call very much," he added, "and the same with President Carter, except that he didn't come to our practices."

A collective giggle rose from the assembled press, and Bryant looked startled. "I wasn't trying to be funny," he said.

Clearly, this was not the time nor place for laughs, but the newsboys could be excused for feeling a little nervous. They are not often in the presence of a living deity.

He sat behind a desk with a wooden rail in front of it—almost like an altar—as he met them in a private trailer reserved for such purposes at every Alabama game. He praised Auburn for "playing their little ol' hearts out," and he accepted the record on behalf of all those players and coaches who had a hand in it at this and his previous stops—Maryland, Kentucky, and Texas A&M.

"Really," he said, "only in the last week have I been aware that so many people who were involved in it [the record] expected it to be done. I had calls and telegrams all week. In that respect, I'm relieved to have it over. Now I just want to go home, have some milk and bread and onions, and watch the game on TV. I hope my granddaughter remembered to turn that thing on," referring to his video recorder.

The day was important and strange and inevitable. No matter how he tries to conceal his sentiments, and whatever they may be, Paul Bryant has now run a course that began at Maryland, in September 1945, with a 60-6 victory over little Guilford College. He was just two weeks out of the Navy, and the fifteen sailors he brought with him were even newer arrivals to the campus.

The president of the United States was Harry Truman, who did not make a habit of telephoning football coaches and can be excused for overlooking Bryant's first one.

Now the legend will leap and grow some more, and the Bryant stories will multiply between now and the week of the Cotton Bowl. A fairly recent one reveals how closely he still attends to the details of his football team. This fall, during two-a-day drills, word reached Bryant from the cooks in the kitchen that many of his players were skipping breakfast.

"Most of us were just too tired to get up," said Warren Lyles, the middle guard, "so we slept in. One morning one of the guys heard a funny knock at his door at 7:30. He shouted and didn't get an answer. He heard the knock again, and he got out of bed and threw open the door so he could unload on whoever was there. But it was Coach Bryant. He just said, 'Son, have you been to breakfast this morning?' He said, 'No, sir, but I'm on my way right now.' Coach Bryant just walked down the hall knocking on doors. None of us missed breakfast after that."

Football teams do not move well on empty stomachs. Bryant wanted the record, and every win it represents, and all that such a thing means. It means more than he will ever admit. You do not often hear a losing coach tell the man who beat him that he was proud for him and that he loved him, as Pat Dye told the Bear Saturday night.

A few minutes before, Dye had told reporters, "He's the greatest coach the game has known. I don't think there's any question about it. If anyone was going to have that record, it ought to be him."

Only Bryant can say for sure why he keeps coaching. But why he keeps winning is no mystery. He recruits superior athletes,

THE TYLER ROSE, THE RYAN EXPRESS, AND THE BEAR

and the legend helps him. He used three quarterbacks against Auburn with no drop-off. A reserve halfback named Linnie Patrick carried the ball only once until the fourth quarter, then spun and twisted for runs of thirty-two and fifteen yards and the touchdown that sent Bama ahead to stay at 21-17.

Bryant has mellowed some, but he still controls the game. Joey Jones, his safety, fumbled fair catches twice. After the first one, Auburn's Chuck Clanton dribbled and kicked the ball thirty-eight yards to the Alabama 5, setting up the touchdown that tied the score at 14-14. The next one gave the Tigers a field goal from nineteen yards out and the lead with two and a half minutes gone in the fourth quarter.

Alabama had a different safety the next time Auburn punted.

Back in the trailer, the Bear was asked what his plans were for the Cotton Bowl. With just the trace of a smile, he snapped, "How the hell could I have some plans for the Cotton Bowl, when I haven't even quit shaking yet from the end of the game?"

The record is his, the power and the glory, and he can afford to be testy with tiresome sportswriters. In fact, he can afford to be anything he wants.

A FINAL TRIBUTE

JANUARY 30, 1983

The heart of Bear Bryant was like a stadium, with room for thousands of former players and coaches and writers and friends. The telephone in the home of Johnny Mitchell, a trusted chum out of the Texas Aggie era, did not stop ringing the day after the jarring news of Bryant's death. "People called from all over the country," he marveled. "They left messages with my wife: 'Tell Johnny we were sorry to hear about Paul.' It was as if they thought he belonged to me."

So he had. In a sense he belonged to all of those who care about the family of sports, about pride and loyalty and excellence—the Scriptures according to Paul W. Bryant. Many were the people and places that claimed him: all of Alabama, and parts of Texas, Kentucky, and Maryland, where he coached. And Arkansas, where he was born.

If one were to ask what made Bryant the driven competitor he was, the answer starts here, with the shabby twelve-year-old boy who helped his mother sell vegetables from the back of a wagon drawn by mules, enduring the taunts of the town kids. Bryant wrestled with more than a carnival bear in his lifetime. Years later, he wrestled with a win-at-any-cost image he once courted but came to dislike. Still, you don't win as often or as long as he did, you don't become Paul ("Bear") Bryant and not pick up labels and some detractors.

It was sudden and sorrowful and, yes, a little eerie when Bryant's great heart stopped beating this week at sixty-nine. He had done everything he set out to do, and more. He became the winningest college football coach of all time. Depending on which poll you believed—and he always believed the one that had Alabama first—he won five national titles. He retired and handpicked his successor, Ray Perkins. And then six weeks after he announced he was stepping down, four weeks after he coached his last game, he died.

THE TYLER ROSE, THE RYAN EXPRESS, AND THE BEAR

According to Coach Bryant, his wife had to be convinced that his retirement was a good idea. They had met as students at Alabama, where Mary Harmon was a campus beauty. (She still is.) Her intuition may not have agreed with his, but now we are left to ponder the order of things.

Some were still trying to figure out why he retired when he did.

Our guess is the Bear had finally reached an age where he no longer wanted to change, as he had done for five decades. The day of the Wishbone was ending. Texas and Oklahoma, among the teams that perfected it, had already gone another way. But a few years ago, Bryant vowed to a writer, "I'll never teach pass blocking again."

Pass blocking is mean stuff. It is the least fun you can have on a football field. So it was simple, really. Bryant made a coaching decision. When he felt Alabama might no longer dominate with the Wishbone—just winning wasn't enough—he stepped down.

There were contradictions in the nature of Paul ("Bear") Bryant that provided his friends, and even his critics, with endless hours of puzzlement. He was strong as pig iron, and yet he cried without shame: after bitter losses, or when he learned that one of his former players was seriously ill, or when the news was good, as when Gene Stallings got his old job as coach of the Texas Aggies. He was like the old-time cowboys, who could brave the hardships of the range and then weep at a painting on a bordello wall.

In the months to come, there will be endless attempts to explain Bear Bryant. Those with a sense of romance and imagination will try to convince the world that he was a sort of Wallace Beery character; that beneath his gruff, gravel surface beat a heart as soft as banana mush.

But his compulsion to win is what most will remember. Some of his most bitter defeats were, in fact, tie games. One year Alabama had raced to Tennessee's 1-yard line, tied 7-7 with a few seconds left. A sophomore quarterback named Ken Stabler threw the ball out of bounds to stop the clock. Unfortunately, for Stabler and Alabama, it had been fourth down. That was how the game ended.

To compound the pain, when they reached the locker room the Alabama players found the old wooden door locked and no one around with a key. They stood there, miserable and impatient and fearful, waiting to see how their coach would react. Suddenly, Bear Bryant sent a powerful forearm shiver into the door, and with a loud snap it split in two. He led his team inside.

Bryant's position on this issue was always clear. His first Texas Aggie team lost a game by three points when he had them try for a touchdown. He was asked if he had considered going for a field goal and the tie. He snapped, "Hell, no. A tie is like kissing your sister."

That line became nearly as well identified with Bryant as Leo Durocher and his immortal "nice guys finish last." Later, with admiration, I asked Bryant how he always managed to come up with such great lines.

He never hesitated. "Aw," he replied, "I heard Jim Tatum say it once at Maryland."

He called himself a field coach, as opposed to those who prefer to draw X's and O's on a blackboard. Whatever he was, the record book establishes him as the greatest of his time, maybe any time. Now he is a mythical figure, a soul brother for Amos Alonzo Stagg, whose victory mark he broke and who practically invented the college game, and Knute Rockne of Notre Dame, the first of the great psychologists, of whom Bryant may have been the last. Clark Nealon, the former *Post* sports editor, remembers as a junior at A&M reading about the death of Rockne in a plane crash in a Kansas cornfield. "When Rockne died," says Clark, "there was sorrow on a national scale. I can't recall a sports figure whose death caused the same reaction until Bryant."

A few years ago, ABC used a hidden camera to pick up one of the Bear's halftime talks for a television special. He didn't say much until it was time to return to the field, and then his voice was a hoarse whisper. "This is great," he told his Crimson Tide. "We're *behind*. If we've got any class at all, now is our chance to find out."

Alabama did rally, but the best they could get was a wild, 37-37 tie with Florida State. There is no record of what he said after the game. Such outcomes bedeviled him, but they will not be his legacy. Winning will. He was Paul ("Bear") Bryant.

With a Little Help From My Friends

HE'S STILL GOT THAT SWING

APRIL 11, 1982

The trouble with Rusty Staub is that you can't tell time by him. No, that doesn't mean he should have a sundial for a face. All we mean is that he has changed little—just a touch through the chest and around the beltline—since he first came to Houston as a freckled, six-foot-two, 190-pound, nineteen-year-old cleanup hitter. Do you want to feel really ancient, sports fans? Do you want to feel like George Burns's older brother? All you need to know is that, with the arrival of the 1982 baseball season, Daniel Joseph Staub, thirty-eight, starts his twentieth year in the big leagues.

As a fiddler on the roof of the press box would say, "I don't remember growing older, when did he?"

Staub has been gone from the Houston baseball scene since 1969—to Montreal, New York, Detroit, Texas, and back to New York—and yet he is part of the sports history of this town as few have ever been. When the Astros traded Staub, they did more than deal away one player. It was like giving up a child for adoption. He was their first handmade star, their first .300 hitter, their first $100,000 bonus baby who survived and produced.

He has been around for nearly twenty years, and Houston still claims him. His home is here. His friends are here. Some of his favorite restaurants are here—not including the one he owns on the East Side of Manhattan, called Rusty's. It is not stretching the truth to say he left his youth here. And now he's quite the visible bachelor-around-town in the nonbaseball months, tending to his real estate investments and helping various charities. For example, the night before he left for spring training, he worked as a celebrity waiter at a March of Dimes benefit dinner.

WITH A LITTLE HELP FROM MY FRIENDS

To understand the special place Staub occupies in Houston, you have to go back to the autumn of 1961. Most of the teams in baseball had dispatched their agents to his native New Orleans, where, as a high-school senior, Rusty Staub had batted .300 on home runs *alone*. Scouts from sixteen clubs were there, or on the way, when Hurricane Carla blew in. It poured for five days. When two Philadelphia scouts were pressed by the home office for a report, they wired back, "He runs good in the rain."

But here came Paul Richards, the Houston general manager, flying through the hurricane—it was like *Hell's Angels,* see, with the scarf and the goggles—to stick $100,000 in Rusty's wet palm. (This later became known as the Louisiana Purchase.) After a year in the minors at Durham, North Carolina, he was batting cleanup in the major leagues.

He was just what a struggling expansion franchise needed: a teenage idol, a symbol of good times and winning teams to come. They would finally come—long after Rusty had left town, seen the lights, and played in a World Series with the Mets in 1973.

Suddenly, twenty years have passed, and he is one of a handful of active players who have been around that long. Pete Rose and Joe Morgan broke in that same year, 1963. This will be Jim Kaat's twenty-fourth year, if the Cardinals keep him; twenty-one years each for Willie Stargell and Gaylord Perry; and twenty-two for Carl Yastrzemski.

The list of iron men isn't long, and the name that was least likely to be there is Rusty Staub. Almost from the start, some said his career wouldn't last—that his ankles were too weak, his feet too tender, and his upper body too big. They were wrong.

He taped his ankles like a football player and, for a time in Houston, wore soccer shoes in the outfield and spikes to run the bases. He never stopped looking for an edge. One year, he even led his team in stolen bases. In 1970, at Montreal, he had twelve steals, two more than Ron Fairly.

In Montreal they nicknamed him *Le Grand Orange.* And, along the way, Staub became baseball's Galloping Gourmet; he opened a restaurant and could cook too. One of his specialties is chicken Cordon Bleu. He once kept $30,000 worth of vintage wine in a closet in his Houston townhouse.

He became the kind of player the scouts, and his admirers, thought he would be: a smart hitter and a leader on every team

WITH A LITTLE HELP FROM MY FRIENDS

that signed him. This year has marked a career change for Rusty Staub. During the winter, the Mets made him a player-coach. Players had been asking his advice for years. At twenty-three, he taught a veteran left-hander named Hal Woodeshick a better way to throw his slider. Woody was a relief pitcher—and a character—on those early Houston teams, then known as the Colt .45s. He figured in what may have been the most embarrassing memory of Staub's career. He won't appreciate our recalling it now. But you get a sense of Staub's pride when you realize that the story still makes him flinch, twenty years later.

Staub was a rookie first baseman when Woodeshick twice picked off a runner. Unfortunately, he also picked off Staub. "Now, the first time was my fault," says Staub. "But the second time, we were playing the Mets, and I told Woody, 'I'm going in on the first pitch, so whatever you do, throw to the plate.' He nodded. I charged in, and the next thing I knew, Woody had gone over to first. The ball whistled past my ear into right field."

Asked to pick the high and the low of his career, Staub says, "I don't think anyone realizes how rough it was for me at first. Some of the players resented the bonus money I got, and the publicity. I was ready for the game, but not for the life. The high spot was winding up as the leading hitter in the 1973 World Series, when I wasn't sure I'd even be able to play."

Rusty hit only .224 as a rookie in Houston. "The fans thought they were getting Stan Musial, Ted Williams, and Mickey Mantle combined," he says. "Then, all of a sudden, they found out that all they had was a nineteen-year-old kid who didn't know a thing."

He always had the swing, and the rest he learned fast. He batted .333 in 1967, led the league at midseason, and finished in the top five as Roberto Clemente won the title. Now he has more than 2,500 hits to show for his twenty seasons, and he is closing in on 300 homers and 1,500 runs batted in. His lifetime average is .280. But you can't judge Rusty Staub on numbers alone. His old teammate, Joe Morgan, once said, "Pete Rose gets a lot of ink, and he deserves it: 'Mr. Hustle.' More people ought to watch Staub. He always backs up the base, runs out every ball. Nobody hustles more than Rusty."

The year the Astros hired Harry Walker as batting instructor, Gene Mauch, then managing the Phillies, made an observation: "The best batting coach Houston ever had is that redheaded kid. Staub made himself a hitter, and he did one hell of a job."

WITH A LITTLE HELP FROM MY FRIENDS

Our friendship dates back to his rookie year. Before his first major-league road trip, his mother—nervous, as most mothers are when a young son is about to leave home—asked me to keep an eye on her unmarried, sheltered, teenage son. At the time, Staub did not smoke, drink, keep late hours, or chase girls. To this day, at least partly as a result of my influence, he still does not smoke.

A few weeks before Staub left for training camp this season, he had dinner with friends at the home of Houston's well-known music-making couple, singer Nancy Ames and pianist Danny Ward. I was there, having covered Staub in those years when he and the Colt .45s were young and struggling and the odyssey had just begun. By the end of the evening, we had talked the equivalent of a book. Ah, the names . . . Dizzy Dickson, John Bateman, Hector Brown, Dave Adlesh, Joe Morgan, Jimmy Wynn, Norm Larker, Dick Drott, Turk Farrell. With each name came an anecdote, or a character insight, or a piece of craziness.

He talked about George Brunet, a vagabond pitcher who played for sixteen or seventeen teams, at least. Once, when the Braves traded Brunet to the St. Louis Cardinals, their publicity man caught hell from his wife after she intercepted a telephone message telling him what time to "pick up that Brunet from Milwaukee" at the airport.

In 1969, Staub helped write a new baseball law by getting traded to Montreal for Donn Clendenon and Jesus Alou. Remember that one?

After Clendenon had refused to report to Houston, the commissioner ruled that the deal must stand because the Expos had built their first-year promotion around Staub, *Le Grand Orange*. For a while, it looked as though we might have to go to war with Canada. In the past, a trade was voided if a player balked. From then on, the rule was *caveat emptor*.

In 1973, Staub helped the Mets—who had won only eighty-two games—to reach the World Series. He delivered key hits and big catches for them, despite a shoulder so painful it forced him to throw underhanded. The Mets lost the Series to Oakland in seven games.

Nostalgia is nice, but it doesn't mean a thing if you don't have that swing. Rusty Staub still has it. Last year, in a strike-shortened season, he hit .317. He will play this season under his fourteenth manager, George Bamberger, and there are some who think Staub will manage a team himself someday. But he is not thinking that far ahead. He is not thinking much beyond his next time at bat. His contract with the Mets expires in 1983. "I'd like to sign one more," he says. "It would mean something to play past my fortieth birthday, to have lasted twenty-two years. Not many do. I don't think anyone thought I could."

Rusty was born on April Fool's Day, 1944. He came along at the end of an era when rookies were barely tolerated, and when he was nineteen, some of his teammates rode him without mercy. In a bar one night, he took the teasing—and the abuse—and with a grin, he said, "It's okay. I'll be here long after you guys are all gone." Rusty Staub kept his word. He usually does.

FIVE HUNDRED WAYS TO WIN OR LOSE

MAY 30, 1976

Was it in or out of character for A. J. Foyt to lend a car for a practice spin to the lady motorist, Janet Guthrie? Was it, or was it not, a male chauvinist thing to do?

Yes and no.

There is that touch of gallantry in Foyt. There is also an instinct for the underdog. That is a nice quality and we admire it, especially in those who never have been one. So when it appeared that certain other drivers were enjoying Ms. Guthrie's problems, A. J. reacted by offering her a ride. What he meant to do, and did, was give her the chance to demonstrate that her failure to become the first coed at the Indy 500 was mechanical, and not personal.

She did it by tooling around the track in Foyt's backup car at a speed of better than 181 miles per hour, fast enough to qualify, if the lap had counted, which it did not. That was all Foyt intended to do and that was enough. He had given Janet a showcase. He is not Hertz, after all. He does not put people in the driver's seat, especially strangers and rookies, whatever their gender. And not in a car worth $100,000. He may be gallant but he is not stupid.

But the gesture was pure Foyt. It had a touch of class. It also reminded everyone that if this is May, it must be Indianapolis, and A. J. is still here, as he has been every May since 1958. It also reminded us that no one can predict what A. J. will do next, sometimes not even A. J.

No one tells him what to do. No one upstages him. Each year at this time, at the Speedway, the mother temple of horsepower, writers and guests move in and out of the garages as though they were model homes. But not where A. J. Foyt works. They walk wide and slow and softly past that space, pausing to see if they can catch a glimpse of that still-boyish Texas trooper's face. Sometimes they simply stand around and listen for the sounds that will tell them A. J. has just taken a bite out of one of his tires.

Either way, they do not loiter long, out of respect for the legend Foyt has become, and for the temper that has grown famous with him. It is an honest temper and he does not often waste it on petty matters. But to interrupt him, while he is tinkering with his car, would be like stopping Dr. DeBakey during surgery and asking if he feels like Mexican food tonight. Or close to that.

Besides, this is his nineteenth Indy 500, and surely he has said it all by now. We know that he does not like starting from the second row when the flag drops Sunday. He has been in poorer spots—thirty-third, for example—but his position on this is quite clear: "You can run in front as easy as you can in back."

One might hesitate to give A. J. credit for the popular boom in auto racing. There are simply too many factors involved to ever break down the points that fine. For the same reason, you conclude that those who claim Babe Ruth saved baseball have always overstated the case. It is like giving King James credit for the Bible.

But Foyt, more than any other driver, as much as any athlete of our time, became the symbol of his sport and a product of its growth. Auto racing has been, for about ten years now, one of the glamour sports, bringing out the leadfoot, the wishful motor jockey in most of us. Tearing around the track, in the helmet and goggles and spacesuit, at speeds faster than a man can think, hanging your hide over the edge—we envy that.

Show folks are attracted to auto racing and that has become a fair indicator of when a sport is in fashion. Offhand, you can think of Paul Newman, James Garner, Steve McQueen, one of the Smothers brothers. All of them have raced—on the track, not on film.

You suspect that Foyt—with his looks, his style, his intensity, and, not the least of it, his ability to survive—is responsible for some of that. He has created new fans and kept them. He was the macho figure for his time, a man's man with a smile that can melt the heart of a prison matron.

WITH A LITTLE HELP FROM MY FRIENDS

There was a story going around a year ago that tells you about Foyt's disinterest in special poses, and also where his head is while he works. The story may not be true—many of the ones they tell about him are not—but this one you tend to believe. He was in the pits at Daytona when Paul Newman strolled over, and they chatted, while a crowd collected. Finally, A. J. began to fidget.

"Lissen, you guys, I gotta go," he said. Then, turning to Newman: "So long, Steve."

As we say, there never has been another quite like him. He is over forty now, still gunning to become the first man ever to win the Indianapolis 500 four times. We have a hunch he will do it Sunday. We have had that hunch before, in the nine years since he won it for the third time, but never quite so strongly as now.

A guy who is kind to lady drivers can't be all bad.

THE PLEASURE OF HIS COMPANY

FALL 1975

As one old pro to another, twenty-one-year-old Marty Howe skated over to the grizzled fellow in the #9 jersey and gave him a rough hug. "Helluva season, Gord," he said.

The fact that #9 had once claimed him as a tax deduction made the words no less touching. Not fresh or flip, just touching. He was really saying, what a swell way to go out, to end a career. It was as if Prince Charles had said to his mother, "Nice reign, Liz."

Then, Mark Howe arrived. For just an instant, #9 thought he detected a tear in the eye of his younger son. Naw. It was probably the reflection of the lights off the ice. "Great," he said, "just great," and he laid his head on the shoulder of his dad.

That was the picture an alert photographer snapped, a fine moment frozen in time. A few feet away, captain Ted Taylor was accepting an enormous bucket called the Avco World Trophy, living proof that the Houston Aeros had won the championship of at least half of the hockey world.

Taylor was thinking about that trophy even before the final game against Quebec. In the locker room, Ted approached Gordie Howe and said, "If we win that thing tonight, it'll be your last chance. Do you want to receive it?"

Gordie shook his head. "No," he said, "you're the captain."

That was characteristic of the Aeros, their success and their class. But trophies are like memories. You only have room for so many. If you treat it right, a photograph, like a good woman, is forever.

A week later, Gordie was telling a friend, "When I saw it in the papers the next day, it just choked me up. It seemed to sum up everything. Mark had his head on my shoulder, and I was looking at something straight ahead."

If we can believe the rumors that have persisted for more than a month, Gordie Howe was looking straight ahead to the presidency of the Aeros, under a new ownership. If that happens, the only father-and-sons act in the history of pro sports will continue on yet a higher level.

That raises another interesting picture, of Gordie sitting across the table from Marty and Mark, negotiating their contracts, trying to drive management's hard bargain.

"I don't see that as a problem," he said, with a straight face. "I would just give them the franchise and then resign."

He thought a moment and then added, "No, someone would have to be in there with me. For one thing, Colleen would be representing them, and she's tough." On occasion, the very blonde, very energetic Mrs. Howe also has represented her husband.

In your normal sports negotiation, Mark Howe would bang his fist on the desk and accuse the club president of being a tightwad, an exploiter of the working class, and a man without heart or human warmth. Marty will announce that he is considering an offer from the World Football League, and their agent, Mrs. Howe, will suggest that if Gordie wants dinner that evening, he should stop off at the Pancake House.

Gordie insists that if such a situation developed, or even one remotely close to it, he would appeal to the fairness and maturity of his sons. Failing that, he would take away their car keys.

It is part of the charm of Gordie Howe that he does not dwell very long, or very seriously, in the world of hypothetical situations. He prefers the one in which he now lives, with its confusions and small glories.

This is a mellow, sunset time for him. Two years ago, he unretired to play on the same team with his sons. That was the second coming. Now we have the second going, and this one, he says, is for keeps. He is forty-seven years old and, except for a token game or two next fall, he has prepared himself to close the book.

Deacon Jones retired from football the other day, saying that "no one has to tell you when, your body tells you." For all his endurance, his remarkable physical qualities, Gordie agrees with that.

"You find yourself sitting in a corner," he says, "wishing you didn't have to put the uniform on. I hated that feeling. It was like that in Detroit before I quit the first time. I'd think, 'Oh, gawd, I wish I didn't have to put this dumb stuff on again.'

"It comes in the practices first. Then, you start feeling that way before a game. It just gnaws at you. Your bruises start to last for two weeks."

He had twenty-seven years of bruises, of banging into bodies and boards that didn't give, of playing the game as well as anyone ever played it. Yet, it isn't easy to part with, as Gordie knows. He tried once and couldn't. But when the bruises heal, the goals and the good times—and the photographs—will still be there.

UECKER GETS A HIT— FINALLY

AUGUST 27, 1978

Bob Uecker was baseball's catcher in the wry, a career irregular who was once banished to the minors by a manager who snarled, "There is no room in this game for a clown."

The manager was the late Chuck Dressen, who considered himself a gourmet cook. When Uecker was a rookie trying to stick with the then-Milwaukee Braves, he watched bemused as Dressen prepared a large vat of chili for friends he planned to entertain in the clubhouse after the game.

When Dressen wasn't looking, Uecker would add a few extra ingredients to the chili, such as cigarette stubs and sand from the players' butt box.

But the manager was wrong. There was, and is, a place for Bob Uecker in baseball. In fact, he still has the view he always had—from behind home plate, although usually two tiers above field level. Uecker's place is in the broadcasting booth, during the week on radio for the Milwaukee Brewers, and on Monday night for ABC television.

Last week he slipped into his buttermilk-colored blazer and joined the ABC crew in Houston, where the Astros won the first of three from the Cubs after losing six straight in Pittsburgh. It was a win Houston badly needed, noted Uecker, since the club was "oh-for-Pennsylvania."

He has created a whole new career for himself by focusing on baseball's quirks and foibles, especially his own. Uecker's span as a big-league catcher was short, six years divided among the Braves, the Cardinals, and the Phillies, with a lifetime average of .200, on the nose.

The Braves released him in the spring of 1968, after he tried to come back from a broken arm he suffered when he fell off a Honda. His case wasn't exactly helped when he got into a brawl in a bar where the Braves did much of their training that spring. He was trying to keep two of his teammates out of a fight. Instead, he wound up getting hit over the head with a beer bottle. They need forty-eight stitches to patch up his forehead.

It is often a poignant, searching moment when a big-league player comes to the end of the line. The Milwaukee manager that year was Luman Harris, formerly with Houston, and this is how Uecker tells it:

"When a player is traded or sold, that's one thing. But when you get cut, well, it's traumatic. It isn't easy for the manager, either, having to break the news to a fellow that he's finished, washed up. I'll never forget the day it happened to me. I opened the door to the clubhouse and Luman looked up and shouted, 'No visitors allowed.'"

In the eleven years since he put away his mitt and picked up a microphone, Uecker says he believes the game and the players have changed. There is less tolerance of the kind of glorious nonsense in which Uecker and his companions indulged. There was the year the movie *Planet of the Apes* swept the land, and two of his St. Louis running mates, Tim McCarver and Ray Sadecki, bought gorilla masks.

"They wore them everywhere," he said. "On the plane, in the clubhouse, in their hotel room. Many a maid went flying out of their room, believe me. Some nights they would take some clothes and make a dummy, stuff it with bedsheets and pillows. Then they'd put the gorilla mask on top and stick a cigar in his mouth and prop him up in one of those big, overstuffed chairs. Now, their room might be on the twentieth floor and mine would be ten or twenty floors below them. But they would carry that thing down the stairwell at four o'clock in the morning and knock on my door. I'd get out of bed and there would be this ape, with a cigar in his mouth, sitting in a chair."

Such stunts helped make the boredom and monotony of life on the road bearable. There was always something. Another year, giving hotfoots was all the rage, pardon the expression. "You'd stick the match between the sole of a guy's shoe, or in his belt, or anywhere," recalls Uecker. "It was kid stuff, but it caught on. Once, when Houston came to Milwaukee, Turk Farrell came over to our bull pen and asked if we had any lighter fluid. I asked him what he wanted with it. 'I'm gonna light up Bragan,' he said. I found some for him, and then we all lined up against the fence to see what happened."

Bobby Bragan was then a Houston coach, and later the manager of the Braves. Uecker and his pals watched, spellbound, as Farrell sat next to the unsuspecting Bragan, casually dousing his shoes with a fine stream of lighter fluid.

"Then he moved away a step and flicked a lighted match at his feet. I mean, Bragan went up in *flames* . . . his shoes, his socks, his pants. Of course, it went right out, but Bragan did quite a dance."

Uecker had a reputation for being a fine defensive catcher, who worked with some great ones—Warren Spahn, Lew Burdette, Bob Gibson, Curt Simmons. But he was so weak as a hitter that one night, when he drew an intentional walk from Sandy Koufax, of all people, he warned the Dodger pitcher that "the commissioner will probably investigate this."

Today, he looks around him and sees not much that's funny, unless you enjoyed Billy Martin's breakdown and a few guys getting punched out. "The players today don't seem as loose," he says. "There is too much money at stake and the owners won't tolerate any horsing around."

Bob Uecker figures he lasted six years on marginal ability. Today, he might not last six minutes. Maybe Chuck Dressen was right, after all.

SPITZ STILL SMOOTH

AUGUST 6, 1978

Mark Spitz was preparing to ascend a rickety-looking metal stairway to the television platform high above The Woodlands pool. John Naber, the gangling gold medalist of the 1976 Olympics, called after him, "Good luck, Mark." Then, before Spitz could open his mouth, Naber added, "I know. Luck has nothing to do with it."

The reference was taken as a kidding one. In his occasional role as an analyst for ABC, Mark will accept whatever help he can get. But once he stood poised on the edge of a pool, no rival ever wished him anything luckier than a broken toe. And that was the way he liked it.

To Mark, winning was an endless battle of skill and cunning. He was telling his companion in the ABC booth, Jim Lampley, how he arrived at Mexico City in 1968 as an overbearing, insecure eighteen-year-old. Where at other events the swimmers walk around the deck before a race, Mark found to his dismay that the eight finalists were locked in a room for the final thirty minutes, where they could stare at the walls or the floor or at one another.

"In 1968, that room lost races for me," he said. "In 1972, it won them for me."

I asked him if he really thought so much of swimming was mental. He pointed to the young men frozen where they sat, all in a row, waiting for the start of the next race. Some had their heads bent. Others stared without seeing at the cool, blue water. "Look at those guys," he said, "sitting there like they were getting ready for a concentration camp. Thinking about things they've thought about a hundred times before. Me, I was always shaking an arm, a leg, something. Trying to get rid of nervous energy. Distracting people."

Six years after he enjoyed an Olympic moment that was pure

gold—seven gold medals—Mark Spitz is not exactly a fish out of water. But he has been in a pool for his own pleasure fewer than a dozen times since he retired. When someone wanted a publicity picture this week at the AAU Long Course swimming championships, he had to borrow a pair of bathing trunks.

The reputation of Spitz lives on, even if his world records do not. The last of them, the last of the seven he set at Munich in 1972, fell a year ago to Joe Bottom, out of Santa Clara and Southern Cal. People still think of Mark as the driven, tense, sometimes-difficult young man who made enough money in one year from endorsements to live comfortably the rest of his days.

But he is twenty-eight, and he showed up at The Woodlands looking relaxed and perfectly aimed and sporting a neatly trimmed beard that made him look like a young Viennese psychiatrist. Someone remarked to Lampley that Mark had improved on the air, and seemed more sure of himself.

"He has improved as a person," said Lampley. "He's grown. He knows how to be civil with people now. He isn't competing anymore."

Spitz travels for ABC and the two or three companies he still represents, sails when he get the chance, and is a partner in a construction company in Los Angeles. When a problem developed one weekend on a unit of townhouses he was building, he peeled off his shirt and began driving nails, reinforcing some supports. Mark is really not as complicated as people want to make him out. He is restless, and he likes to get things done.

But he doesn't miss the competition, and he misses the glory less than he thought he would. He knows his time on the stage has passed. "There are very few people around now that I swam against," he said. "There are girls here who were six years old when I won my medals in 1972. By the time you've been out of it six years, a new generation has taken over."

I remember a speaker at a banquet making that point once, how quickly the names and the numbers change. "Today," the speaker said, "little thirteen-year-old girls are breaking the world records of Johnny Weissmuller. And do you realize who he was?

"That man was Tarzan of the Apes!"

Spitz never went swinging through the jungle on a vine. The movie career he once wanted never got off the ground. But he knows who he is and seems to feel fairly good about it. Like Britannia, he once ruled the waves. The headline writers at

Munich dubbed him "Mark the Shark," and the name seemed to fit like the skin-clinging suits swimmers wear today.

Each year, they seem to be younger and stronger and the times quicker. Now they are into pumping iron, her as well as him, a trend that leaves Mark uncertain. "My heart used to get palpitations," he said, "if I just walked past a barbell."

A young lady padded past, her feet bare and her hair wet, with shoulders like Joan Crawford in a suit coat. Mark Spitz frowned and said, thoughtfully, "I guess it depends on the individual."

BACHELOR BO NO MO'

JANUARY 26, 1969

When we last looked in on Bo Belinsky, the wandering left-hander was sunbathing on the palm-lined shores of Cocoa Beach, in the shadow of Cape Kennedy, where his fellow Americans were preparing to explore the moon.

At the time, Bo had applied for a transfer. He wasn't asking for the moon, he only wanted Hawaii, where he would flee with a luscious bit of luggage named Jo Collins (39-24-38).

In this depraved world, when all a man asks is simply to pitch in an island paradise, in the company of a former Playmate of the Year, you conclude that his requests are indeed small.

Happily, Bo got his wish, and now the story has taken a charming turn. This week Bo and Jo passed through Houston, having escaped from Venezuela where Belinsky had pitched his heart out all winter, in return for which the fans threatened his life.

More about that harrowing experience later.

The major news is that their visit to South America served as a wedding trip for the famous couple. Yes, you cynics, romantics, and just plain sports fans out there, Bo Belinsky, baseball's most celebrated Romeo, is a bachelor no more.

Bo and Jo were married quietly, in part for reasons of privacy, but also one supposes because there was no way of telling how the working girls of America would sustain this shock.

I mean, Sandy Koufax has taken the plunge, and now Belinsky. It is getting down to the real diehard bachelors, Joe Namath and Rex Morgan, M.D.

Having been drafted by the St. Louis Cardinals, given yet another chance to grab baseball's brass ring, Bo sees his new domestic status as a definite plus.

"Now that I'm married," he says, "maybe there won't be so

much slanderous stuff written about me. Don't get me wrong. I always went along with it. But I'm tired of it, of the image thing. For my part, I felt the writers were kidding me, and I was kidding them. They'd say, 'A thousand girls?' And I'd say, 'Sure, ten thousand.' "

From time to time in his career, Bo would amuse himself by announcing that he was a new man, he had seen the light and would henceforth lead the existence of a Trappist monk.

But eventually Bo would be struck by the irony of his personal conflict. On occasions when he would stay up until nearly dawn, chasing the bright lights, he was apt to go out and pitch himself a runless beauty of a game. Other times he would watch television, retire early, sleep eight hours, and then wake up with a sore throat and get bombed.

Bo would consider the ravages of rest, and go back to his old style of living.

Yet if Belinsky, now a respectable married man, insists that his capers were exaggerated and his legend overblown, far be it from us to dispute him.

We have refrained from reporting this incident in the past, for fear of hurting Bo's reputation. But now it can be told. Once, when the devil-may-care southpaw was the property of the Houston Astros, he invited your country cousin here to join him for a swinging night in Los Angeles, a small mining town in the West.

Splashing on roughly half a gallon of Brut aftershave, I nervously accepted his invitation. Whereupon Bo slid behind the wheel of a borrowed, mint-green Caddy convertible, and we tooled off into the beckoning night. Forty minutes later, we arrived at the home of an old friend of his, where we consumed our weight in Italian food and after which Bo fell asleep in front of the television set.

Still, everyone is entitled to an off night.

To her credit, his bride is undisturbed by his notoriety as Playboy of the Western World. "In the first place," says Jo, "when I met Bo I realized that he wasn't as wild as he was made out to be. Now I think he has settled down even more, and he's serious about his future. I think it will help his pitching."

Looking back, Bo tends to agree with the advice of Satchel Paige, who decided long ago that the social ramble ain't restful. "I didn't run around all that much," he says. "It went in spurts.

Sometimes I'd go along for six weeks being calm. Then I'd snap, and when I snapped, I'd make the scene."

If there are some popular misconceptions about this retired bon vivant, it seems obvious that Bo helped create them.

He was tickled to discover that, when the Cardinals drafted him, most newspaper accounts referred to him as Robert Boris Belinsky. It develops that he has no middle name.

"Writers would ask me what Bo stood for," he explained, "and I'd tell them Robert, but they couldn't accept that. So I'd say it was short for my middle name, Boris, and that made them happy."

He grinned, and let the name trip off his tongue. "Boris Belinsky . . . you know, I kinda like it myself. Sounds like the first Russian commissar to pitch in the big leagues."

What they were calling him in Venezuela, at the time of his hasty exit, was not quite so appealing. It is probably just as well that Bo understands little Spanish.

As you recall, after moving on from Cocoa Beach to Hawaii, Bo and Jo followed the sun to Caracas, where he had been engaged to pitch in the winter leagues.

"Until the trouble started," says Mrs. Belinsky, "the fans loved him there, they really did. He was a great drawing card, and if they had just let him pitch, they would have won the pennant."

"The trouble," as Jo refers to it with delightful feminine understatement, began after Bo was credited with his eighth win. He now needed just two more to qualify for a bonus of $1,000 promised him by management.

At this point Bo found himself in stir for ten days, unused and all but unnoticed by his manager, Napoleon Reyes, a little fellow with a large, round tummy who wears his cap sideways. He looks like a character drawn by Al Capp.

Bo got the impression, heaven knows how, that he was being sidetracked so his team, Magallanes, would not have to cough up the additional scratch. Feelings became more bruised when Bo publicly supported a player whose contract the club tried to break, after which he declined to pitch with a tender arm in a game already lost.

By the time the manager and the owner got through barbecuing Bo in print, he had the feeling his life was worth a few cents less than a tortilla.

"We received some threatening phone calls," says Jo, "and

some fans even banged on our door. There was no way that Bo could have gone back out on that mound without someone taking a shot at him."

"The fans get pretty emotional down there, anyway," added Bo. "When we were in a losing streak, one guy tried to commit suicide. Slashed his wrists."

This was in their suite at the Ramada Inn, on the Gulf Freeway, many miles and a few hours from the bricks and bottles and fireworks of the Caracas ballpark.

"It's quite a sight," said Jo, "to see uniformed soldiers carrying machine guns standing in the aisles."

"Yeah," said Bo, "but when the shooting starts, they hide their guns, roll up their sleeves, and try to pass for civilians. The only ones you can count on are the *Guardia Nacional.* That's their elite force, the National Guard."

Their plane tickets confiscated by the ballclub, Bo and Jo packed up one night and slipped out to the airport, peeking nervously over their shoulders. They told the airline they had lost their tickets, purchased new ones, and flew to Houston. To celebrate their departure, Bo filed a $33,000 lawsuit against the ballclub for slander and related grievances.

It was altogether a mad escapade, quite in character with the old Bo Belinsky. As for Jo, she left Caracas with mixed feelings. The women there wear dresses well below the knee, and when Jo would walk down the boulevard in her miniskirts, the men would pour out of stores and buildings and trample each other in the streets. The government nearly declared her a traffic hazard. Also, she could not find a restaurant that served good Mexican food.

The old Bo Belinsky was once America's guest, dividing his time with friends in Los Angeles or Las Vegas or Hawaii, leading a life of sweet irresponsibility. This week he paused in Houston to visit another old pal, Arlie Taylor, who manages the Gulf Ramada, and to adjust his living style to suit the new Bo Belinsky.

When he speaks in terms of settling down, he means taking his home to where his friends are. So Bo is thinking of purchasing a house trailer, to be decorated with tasteful elegance by Finger Furniture Company, another Houston contact.

He did not win a great many games here, but he met a number of people who found him to be an engaging, low-keyed, poetic sort of fellow, and they will be rooting for him to hit it big in

WITH A LITTLE HELP FROM MY FRIENDS

Saint Louis. The curious thing is that in the view of most authorities, Bo has always possessed a major-league arm.

He may or may not have lost some heavy support among women, whose attraction to Bo was never exaggerated. They were captivated by his smoldering eyes and deep, purring voice, which sounds, according to one sweet thing, "as though between each word he were dragging on a cigarette."

But Bo has removed himself from circulation now, and assumed the kind of responsibility he had avoided for thirty-two years. You recall the day he quit the Houston Astros camp where Saturday night curfew was 1 A.M., two hours earlier than Bo cared to return to his couch of virtue. He had a date with Jo and he did the only thing a gentleman could. He jumped the club. Most guys would gladly have given up their citizenship.

And it all turned out splendidly, proving that you cannot put a stopwatch on love. Even in baseball, it is bigger than time and space.

BUBBA WHIPS POVERTY

JANUARY 16, 1971

MIAMI BEACH—In his pursuit of excellence, Bubba Smith is motivated by something outside of time, above price, and beyond love. It is called money.

This is especially important Sunday, when Bubba's Baltimore playfellows encounter Dallas in that cosmic event known as the Super Bowl. At stake will be $15,000 to each winning player, and half as much to each loser. *Viva la difference,* says Bubba Smith, in his native French.

Now you must understand that Bubba Smith does not hate the Dallas Cowboys, or even Rayfield Wright, who will oppose him across the line of scrimmage. The Cowboys are good citizens who pay their taxes, treat their parents with respect, do not kick small dogs, worship one God, and never squeeze the Charmin. His attitude toward them can be summed up in one thought: "They are in my way. In the way of my championship ring, in the way of my money, in the way of everything."

One is advised not to get in the way of Bubba Smith, who is six-feet-seven and 290 and has been mistaken on occasion for the Pan Am Building. Bubba is also a great man, and if you continue reading you'll discover why.

To begin with, there is a startling amount of depth to him. He possesses a quality called "street smartness," which has nothing to do with education.

When he graduated from a black high school in Beaumont, Bubba had never, not once, spoken to someone whose complexion was white. So he enrolled at Michigan State, and he had one request: He wanted a roommate who was white and didn't play football. He got him, a student from a small, insulated town in upper Michigan who had never, in his life, so much as seen a black person except on television.

"I wanted to find out what was going on," says Bubba, "why

WITH A LITTLE HELP FROM MY FRIENDS

there is so much animosity around, why people can't live together. We used to rap far into the night, me and him, and I found out part of the answer. People got to talk to each other."

Now that is what makes the Baltimore defensive end a deep and thoughtful fellow, but it isn't what qualifies him as a street-smart guy. This is:

In four years of playing professional football, and playing it fiercely, Bubba Smith has never cashed a paycheck. Not one. He doesn't even know the amount that appears on the face of them.

"They go right to my momma in Beaumont," he says, "and she deposits them directly into the bank. I never even see 'em."

Idly, we asked Bubba what he lived on. "Fringe money," he replied. "What I pick up from speaking engagements, TV dates, public appearances, endorsements, things like that."

But what about his social life? Contrary to romantic belief, the best things in life, such as girls and other goodies, are not really free.

"I am single," said Bubba, as though that explained much of it. "I have a pad in Baltimore that used to be two apartments. They knocked out a wall. The furniture is plush. It cost me nothing, through friends and deals.

"I seldom pay for food and drinks. The chicks I date enjoy cooking for me, and when they want a night out, I let them come over to my place, and they can cook the meal there. When we hit a nightclub, someone always says, 'Can I buy you a drink?' I never refuse."

Clearly, at the game of free enterprise, Bubba could give lessons to your old-time international tennis bums.

"I have a lot of clothes," he goes on. "I love clothes, but I don't blow big money on them. Four of the chicks I date sew. I bring them the material, and they make my wardrobe for me. I can't buy off the rack, anyway."

As we take inventory now, we find that Bubba has one squad of ladies to feed him and another working in the quartermaster corps. He is a one-man army.

But what about those little endearing gestures that mean so much to women, we persisted, such as diamond bracelets. Don't you get involved?

"Not to that extent," he replied. "They must love me for myself, not for my money. The last time I bought a girl a present was

WITH A LITTLE HELP FROM MY FRIENDS

in the ninth grade. It was a little necklace, a locket. Later, we broke up, and eventually she got married."

You conclude that love is just one heartbreak after another. Having invested his cookie money in a necklace ten years ago, only to have the girl betray him, Bubba won't be hurt like that again.

Bubba insists that he doesn't know the exact amount of the treasure now socked away in a Beaumont bank, but it figures to be well over $100,000. It will sit there gathering interest, or dust, until he gets the urge to settle down, or buy a farm, or cover whatever family needs might arise. Money is important to him, not for the sheer joy of accumulating it, but for the freedom and security it can buy.

"I've seen it all happen too many times before," he says. "My father was a high-school coach in Beaumont, and he coached eight or nine players who made it to the pros. I've seen 'em go through money. I saw Ernie Ladd do it. I just refuse to let it happen to me."

Bubba is hoping to add fifteen big ones to his antipoverty fund Sunday, another paycheck not to cash. While his teammates invest fortunes in alligator shoes and wide ties, on Chateaubriand and vintage wines, he quietly goes his way as America's guest.

As we talked, Bubba ordered a grilled-cheese sandwich and a Coke. The bill came to $1.53. I picked up the check. It made me feel good. It was like giving to the United Way.

NAMATH ERA ENDS QUIETLY

FEBRUARY 5, 1978

His style and skill made him a star. But five words made Joe Willie Namath a legend: "We'll win. I'll guarantee it."

That promise was spoken on the eve of Super Bowl III, at some kind of mom-and-pop banquet in a suburb of Miami, Florida. Only three writers had bothered to show up, and no one seemed to make much of a fuss that night over Namath's prediction. He had been saying it all week, that the New York Jets, a 17- to 19-point underdog, would unfrock the almighty Baltimore Colts. People had been falling down in helpless fits of laughter, reviving only long enough to increase their bets on Baltimore.

I didn't even consider that boast to be Namath's best line of the evening. During the after-dinner speeches, Larry Grantham, the solid and serious Jets linebacker, had asked for a round of applause for the players' wives, who had sacrificed so much during the season. Then, Namath went to the mike and asked for a hand for the single girls of New York, "who sacrificed just as much and complained a helluva lot less."

Of course, as football historians so well have documented, Joe Namath did deliver on his guarantee. The Jets, with Broadway Joe running the attack with nerve and precision, plundered the Colts 16-7 in what may have been the most important pro game ever played. It established the upstart American Football League as the equal of the old, established tribe, and ushered in the golden age of national exposure and television riches.

That Joe Namath was the symbol of that achievement, no one can really doubt. In the steaming, delirious New York locker room, in Miami's Orange Bowl, Weeb Ewbank was asked if he had really believed his Jets could bring it off.

A portly, grandfatherly type, the old coach said, yes, he had made up his mind that very morning, after leaving church services.

He had paused on his way out, and, after complimenting the minister on his sermon, decided on an impulse to ask the question that was on the minds of millions of fans across the country.

"Reverend," he asked, "who do you think will win the Super Bowl this afternoon?"

According to Ewbank, the preacher lifted his eyes, extended his palms, and said, "Whomsoever the Lord nameth."

Indeed, Joe Namath was the chosen one in those years, a drawing card when the AFL needed one to survive. The tributes are coming now, in the wake of his not-unexpected retirement last week. Many of the stories make a point of saying that Joe Willie was not very well understood. I never quite saw it that way. I thought he was remarkably easy to understand. There was little mystery to him at all.

He liked pretty girls, preferably blondes, Johnny Walker Red, soft llama rugs, restaurants where the waiters spoke with an accent, and friends who did not try to analyze him. No football player in history, including Red Grange and O. J. Simpson, was marketed more effectively than Namath. Deep in his gypsy soul, Joe wanted to think that material things didn't matter, that if someone wanted to melt his heart, they should do so with violin music. But he made a lot of money, enjoyed it, and—for what he gave to the sport—earned every dime.

His place as a quarterback will be hard to evaluate for the record book, partly because of the physical problems that haunted him. He will present one of those cases in which people can only guess at what he might have done if his legs had remained sound. You tend to feel the same way about Mickey Mantle. On ailing legs, Mantle made it into the Hall of Fame. With healthy wheels, he might have joined Ruth and Cobb as three of a kind.

His friends are fond of claiming that Joe "never changed." Baloney. All of us change. Joe did, in many ways for the better. He went through a wild period of Fu Manchu mustaches and big business deals and tacky movies. He went through a period of not talking to the press. He retired three or four times and once, for revenge, he called a news conference at 9:30 in the morning.

But he grew in taste and class. He didn't play a down the last two months of what would be his last season, but he never complained, never stirred the kind of trouble that one in his position could easily have done.

So the Namath career ended in irony. In Los Angeles, he wound up on the bench with the best football team he ever knew, after all those seasons of fighting for his life in New York. Back in training camp, Joe had roomed with Pat Haden, the young Rhodes Scholar who would end up taking his job. Haden was asked what their social life was like.

"On a typical night," he says, "we make a bowl of popcorn and watch the 11 o'clock news. Then we watch Johnny Carson and go to sleep after the monologue." You reflect that Namath must have made a pleasant roommate, especially if one doesn't mind the smell of Brut.

Joe may or may not have slowed down off the field. But as a quarterback, he was nearly immobile. No one ever threw a straighter pass, tried harder, or made fewer excuses. But at the money he commanded, no one needed a backup passer.

Many athletes have a fear of getting out too late, exceeded only by their fear of getting out too soon. Namath didn't overstay his time. He was entitled to one more shot with a winning team. Too bad the script didn't play.

I covered his last college game, a 21-17 loss to Texas in the Orange Bowl on New Year's Night, 1965. The next day he would sign his famous $400,000 contract. Steve Sloan started for Alabama. Joe had knee hurts even then. I do not remember a more electrifying moment than when Namath came off the bench, in the second quarter with Alabama two touchdowns behind. The crowd went berserk as he trotted onto the field, slowly, his white sneakers glowing in the lights. Alabama missed by a yard of winning the game and the national title. Texas stopping Namath twice on the goal line. In the years to come the pain lingered, but Joe had an honest answer to the obvious question: "No, I didn't score. But I sure as hell got over the goal line."

A BONUS FROM BERRA

DECEMBER 3, 1985

NEW YORK—In everyone's life there is a summer of 1942. That was the year Yogi Berra signed with the New York Yankees for a bonus of $500, a world war ago, two generations ago, and still he remembers it as though only a fingersnap of time had passed.

The reason he remembers is that the money came hard. And because of it, he almost walked away from this dream he had of being a professional baseball player. Yogi was seventeen that summer, even then proud and competitive.

The year before, the St. Louis Cardinals had signed his best friend, Joe Garagiola, out of a tryout camp both had attended. Both were catchers who batted left-handed. The Cards paid Garagiola $500 to sign. They offered Yogi a contract but no bonus. It almost killed him to do it, but he turned them down.

"I wasn't jealous of Joey," he says, even now his face clouding up at this long-ago affront by his hometown team. "I was glad for him. But I knew I was worth it, too. I wasn't gonna play unless I got it. For one thing, I knew it was gonna be hard enough to talk my folks into letting me go."

Even the St. Louis Browns took a pass on the kid with the squat body and the odd gait. Then the Yankees came along, and a scout was impressed that Berra never asked what his salary would be. They said sure, he could have his $500 bonus, and off he went to play for the Norfolk Tars in the Piedmont League. When he signed the contract, he learned he would be paid $90 a month.

And that was fine with Yogi. What wasn't so fine was that the Yankees played games with him on the front money.

"They said I wasn't supposed to get it unless I finished the year with the club. Well, I got it at the end of the season," Berra

WITH A LITTLE HELP FROM MY FRIENDS

said. "But I learned a heckuva lesson. My take-home pay was $35 every two weeks. I could have made more than that shining shoes at the bus terminal. I had to write home to Mom to send me a little money so I could eat. She would send me a money order for ten bucks, and she would always write, in Italian, 'Don't let your father know you're hungry, or he will make you come home.'

"After that, I made up my mind that for as long as I played ball, I would get everything I thought I had coming to me." Slow grin. "I think I did pretty good."

The story produced an interesting sequel or two. Just after Yogi signed with the Yankees, he received an urgent telegram from Branch Rickey. It was Rickey, as general manager of the Cardinals, who had decided Berra was not worth $500. Now he had quit the Cardinals and taken over the Brooklyn Dodgers, and he wanted Yogi to report to their big-league camp the next summer—for a bonus. Too late. Yogi was a Yankee.

After a year at Norfolk, Yogi joined the Navy, saw action on an LST, was in the thick of the D-Day invasion, and came home with a bunch of medals. By 1946, he was home and appeared at the end of the season with the Yankees. Garagiola was in the World Series that year with the Cardinals. And what were the odds that two kids from the same block would wind up catching for two big-league teams?

Years later, Garagiola practically invented a nightclub act around the fact that he and Yogi grew up together in St. Louis. The Berras lived at 5447 Elizabeth Avenue, the Garagiolas at 5446, on what was known as "Dago Hill."

Joe would always get laughs on the banquet circuit when he told his audience, with the air of a man explaining something quite complicated, "A lot of Italian families lived on that hill, you see, and that is the reason it is called Dago Hill."

It was in the first half of a doubleheader on a Sunday in late September 1946 that Berra's name first appeared in a Yankees box score—the first of more than 2,000. He caught nine innings against the Philadelphia A's, and no one stole on him. He had a single and a homer and drove in two runs against a pitcher named Jesse Flores. The Yankees won, 4-3.

The Yankees' batting order that day consisted of George Stirnweiss, second base; Tommy Henrich, first base; Bobby Brown, shortstop; Joe DiMaggio, center field; Charley ("King Kong")

Keller, left field; Bill Johnson, third base; Johnny Lindell, right field; Berra catching and Spud Chandler pitching.

"Of considerable interest," Harold Rosenthal in the *New York Herald-Tribune* wrote, "was the appearance of several recent Yankee acquisitions. Bobby Brown, Newark's hard-hitting shortstop, made his debut, as did Larry Berra, the Newark catcher."

With his five-foot-eight frame and his long arms and happy Halloween face, he was immediately labeled a character. Actually, he was not yet either a character or a polished catcher. Bill Dickey helped make him a catcher, and his own unbridled spirit and his wrong way with words made him a character.

In his New York heyday, he was introduced to Ernest Hemingway at a party at Toots Shor's. When he returned to his table, he was asked what he thought of him. Said Berra, "He's quite a character. What does he do?"

"Well, he's a writer," someone said.

"Yeah?" Yogi asked. "Which paper?"

He outlasted them all, of course. All of the players, Hemingway, even the *Herald-Tribune*. Casey Stengel would not appear on the scene until 1949, and he would say years later that his two greatest players were DiMaggio and Berra.

Houston will get its money's worth when he joins the Astros' coaching staff for 1986. True, fans don't buy tickets to watch a first-base coach think or a bull-pen coach sit. If they did, someone would have stuffed and mounted Babe Ruth long ago and propped him up next to the water cooler.

But Berra is a piece of baseball history, and it isn't easy to find a living immortal these days. Wherever they use him—in the coaching box or sitting next to Hal Lanier—he will help the team just by being Yogi.

Success never spoiled him, his or anyone else's.

He was the catcher the day Don Larsen wrote his name into baseball legend in 1956 with the only no-hit, no-run, perfect game in World Series history, the most dramatic game ever pitched.

In the crowded and tumultuous Yankee clubhouse, a writer approached Berra for some deathless comment. "Well," Yogi said, bumming a cigarette, "what's new?"

Letters From Lefty

SPRING TRAINING

MARCH 19, 1962

(With apologies to Ring Lardner, this is the kind of letter today's rookie ballplayer might write from spring training.)

Apache Junction, Arizona
March 19, 1962

Dear Alice,

Well, we started our practice games this week and none too soon, as I was getting mighty tired of the routine around here. We would spend all morning running and doing knee bends, and then in the afternoon we would sit outside the hotel and watch the cracks in the ground widen.

One of the coaches, Jim Busby, leads us in exercises every day for an hour. No kidding. Busby is the only man I ever saw who looked as though he enjoyed touching his toes while keeping the knees straight. You have to like the feel of your toes a good deal for this.

Alice, you wanted to know what us big-league baseball heroes did in our spare time, and I'm going to tell you. Mostly we complain. You have heard of towns where they roll up the sidewalks at 7 P.M.? Well, there *are* no sidewalks in Apache Junction. This place just doesn't swing.

We are far removed from the simple pleasures of life, such as a drive-in movie (eighteen miles away) or a dog track (thirty-five miles). You have to go to Phoenix to see the greyhounds run, but a bunch of us are going tomorra night. It will be the first time for me and I am certainly looking forward to it. As I understand it, they turn a rabbit loose and the dogs chase it around the track. For many years the rabbits have tried to arbitrate this dispute, but to no avail.

It is even a forty-five-minute drive from here to the statue of Tom Mix on the highway to Tucson, in case you would like to stop and pray.

Now, I'm not knocking the place, understand, but you can sit on the doorstep of our hotel, the Superstition Ho, and see the entire town, including suburbs. They tell me the population has tripled in less than a year to over 5,000, but I suspect that they must have counted all the burros.

Apache Junction has one drugstore, two gas stations, a laundromat, a supermarket, thirty-three real estate offices, and one saloon, the Red Garter, where some of the Colt .45s do their serious training. The baseball field—named Geronimo Park after you-know-who—is built in the shadow of Superstition Mountain. Out here, everything is built in the shadow of a mountain, even other mountains.

Legend has it that the famous Lost Dutchman gold mine is still hidden away in those mysterious hills beyond right field. Since 1900, at least fifty persons have died violent deaths there—in the mountains, that is, not right field, though we have had one or two close calls this spring. The fifty croaked while searching for the Dutchman's gold.

Alice, you remember the movie in which Humphrey Bogart was a grizzled old prospector, and in one scene he was crawling on his hands and knees in the desert, with an empty canteen in one hand and his lips chapped? Well, that's what Apache Junction is like.

They got eight varieties of cactus out here, which is the sort of information that doesn't help you much if you sit on one. The land is dry and pebbly and thick with sagebrush and you run across a lot of bleached bones. Cows, I think. So far I have heard only one fellow speak kindly of the place and that was Clint Courtney, the hard-bitten old catcher who is on our minor-league coaching staff. "I lak it heah," he said the other day, while picking his teeth with a cactus needle. "A man orter be able to keep his mind on baseball."

The ball park is a mile from our hotel, and Dick Farrell, who used to pitch for the Phillies, always takes the shortcut across the sage and underbrush. Along the way, he shoots at various objects with a .22 pistol. I predict that Farrell will be the first guy in camp to lose a toe.

So far Turk, as we call him, has shot four jackrabbits, two lizards, one snake, one quail, and more than a hundred beer and whiskey bottles. "That's a lot of bottles," chortled Farrell. Our manager, Harry Craft, said the same thing, only in a suspicious tone of voice.

Apache Junction grows on you though, Alice, like some sort of fungus. They had a parade out here for us, and it was really something. You remember the one they had in New York for John Glenn, the astronaut, with the confetti knee-deep and people jammed together like suits in a closet? Well, this one had more folks in the parade than watching it.

They say if you can play ball here, you can do it anywhere, including the deck of an aircraft carrier in a tropical storm. The Arizona desert has the highest, bluest sky in the world, and some of our outfielders complained that they could not follow the ball. "Tut, tut," said Al Spangler, who majored in math at Duke. He would merely allow for the force of impact and the rate of descent and he would catch the ball while making change for a $20 bill. So the first game we play, one fly drops at Al's feet and another falls behind him. He explained later that he forgot to figure on the curvature of the earth.

Well, Alice, it is too early to get nervous and I do not want to upset you, but I don't think I am going to make the club. Luman Harris, one of our coaches, came by my room yestiddy and suggested that I not send my laundry out. I think he was trying to tell me something.

Wish I had Wally Wolf's money. I would tell them to go fly a kite in an electrical storm. Wally is the pitcher from Southern Cal who got a hundred grand for signing. Wally says he is going to give it one more year and if he doesn't make the Colt .45s, he is going to buy the club and hire himself as general manager.

A very dramatic thing happened on my first day in camp, Alice. You know how it is in the storybooks. A young kid my age, nineteen or twenty, I forget which, goes to big-league training camp and he ends up with a locker right next to some famous ballplayer that was his boyhood hero. Well, guess what happened to me? I walked into the clubhouse and looked at the name tags over the lockers, and I never heard of ANY of these guys.

You Know Me, Alice
Lefty

HOLDING OUT

FEBRUARY 24, 1963

To: George Kirksey
Vice President, Houston Colt .45s
From: Lefty
Subject: Wages

Dear G. K.,

I would have written you sooner but I laughed so hard at the last contract you sent me that I hurt my side, and it was very painful to try to hold a pencil.

I see in the papers where all the pitchers and catchers are out in Apache Junction, except me and Merritt Ranew. Frankly, I would like to be out there with you, as I could use the rest. But as you know, Alice and I plan to get wedlocked, and whoever said two could live as cheaply as one must have been thinking about goldfish.

Really, George, I did not expect a very large salary. But don't you think a dollar and fifty cents an hour is a little ridiculous?

You keep mentioning last year. Why do you do that, George? You do not strike me as the type of person who always lives in the past. I realize that I had the worst earned-run average on the club. I know I gave up the most walks, hits, home runs, and wild pitches, and broken shoelaces.

But what the heck, nobody is perfect.

Why don't we talk about next year instead, and all the wonderful games I plan to win for the Colt .45s? For one thing, I am in the best shape of my life and I am completely over that football injury I suffered last November. (I fell off a bar stool watching the Aggie-Texas game on television.)

I am working out daily, running two laps around the house to open up the pores. One must be careful not to get overtrained. I read about a farm boy in New Jersey who lifted a young cow daily for several months. He finally quit on the advice of his doctor, though I have an idea that sheer boredom had something to do with it.

Anyway, if you will look it up, you will find that I was a hard-luck pitcher in 1962. In eleven of the games I started, the club failed to score half as many runs as I gave up. "Lefty," the folks at home keep saying, "if it wasn't for bad luck, you wouldn't have no luck a'tall."

Now, George, I'm twenty-two-and-a-half years old and getting to the point where I must think about the future. I have a real good job here in Point Desolate, working in my Uncle Philo's feed-and-grain store. Last month we sold over 3,000 pounds of chicken feed, and, as we say around the store, that ain't money. Ha, ha.

I hate to admit this, but I am growing homesick for Apache Junction. I was sitting on the porch the other night, swatting flies and stringing them up by their fuzzy little legs, as an example to other flies. And I got to thinking about how nice it is out there this time of year. Haven't had any more trouble with the Apaches, have they?

Some of the guys run the place down a lot and call it the poor man's College Station. But remember Eddie Olivares, the rookie outfielder from Puerto Rico? He brought his bride to Apache Junction for their honeymoon last spring. Boy, I bet Niagara Falls trembles at the news. Eddie broke his leg the second week of camp and missed the entire season. But I don't guess they can blame that on Apache Junction.

I got to thinking about the 1962 season, our first in the big leagues, and you know what really stood out in my mind? No, not us losing less than 100 games, which was truly a grand achievement. No, not Farrell throwing a spitter to Stan Musial or hitting Willie Mays with pitches twice in one game. Or Bob Cerv getting thrown out at home trying to score from second on a triple.

They were all great thrills, of course. But the day I'll never forget was the one in Los Angeles when Hal Woodeshick won the West Coast cow-milking championship from Lee Walls of the Dodgers. Woody darn near filled that pail up, and it was a sight to see him sitting there on that little stool, squeezing his way to victory. Woody had the situation well in hand, so to speak.

George, I am surprised at you. In your letter you said that you heard some of the boys like to hit it up at the soda fountain once in a while, and you asked me if I drink. I just want you to know that if I have to drink to make this ballclub, I'll give up baseball.

But back to the contract. Now you said that you would gladly give me a raise if it was up to you, but of course it isn't your money and so it isn't up to you, and so forth. You also quoted Mr. Richards as saying if I didn't like the contract I could lump it, and he would trade me to the Mets for an electric fan, to replace the one that Norm Larker kicked one night in the dugout and broke.

However, having a keen sense of humor, I let bygones be bygones. We really aren't so far apart. Make it $1.75 an hour and I'll see you at Geronimo Park.

You Know Me, George
Lefty

IN THE BULL PEN

MAY 3, 1964

Houston, Texas
May 3, 1964

Dear Alice,

Well, here it is the third week of the season and I haven't pitched yet, which you probably noticed from looking for my name in the box scores and not finding it. So the other day I up and asked Harry why, and he said he'd like to use me but he's afraid I'd pitch a good game and mess up his starting rotation.

I can certainly see Harry's side of it, but you know me, Alice. I'm a feerse competitor. I haven't pitched in thirty-one days now, and I'm afraid I'll lose my sharpness.

Sometimes I think there is no justice in baseball. Like last week Ken Johnson lost a no-hitter and *Cincinnati* protested the game. It had to do with one of the umpires changing a decision, which didn't matter anyway, since the Reds won, 1-0. I do believe that Kenny had a prior claim, as the insurance adjusters say.

Anyway, even though I'm not pitching right now, I'm still helping the club. I do this by kidding the guys and getting their minds off their troubles.

You may have read that Jimmy Wynn has been having some problems in center field. One night he dropped a fly ball, misjudged another, and made a bad throw. So the next day before the game, his glove was on the grass and somebody accidentally stepped on it with his spikes.

"Well," says I, "there goes the pennant."

The fellows all get a big bang out of my sense of humor. Al Spangler says that when I pass on to the one great diamond in the sky, I should donate my brain to *Mad* magazine.

Well, Alice, this was the week that was, and what it was, was awful. We beat the Dodgers once in four games, then the Cubs come and stomp us, 11-3 and 9-0. I have a feeling I may get to pitch soon, because I heard Harry say that if this keeps up, he may suit up one of the writers, and I'm sure he'd use me before one of them, if only out of loyalty.

When you're going bad, Alice, even the parking-lot attendants get on you. The other day, John Bateman, Rusty Staub, Steve Hertz, and me went to a hospital to visit a sick kid. On the way, we stopped off for lunch, to keep our stren'th up, and when we pulled into the parking lot, Bateman says to the attendant, "We got a baseball in the front seat. Keep your eye on it."

"Who hit it?" he asked. "A Dodger?"

"No," said Bateman. "Staub."

"Staub?" repeated the attendant. "When was the last time Staub hit a ball?"

Rusty really got a laugh out of that.

Things are bound to get better for us, though. We leave after today's game for a road trip that takes us to San Francisco, Los Angeles, and Chicago, which are my three favorite cities. They have a lot of culture in San Francisco. A bunch of us went to a museum there once, but all the signplates were in Latin, which for the average baseball player can be very boring.

You asked me to tell you about some of the amazing Colt .45 players, Alice, the behind-the-scenes stuff that you can't get in the papers. I know you especially wanted to know about Bob Aspromonte, but I thought that instead I would tell you about our clubhouse man, Whitey Diskin, which I know you will find interesting and sort of different.

Whitey is one of our unsung heroes. In the old days, a clubhouse man was mostly in charge of water buckets and toothpicks. But now he belongs to that great American institution, the small-business man. His business is run on credit.

He takes care of our equipment, packs the gear on road trips, sees that the uniforms are laundered, and merchandises to the players such items as they demand during the course of a day—chewing tobacco, gum, Cokes, sweatsocks, etc.

It is strictly on the honor system, and twice a month, when we get our paychecks, we settle up with Whitey. Of course, some risk is involved. At the various cutdown periods, Whitey must watch the door carefully, lest some departing player, his memory dulled by the grief of going to the minors, forgets to settle his tab.

Once one of the Colts—I think it was Turk Farrell—agreed to name Whitey as the beneficiary on the flight insurance the club provides, if Whitey would carry him free on the swindle sheet all year.

Whitey, overwhelmed by the sentiment of the proposition, was about to agree—when it suddenly occurred to him that he would be flying on the same plane.

Whitey has hair the color of cotton, what's left of it, thick glasses, and the look of a leprechaun. He's a real sentimental person, and any day now, he will remind the rookies that Mother's Day is coming up soon, and to send something home besides their laundry.

Alice, the folks back home keep writing in to tell me what I should do with the Colts. This flatters me. But they will be shocked to learn that no one at Colt Stadium has ever asked me anything, except once a fire marshal asked me not to block the aisle.

That was when I was talking to a Triggerette one night before a game.

Tell your pa that I do think his idea has a lot of merit, the one about letting right-handed hitters run to third base and then to second, first, and home. I agree with him that a left-handed batter has a big advantage, since he is a yard closer to first base, and his very swing starts him in the right direction, while the right-handed hitter ends up facing third base. It doesn't seem fair.

By letting the right-handed hitters run to third, instead of first, it would also speed up the game, because in the case of some Colt base runners, this would make a difference of from two seconds to five minutes.

I also agree with him that there might be some confusion if, say, the bases are loaded and a right-handed hitter is at bat, but I do think that the club owners could work this out if they really wanted to.

Well, got to sign off now. I'm in the bull pen today and it's my turn to go buy the snow cones.

You Know Me, Alice
Lefty

RATING THE FANS

SEPTEMBER 6, 1964

Pittsburgh, Pennsylvania
September 6, 1964

Dear Alice,

The season has now reached that stage where playing each game becomes a reluctant duty, like carrying out the garbage. You feel tired all the time. Your feet hurt. The plane flights last too long, and you have read everything in the magazine rack, including the writing portfolio, three times.

The television set in your room receives only horizontal lines. The days grow shorter, the crowds smaller, the laughs fewer and farther apart.

You need an incentive just to keep going, and fortunately Paul Richards has given us one. He called a meeting of all the Colt .45 players and he told us if we did good we might get traded.

As I see it, Alice, this has not been a good year for us pitchers. Bo Belinsky punched a sportswriter and instead of a medal, like he deserved, they gave him a suspension. The Giants called up a Japanese rookie and when somebody asked if he was excited, he answered, "Not velly."

Sandy Koufax hurt himself. Warren Spahn grew old. Turk Farrell went through half of June, July, and August with a total of one win, including ties.

And you have heard of gopher balls ruining a pitcher? Well, out in California the right fielder on a little-league team was bit by a real gopher. Now that's what I call hard luck.

This has been another difficult week for us, Alice. Danny Coombs caught his necktie on the door of his hotel room this morning, and since the bus was ready to go, we had to leave him behind. In Philadelphia the other day, Hal Woodeshick was kidnapped by a gang of Brownie Scouts looking for the Beatles. They released him when they found out what it costs to feed him.

On the top of that, we've lost seven of our last nine. If it isn't one thing, it's another.

Baseball players are a strange breed, Alice, but baseball fans are stranger. As a relief pitcher who seldom pitches, I am something of an authority on the subject. We sit out there in the bull pen in the various and sundry parks, making chitchat and occasionally exchanging a new baseball for a sliced-chicken sandwich. This way, you get to know the fans.

I am often asked how I would rank the fans around the league, and my answer is that the best way to rank them is alphabetically. I do not know how else to do it.

Do you rank them on loyalty? The Met fans are in a world of their own. On good manners? The Phillie followers are dead last. On knowledge of the game and appreciation of good plays? You got to go for the Cub rooters.

Or do you judge it, as I am tempted to do, on which park has the best-looking women? Dodger Stadium, then.

You know me, Alice, always clowning. But for your own amazement, I'll tell you a little about the fans around the league, listing them according to how they score overall in five categories: team support, knowledge of the game, fairness, good manners, and pretty girls:

1. Chicago. They stick by a loser, which is all they have had in ten of the last eleven seasons. All a Cub fan asks is eighteen inches of plank with a number on it. They are the old-fashioned kind who don't leave until all the cushions have been picked up. The men sit out in the bleachers with their shirts off and sun themselves, which is good for the pores.
2. New York. The Met fans are a bigger attraction than the team. They have grown slightly more refined, without losing their zest, since moving from the Polo Grounds to Shea Stadium. They are known as the New Breed, and also as the little old signmakers.
3. Saint Louis. The most diehard and the most argumentative fans in the league. Notorious front-runners, but also very sentimental. They have been known to weep over a baseball card with Alpha Brazle's picture on it.
4. Los Angeles. The fans of the Dodgers seem to be mostly comedians. I mean, this is the way they make their living. Every night you see famous comics in the stands, such as Danny Kaye, Milton Berle, and Walter Winchell. One gets

the impression that not all Dodgers fans are sincere, because many of them go to the game to be seen as much as to see. You gaze around the crowd with a pair of binoculars, and you find yourself looking into another pair of binoculars. Very disconcerting.

5. San Francisco. As fickle as the winds that inhabit Candlestick Park. But any fan who will wear a fur parka in thirty-degree weather, in August, to see a baseball game has got to be loyal. They play a nice selection of music over the loudspeaker, if you like "I Left My Heart in San Francisco."
6. Philadelphia. They have the best and worst of fans. The problem is that they understand the game too well. They boo everything except "The Star-Spangled Banner." Have been known to shower opponents with ice, rotten fruit, and any items not nailed down. Last week they booed Richie Allen and applauded Don Larsen, who pitches for Houston.
7. Milwaukee. Once the best in the league, now near the bottom. Made a slight comeback at the box office this year, and for five innings are among the best fans in the league. But some fans guzzle beer for two hours, and by late in the game, the ushers have their hands full.
8. Houston. Our fans leave the games earlier, boo less, and dress better than anybody. Are not yet knowledgeable, but learning fast. Smokey Burgess of the Pirates claims that Houston fans make the most vicious personal remarks against opposing players. Did somebody out there call Smokey fat?
9. Pittsburgh. The Pirate fans have lost interest, a condition due in part to the dreariness of Forbes Field, which was outmoded twenty years ago. Teenagers rioted during a game early in the season, after listening to the music of a Beatles-type combo. Can you blame them?
10. Cincinnati. Everywhere you go, you hear people say, "Our town won't support a loser." The Reds are drawing poorly this year with a contender, so where does that leave Cincinnati?

Incidentally, every park in the league has a rule barring known gamblers. This is to make room for the thousands of unknown gamblers who attend games.

You Know Me, Alice
Lefty

SOME FORGETTABLE MOMENTS

OCTOBER 2, 1965

Houston, Texas
October 2, 1965

Dear Alice,

Well, we play our 162nd game Sunday, and Luman Harris says if we win we can have the rest of the year off.

The Domed Stadium had a great season, but the Astros didn't do so hot, although we did discover some promising new talent like Robin Roberts. Also, Joe Morgan and Larry Dierker. We played the last two months of the season on heart alone, plus an occasional aspirin.

I can't in good faith say I'm sorry to see it end, but I will miss the guys on the club. Like Ron Brand, who is always joking. "Lefty," he says to me the other day, "you are so poorly coordinated, I bet you can't take a shower and sing at the same time."

I guess William Shakespeare—he was a writer, Alice, but I don't know for which paper—described baseball best when he said, "Age cannot wither her, nor custom stale her infinite variety."

I'm not sure what that means, but the 1965 season certainly had a lot of variety.

This was the year when baseball moved indoors and faced the most serious threat in its history: The possibility that a game might have to be called on account of sun. Remember, Alice? In the daytime you couldn't follow a fly ball in the Dome, because of the glare from the Lucite panels. A few outfielders nearly gave their lives to the cause, but they finally painted the glare away with an ocean of whitewash.

LETTERS FROM LEFTY

This was the year when his pride wouldn't let Warren Spahn quit, but a broken hip forced Casey Stengel to retire because "I can't walk out to the mound and change pitchers anymore." Jim Maloney of the Reds hurled two no-hitters and broke even. New York beat him the first time, in extra innings, and later Maloney said, "I have nothing to be proud of. All I did was lose to the Mets."

The year began in Florida, Alice, in spring training, where the games mean nothing because the pitchers are ahead of the hitters. Or are the hitters ahead of the pitchers? I forget which.

Over at Saint Pete, there was a guy with the Mets who thought he was Napoleon. Danny Napoleon, a rookie outfielder. "He'll be okay," said Stengel, "if he keeps his hand out of his shirt."

There was great optimism in the camp of the Astros, although no one knew why. Then, suddenly, we were home to open the season, squinting up into the glare but eager to get started in the modestly furnished playpen that Judge Roy Hofheinz invented, borrowing some of his ideas from the early Romans and a few from *Popular Mechanics*.

Well, Alice, we have reached that point where it is traditional, I think, to look back over the season. I went back through my diary and jotted down a few of the high and low points, which follow herewith:

April 9. The Dome opens with a three-team exhibition series involving the Yankees and the Orioles. Joe Pepitone of the Yankees announces, proudly, that he got the first error by an Italian in the Domed Stadium.

May 1. The Astros whip the Cubs, 6-1, for their tenth-straight victory. General Manager Paul Richards has to caution the fans, who are growing hysterical and trying to order World Series tickets. "We will lose a few before the season ends," predicted Richards. And sure enough, we did.

May 21. In an interview, San Francisco's Masanori Murakami corrects a report published earlier in Houston that his favorite songs are "Horro Dorry" and "Up a Razy Liver." Murakami says his favorite song is "Wouldn't It Be Rovery."

June 14. The Dome begins to look like Grand Central Stadium. Astros send away Ken Johnson, Al Spangler, and Hal Woodeshick; bring in Lee Maye, Jim Gentile, Ron Taylor, and Mike Cuellar. "Now don't feel that you HAVE to make a lot of trades," a nervous Judge Hofheinz tells Luman Harris. "The stadium will carry us until 1967." Answers Luman, "Maybe so, judge, but my contract only runs through 1966."

July 8. Li'l Joe Morgan hits 6-for-6 against the Braves, including two homers, four runs scored, and three runs driven in. Naturally, the Astros lose in twelve innings, 9-8.

July 10. Houston becomes the seventh National League club to hire aging slugger Frank Thomas. "It's nice to know that someone still wants you," says Thomas.

July 29. "I've heard of guys going 0-for-15, or 0-for-25," complained a slump-ridden Bob Aspromonte, "but this is ridiculous. I'm 0-for-July."

August 10. Ex-Phillie Robin Roberts shuts out Philadelphia, 8-0, on four hits in his first start for Houston. Didn't you know he would? Couldn't you feel it?

August 31. Frank Thomas hits two home runs in his last game as an Astro, then is sold to the Braves. "It's nice to know that someone still wants you," says Thomas.

September 2. Casey Stengel, his retirement announced earlier in the week, bids good-bye to the Mets and to the writers who had come to love him. And of all the zillions of stories and mental pictures, this is the one that sticks: After the Mets played a twenty-four-inning marathon against the Giants in 1964, in the second game of a doubleheader, Stengel sat quietly in the clubhouse. Suddenly, he leaped for the ceiling. "I just wanted to see," he said, "if I'm still alive."

September 10. The day we lost the pennant. Don Drysdale beat us, 5-2, and the Astros are eliminated from the race. Other eight contenders breathe easier.

September 28. Writers upset the Radio-TV boys, 6-1, in a preliminary game that the fans seemed to enjoy. That is, no one got sick. Nellie Fox gave some sound advice to one citizen-infielder: "If the ball is hit to you slow, charge it. If it's hit hard, let it go by."

September 30. Cardinals eke out 19-8 win. Some fans suggest that the Judge put the glare back.

October 3. Keep the motor running . . . have a good winter, fellows, and hold out for more money.

You know Me, Alice
Lefty

LEFTY SAYS GOOD-BYE

MAY 5, 1966

Houston, Texas
May 5, 1966

Dear Alice,

I got a lump in my throat the size of a medicine ball. I have been traded to New York, and I cannot stop the tide of nostalgia that washes over me. It is not exactly like being waived out of the world, but you never know.

How can I ever forget those wonderful hours I spent in the Houston bull pen, listening to Jim Busby lecture on how to hit behind the runner. Or the friends I made, the good times we had, the many umpires we bit.

But it had to come, of course. Nothing goes on forever except the rent, income taxes, crabgrass, and Satchel Paige. At least I am glad that I stayed long enough to see the Astros on the ascendancy, whatever that is. I can remember, a few years ago, when playing for us or the Mets was considered a fate two times worse than death. Once, an infielder for the Mets delivered an ultimatum to the front office. "Trade me or bench me," he said, and that's the way it sort of was with the Colt .45s, which is the name we went by in those days.

But we are poor and feeble no more, Alice, or so it seems. We are so high up in the standings (third place) that our noses are beginning to bleed.

When I attended my first spring-training camp at Apache Junction, in the Arizona badlands, the biggest name on the roster was Bobby Shantz, the one-time glory tot of the old Philadelphia A's. Now it is Mike Cuellar, a wandering left-hander whose name most fans can't even pronounce (it is KWAY-ar).

Mike has won three games without a loss, and he has been getting his picture and large strings of words about himself in all the papers. He deserves them, and the other day I told him so. "Tank you, Mike," he said. (He thinks everyone is named Mike.)

It may not be possible to turn time backward in its flight, Alice, but we can try.

In my mind, the Houston National League baseball team was born in October of 1961, the day the Astros shelled out $125,000 to draft Joey Amalfitano as their premium pick from the Giants. When asked his reaction, Joey replied, "I may have to increase my insurance. I'm worth more than I thought."

It is hard to realize, but from the original list of rejects and renegades that suffered through the first Apache Junction camp, only four of us were left—me, Turk Farrell, Bob Aspromonte, and Bobby Lillis.

Trouble usually comes to those who attempt to harness certain erratic natural forces, such as lightning and the sea and Turk Farrell. But Turk has made a grand contribution to the Houston story, and he will always remain my favorite Martian.

I remember him beating the Phillies in an extra-inning game that went into the wee hours, and proudly announcing in the clubhouse, "Nobody beats the Turk after midnight."

And there was the time Farrell threatened to cancel his "prescription" to the paper if a certain writer didn't quit ripping him in print.

What we had on the club in 1962, Alice, was spirit and unity. I can still hear Jim Campbell telling Norm Larker, "Dumbo, if it wasn't for baseball, you'd be selling apples on a corner."

Times change, games are won and lost, people come and go, we laugh and weep and yawn, and what it adds up to is this: All the world is a stage, with matinees on Sunday and a day-night doubleheader on Saturdays.

We've had some int'resting fellows on the ball club, and it has been a pleasure knowing them. Once we had our own chaplain, Russ Kemmerer, *an ordained Methodist minister* who was always trying to improve his mind. He read copiously in the works of Funk and Wagnalls and other light novelists.

We've had some characters—Turk, Dizzy Dickson, NoNeck Williams, John Bateman—and we've had some famous ones. Shantz, Don Larsen, Pete Runnels, Johnny Temple, and Nellie Fox, who had known great moments. They came to Houston to try to wake up the echoes, and in a way they did.

LETTERS FROM LEFTY

We had infielders who covered as much ground as a water bucket, outfielders who could drop any ball they reached, and hitters who couldn't hit. We had noisy ones and quiet ones, like Joe Gaines, who never spoke except to make a kind of clicking sound with his teeth when he got hungry.

And now we have young ones with a future, like Joe Morgan, Jimmy Wynn, Sonny Jackson, Rusty Staub, and Larry Dierker, who are studded with talent like a ham with cloves.

What I will miss the most, I guess, is the good conversation on the bench. Me and Aspro and the other handsome young bachelors would sit around discussing the weighty issues of the day, such as whether or not airline hostesses should be compelled to retire upon reaching the age of thirty-three.

And I hate to leave the Dome, of course, where over two million fans watched us play last year. The Judge isn't worried about the attendance this year, either, saying that the Dome will draw well for all eternity. This is based partly on the population explosion, and I guess it is true. Just the other day, four people exploded in Cleveland, one of them while carrying a plate of soup.

I really ought to write a book, but then they would want to make a movie out of it and who would play Farrell? Look after Grady Hatton and the Astros for me, and if you need any tickets, just write Bill Giles.

You Know Me, Alice
Lefty

BACK HOME AGAIN

FEBRUARY 18, 1967

Houston, Texas
February 18, 1967

Dear Alice,

This was the week I came home. After roughing it for nine months in the wild country around New York City, I've come back to Texas, back to the civilized world.

I have been traded back to the Houston Astros by the Mets in exchange for a snowplow, a life-size portrait of Lamont Cranston, and $17 in cash. Frankly, I was surprised that the Astros gave up that much for me, but I understand Grady Hatton is desprit for left-handed relief pitching.

Of course, there is much about New York I will miss. Like lunch at the Four Seasons with Joey Heatherton. Running barefoot through Joe Namath's llama rug. Standing on the floor of the Stock Exchange and putting J. Paul Getty onto a good thing.

But what the heck, Alice. I'm glad to be back where folks laugh and smile and say "pardon me" when they knock you down a manhole. Not that Houston hasn't changed some. I am going to withhold my judgment about these topless nightclubs until I take a closer look at the situation.

I was real proud of the Astros last year. They came within a hair of finishing in seventh place. All they would have had to do was win eleven of their last eight games.

Anyway, it sure will be swell to see my old cronies, such as Turk Farrell, Bob Aspromonte, Rusty Staub, Jim Wynn, and the Frenchman, Claude Raymond.

The word is out that I am to room with Farrell, and I am really looking forward to it. Turk is none too bright, but he has a heart of gold. He is the kind of person who, if you ask him, would help raise money for the widow of the Unknown Soldier.

LETTERS FROM LEFTY

Most of the boys are already on the scene in Cocoa, but I don't report for spring training until the first of March. Frankly, I am in no haste to get there. Cocoa is so small that the head of the Mafia is a Filipino.

As you may recall, Alice, I hired out to the American Football League staff in the "off-season," as they refer to it in baseball. Three weeks after I got there, the AFL merged with the NFL, and now all the problems the leagues had have been settled, with the exception of who gets custody of Toots Shor.

There are things about New York I never did come to terms with, such as the fact that they don't have any *grass*. The parks are so small, Alice, that one night I got mugged by a midget.

As you know, most of my friends are the kind of people you would love to have for a stranger. One of them is Charley Callahan, the Miami Dolphins publicity man who worked for many years at Notre Dame, where he became a legend in his own time, or shortly thereafter.

Charley's heart still belongs to the Fighting Irish, and he is inclined to pick up a telephone at odd hours and share his emotions with various pals around the universe.

On one occasion last season, he placed a *collect* call at 3 ayem to George Ratterman in Oakland, where the one-time Notre Dame star was preparing to do the color on an AFL telecast. It was the night after Notre Dame crushed Oklahoma, and Charley was overcome with a combination of joy and Scotch.

"George," mumbled Callahan, "I just wanted to tell you that I have decided to name you the quarterback on my all-time Notre Dame team."

"That's nice of you, Charley," said Ratterman, sleepily, "but to what do I owe this honor?"

"To the fact," said Callahan, "that Johnny Lujack wouldn't accept the call."

I must stop now, as it is time for my yoga lesson. I will drop you a line from Florida. Meanwhile, I wish you would thank those people who were kind enough to say they were glad to see me come back. As his son said to William Tell, it is nice to be missed.

You Know Me, Alice
Lefty

GOOD-BYE, DIAMOND JIM

MARCH 26, 1968

Cocoa, Florida
March 26, 1968

Dear Alice,

The other day someone tacked a sign to the wall of our clubhouse that said, TEAMWORK IS THE ANSWER. And under it some clown had scribbled, WHAT IS THE QUESTION?

Well, you can call it teamwork or hustle or plain old vitamin C, but we got a better attitude this spring. At least that's what Spec Richardson keeps telling everybody. Maybe he really believes it. Or maybe he wants us to believe it. Anyway, Alice, the credibility gap seems to be getting smaller.

All I know is this. We never had much pride before on the Houston Astros. Most of us were playing because of our boyhood idol. For money. Someone would ask a guy how the game came out, and he would answer, "I went 1-for-4."

It doesn't seem to be that way this spring. We won eight in a row during one stretch, and the way everybody acted, you would have thought these games really counted. I just hope we haven't reached our peak too soon, with the season not yet started and all.

One day Loel Passe, who has never lost a game in the Astro radio booth, looked down from the press box as the players loosened up before a game. "By golly," said Loel, "look at that . . . doing a few pickups. The human body getting into tone . . . and then you send your charges onto the field."

He paused momentarily, chortled, and then exclaimed, "Yessir, it's the year of the Astros. We're going to finish in the first division for sure, and we may just win the pennant. By golly, I really believe that."

Now don't let yourself get excited or overheated, Alice. Loel always talks like that. It doesn't necessarily reflect the opinion of the sponsors, or even the ballplayers.

As for old Buster here, I am having a great spring, although not as good as Bo Belinsky, who is spending his at the beach with Jo Collins, a former Playmate of the Year. Jo began her career as Miss September, and apparently this is where Bo will be ending his. As they say in the song, "The days grow short when you reach September."

Just to bring you up to date, you can tell the girls at the dime store to brace themselves. It sure looks like the club will trade Bob Aspromonte.

A deal also may be cooking for John Bateman, and I sure hate that, as they just don't hardly make them like John anymore. He was reminding everybody that this was National Burlap Week, so you should help an old bag across the street. John says that the other night he saw the movie, *The Boston Strangler*, and he got all choked up.

You know me, Alice. I'm just a naïve kid at heart, but it does seem to me that the news out of Florida is getting wilder. Over in West Palm Beach, a housewife from New York is a student in a school for umpires.

Can you beat that? They say that she has run into problems nobody ever dreamed of before. For one thing, she can't seem to find a chest protector that fits her. I have no idea what her measurements are, but I imagine the tailor's dummy for the average male umpire would run 38-48-42.

What is more, when the president of the school bawled her out one day, she blushed, and moisture formed in her eyes. You have to be concerned for her future in baseball. I mean, she had been exposed to nothing harsher than words of reproof from the school's kindly old prexy. She wasn't being addressed by, say, Leo Durocher or Eddie Stanky.

Of course, it isn't all just fun in the sun. The old and the injured are the drama and fragrance of spring. The drama is their struggle to survive. The fragrance is fear.

Scarcely a team is without one or the other . . . an Eddie Mathews or an Ernie Banks, a Richie Allen or a Jim Lonborg.

In the spring you read the little squibs on the sports page to see who got released, and who went back to the minors. It is a little like reading the obituary columns.

Today the Astros gave Larry Sherry his unconditional release.

It wasn't too very long ago that Larry kept coming out of the bull pen for the Dodgers, winning a World Series for them and getting himself showered with gifts.

Remember Diamond Jim Gentile? He's on the Albany roster this spring, in a Class A league. And Bo, who once pitched a no-hitter as a rookie, is still waiting to see if any club wants him.

You wonder where it went for those who lost the edge in the high noon of their careers.

Oh, well, Alice, this is no time to get sentimental. Let the music play. This is the month to dream, and right now the club looks stellar. If they threw a wet sock up there, Rusty Staub would hit it. Norm Miller and Ivan Murrell have been knocking holes in the fences. The kids, Hal King and Hector Torres, appear ready for a long ride. The pitching has been beautiful.

Meanwhile, at Saint Pete, Gil Hodges says he doesn't care if the Mets lose them all in Florida, and they have tried to oblige him. Gil wants to use as many players as he can, in order to get acquainted with the warm bodies on his roster. "Familiarity," someone predicted, "will breed contempt."

You Know Me, Alice
Lefty

Index

A

Aaron, Hank, 26, 33
Abbott and Costello, 183
Abdul-Jabbar, Kareem, 64-67, 76, 78, 80, 83, 137-138
Adams, Bud, 90, 98-101
Adler, Bill, 144
Adlesh, Dave, 215
Agee, Tommy, 194
Alcaraz, Luis, 5
Alcindor, Lew. See Abdul-Jabbar, Kareem
Alexander, Grover Cleveland, 33
Ali, Muhammad, xviii, 38-40, 41-43, 44, 47-49, 53-55, 58-61
Allen, Lucius, 67
Allen, Mel, xvii
Allen, Richie, 7, 255, 265
Allen, Woody, 78, 164-166
Alou, Jesus, 215
Alworth, Lance, 31
Alzado, Lyle, 112
Amalfitano, Joey, 6, 260
Ames, Nancy, 215
Andre the Giant, 48-49
Argovitz, Jerry, 134
Ashby, Alan, 10, 19, 68, 191
Aspromonte, Bob, 5, 7, 251, 258, 260, 261, 262, 265
Auerbach, Red, 72, 81
Autry, Gene, xviii

B

Bacall, Lauren, 164
Baer, Max, 55
Bailey, Mark, 10
Bailey, Pearl, 78
Bamberger, George, 215
Banks, Ernie, 265
Barber, Red, xvii
Bass, Kevin, 22, 23
Bass, Mike, 110
Bateman, John, 9, 215, 251, 260, 265
Beathard, Pete, 103
Beery, Wallace, 209
Belinsky, Bo, 8-9, 136, 229-233, 253, 265, 266
Belinsky, Jo Collins, 229-233, 265
Bellard, Emory, 97, 160
Belotti, George, 99-100
Berbick, Trevor, 41, 42, 44, 45, 58, 59, 60, 61
Berle, Milton, 254
Berra, Dale, 153
Berra, Yogi, 32, 240-242
Berry, Raymond, 115
Biles, Eddie, 94, 102
Bilko, Steve, 3
Bird, Larry, 71-73
Blaik, Earl, 200
Blake, Robert, 122
Blanda, George, 99-100, 103, 104, 199, 201

Blount, Sherwood, 129
Blue, Vida, 33
Bogart, Humphrey, 40, 164, 245
Bonilla, Juan, 32
Boone, Bob, 20
Borgnine, Ernest, 99
Bottom, Joe, 227
Bradley, Bill, 78
Bragan, Bobby, 225
Brand, Ron, 256
Brandt, Gil, 116
Brazle, Alpha, 254
Brown, Bobby, 100-101, 241, 242
Brown, Hector, 215
Brown, Jimmy, 165, 181
Brown, John Y., 143, 144
Brown, Larry, 79
Brown, Lincoln, 143-144
Broyles, Frank, 86-88, 96, 199, 200
Bruce, Bob, 7
Brunet, George, 215
Bruno, Frank, 57
Bryant, Mary Harmon, 209
Bryant, Paul ("Bear"), 96, 103, 141, 177, 199-203, 204-207, 208-210
Buford, Don, 194
Burdette, Lew, 225
Burgess, Smokey, 255
Burns, George, 212
Burton, Richard, 53
Busby, Jim, 244, 259
Butler, Brett, 32
Bystrom, Marty, 20

C

Cabell, Enos, 9, 153
Calhoun, Jeff, 23
Callahan, Charley, 263
Campanis, Al, 145, 146
Campbell, Christian, 188
Campbell, Earl, 93, 180-182, 183-185, 186-189
Campbell, Hugh, 133, 153
Campbell, Jim, 260
Cantinflas, 136
Capp, Al, 231
Carew, Rod, 33
Carlton, Steve, 17, 198
Carson, Johnny, 127, 148, 194, 239
Carter, Gary, 23, 24
Carter, Jimmy, 176, 205
Casals, Rosie, 151
Cedeno, Cesar, 8, 9
Cerv, Bob, 34-35, 248
Cey, Ron, 15, 33
Chamberlain, Wilt, 72
Chandler, Spud, 242
Chaney, Don, 67
Chaplin, Charlie, 12
Charles, Ed, 194-195
Charles, Prince, 220

INDEX

Chase, Chevy, 47
Chavez, Judith, 176
Clanton, Chuck, 207
Clay, Cassius. See Ali, Muhammad
Clemente, Roberto, 33, 214
Clements, Bill, 128-129
Clendenon, Donn, 215
Cobb, Ty, 28-29, 33, 153, 238
Coleman, Ronald, 161
Collins, Bobby, 128
Collins, Jo. See Belinsky, Jo Collins
Collins, Tony, 115
Connick, Doc, 126
Connors, Chuck, 48
Coombs, Danny, 253
Cooper, Henry, 55
Corcoran, Larry, 192
Cosell, Howard, 53-55, 152, 156-158, 164-166
Courtney, Clint, 245
Covington, Wes, 177
Cowens, Dave, 143
Craft, Harry, 6, 246, 250, 251
Cranston, Lamont, 262
Crawford, Joan, 228
Crosby, Bing, 86
Cross, Irv, 112, 144
Crow, John David, 205
Cruz, José, 9, 16
Cuellar, Mike, 257, 259-260
Cuevas, Pipino, 59
Curry, Bill, 89-91

D

D'Amato, Cus, 46, 57
Dangerfield, Rodney, 129
Dark, Alvin, 146
Daugherty, Duffy, 200
Davis, Al, 117, 185
Davis, Bob, 103
Davis, Glenn, 10, 153
Davis, Mouse, 133-134
Dawkins, Darryl, 79-80
Dawson, Len, 117
De Niro, Robert, 129
Dean, Dizzy, 26-27, 33
DeBakey, Dr. Michael, 218
DeMille, Cecil B., 40
Derek, Bo, 175
Deshaies, Jim, 22
Dickey, Bill, 242
Dickey, Lynn, 103
Dickson, Dizzy, 215, 260
Dierker, Larry, 8, 191, 192, 256, 261
Dietzel, Paul, 199
DiMaggio, Joe, 32, 71, 241, 242
Diskin, Whitey, 251-252
Ditka, Mike, 115
Dodd, Bobby, 200
Donahue, Phil, 173
Doran, Bill, 10
Dorsett, Tony, 143, 180
Dowd, Barry, 69
Dressen, Chuck, 223, 225
Drexler, Clyde, 81
Drott, Dick, 215
Drysdale, Don, 258

Dundee, Angelo, 42
Durocher, Leo, 8, 69, 210, 265
Dye, Pat, 204-205, 206
Dykstra, Lenny, 23
Dylan, Bob, 55

E

Eason, Tony, 115
Eisenhower, Dwight D., 60, 83, 105, 112
Ellis, Jimmy, 58, 165
Elway, John, 125
Evers, Hoot, 3
Evert, Chris, 150, 174
Ewbank, Weeb, 107, 109, 237-238
Ewing, Patrick, 78

F

Fain, Ferris, 33
Fairly, Ron, 213
Farrell, Turk, 6, 26, 32, 215, 224-225, 245-246, 248, 252, 253, 260, 261, 262
Fehr, Don, 131
Feller, Bob, 27, 146, 192
Ferguson, Joe, 15
Fernandez, Sid, 196
Ferris, Boo, 33
Fidrych, Mark ("The Bird"), 2, 136
Fisher, Eddie, 53, 105
Fitch, Bill, 76
Flores, Jesse, 241
Flores, Tom, 117
Flutie, Doug, 174
Flynn, Errol, 108
Ford, Dan, 205
Ford, Gerald, 47, 126
Foreman, George, 59
Forsch, Ken, 10, 20
Forsythe, John, 165
Fountain, Pete, 118
Fouts, Dan, 32
Fox, Nellie, 8, 33, 258, 260
Foxx, Jimmie, 29
Foy, Joe, 33
Foyt, A.J., 217-219
Franklin, Alvin, 80
Franks, Herman, 165
Frazier, Joe, 38-40, 58
Frazier, Walt, 78
Fry, Hayden, 173
Fryar, Irving, 116
Fuller, Leon, 205

G

Gaines, Joe, 261
Galindez, Victor, 55
Gallagher, Jack, 49, 160, 161
Garagiola, Joe, 7, 240, 241
Garner, James, 218
Garvey, Steve, 15, 16
Gaspar, Rod, 193, 194
Gehrig, Lou, 3, 32, 35
Gentile, Diamond Jim, 3, 257, 266
George, Phyllis, 142-144
Geronimo, Cesar, 32
Getty, J. Paul, 262
Gettys, Reid, 80

268

INDEX

Gibson, Bob, 225
Gilbert, Chris, 160
Giles, Bill, 261
Gillman, Sid, 31, 93, 96-97, 99
Gleason, Jackie, 76
Glenn, John, 246
Gooden, Dwight, 153, 198
Goosen, Greg, 3
Gorman, Tom, 13
Gould, Elliot, 165-166
Graham, Otto, 90
Grange, Red, 238
Grant, Bud, 109
Grantham, Larry, 237
Green, Dallas, 20
Greenberg, Hank, 3
Gregg, Forrest, 111
Grier, Rosey, 178
Grizzle, Jim, 86
Gross, Greg, 20
Grote, Jerry, 8
Groza, Lou, 90
Guthrie, Janet, 217

H

Haden, Pat, 239
Haggard, Merle, 188
Hagler, Marvin, 50-52
Haley, Bill, 105
Hall, Tom T., 159
Hamilton, Milo, 198
Hannah, John, 115, 116
Harper, Smokey, 201, 203
Harris, Del, 137
Harris, Luman, 224, 246, 256, 257-258
Hartung, Clint, 33
Hatcher, Billy, 22, 23
Hatfield, Ken, 87
Hatton, Grady, 261, 262
Hayes, Elvin, 64, 66-67, 76, 83
Hayes, Woody, 98, 200
Hayman, Conway, 187
Hearns, Thomas, 41, 43, 59
Hearst, Patty, 148
Heatherton, Joey, 262
Heep, Danny, 196, 198
Henrich, Tommy, 241
Heist, Al, 6, 32
Heldman, Gladys, 150
Helfer, Al, xvii
Hemingway, Ernest, 242
Hemsley, Rollie, 29
Henderson, Hollywood, 94
Hernandez, Keith, 153
Herskowitz, Brian, 167, 168, 169
Herskowitz, Steve, 162-163, 167-169, 203
Hertz, Steve, 251
Herzeg, Ladd, 184-185
Hilton, Nicky, 53
Hirt, Al, 118
Hitchcock, Alfred, 71
Hodges, Gil, 12, 266
Hofheinz, Judge Roy, 6, 7, 9, 257, 258, 261
Hogan, Ben, 32
Holmes, Larry, 41, 42, 44, 59, 60, 152
Holyfield, Evander, 57

Hooker, Fair, 31
Hornsby, Rogers, 29, 33
Howard, Frank, 191
Howard, Trevor, 42
Howe, Art, 10, 15, 16, 17, 18
Howe, Colleen, 221
Howe, Gordie, 220-222
Howe, Mark, 220, 221
Howe, Marty, 220, 221
Hubbell, Carl, 33

I

Iglesias, Julio, 133
Inoki, Antonio, xviii, 47-49
Ivie, Mike, 2
Izenberg, Jerry, 59-61

J

Jackson, Andrew, 110, 119
Jackson, Jesse, 129
Jackson, Jumping Jackie, 81
Jackson, Sonny, 8, 261
James, Craig, 115
Jamison, Al, 99
Jarvis, Pat, 198
Jenkins, Ferguson, 33
Johnson, Bill, 242
Johnson, Charley, 103
Johnson, Dave, 24, 194
Johnson, Jack, 61
Johnson, Ken, 7, 250, 257
Johnson, Walter, 192
Jones, Cleon, 194
Jones, Deacon, 221
Jones, George, 188
Jones, Joey, 207
Jones, June, 134
Jones, Parnelli, 174

K

Kaat, Jim, 213
Kalas, Harry, 161
Kaline, Al, 3
Karloff, Boris, 40
Kaufman, Jim, 140-141
Kaye, Danny, 254
Keller, Charley ("King Kong"), 32, 241-242
Kemmerer, Russ, 9, 260
Kerr, Deborah, 99
Kieseling, Walt, 106
Killebrew, Harmon, 33
Kiner, Steve, 110
King, Billie Jean, 148-151
King, Don, 56
King, Hal, 266
Kirksey, George, 247-249
Kissinger, Henry, 55
Knepper, Bob, 22, 24
Knight, Ray, 23
Koosman, Jerry, 194
Koufax, Sandy, 33, 192, 198, 225, 229, 253
Koy, Ted, 160
Kramer, Jack, 150
Kramer, Jerry, 111
Krauss, Barry, 202

INDEX

L

LaCorte, Frank, 20
Ladd, Ernie, 99-100, 236
Lafitte, Pierre and Jean, 119
Lammons, Pete, 109
Lamonica, Daryle, 103
Lampley, Jim, 226, 227
Lancaster, Burt, 99
Landestoy, Rafael, 16
Landry, Tom, 109
Lanier, Bob, 76
Lanier, Hal, 5, 242
Lardner, Ring, 244
Larker, Norm, xvii, 215, 249, 260
Larsen, Don, 8, 242, 255, 260
Lawson, Earl, 177
Layne, Bobby, 91
Leahy, Frank, 200
Ledbetter, Harry, 140
Lee, Jacky, 103
Lee, Pinky, 193
Lemm, Wally, 101
Lemongello, Mark, 32
Lemons, Abe, 68-70
Leonard, Sugar Ray, 41-43, 50-52
Leppert, Don, 68, 69
Letterman, Dave, 127
Lewis, Guy, 65, 81, 82-83
Lillis, Bob, 5, 260
Lincoln, Abraham, 199
Lindell, Johnny, 242
Lindsey, Jim, 87
Lippett, Ronnie, 116
Lipscomb, Big Daddy, 31, 131
Liston, Sonny, 59, 60
Little, Bill, 160, 161
Lloyd, John, 174
Lombardi, Vince, 108
Lonborg, Jim, 265
Long, Dale, 33
Louis, Joe, 39-40
Lucas, John, 130-131
Luckman, Sid, 202
Lujack, Johnny, 263
Luzinski, Greg, 19
Lyles, Warren, 206
Lynn, Fred, 174

M

Mack, Connie, 6
Madden, John, 113
Maddox, Gerry, 20
Madonna, 77
Malone, Moses, 137
Maloney, Jim, 257
Manilow, Barry, 113
Manley, Dexter, 125
Mantle, Mickey, 7, 32, 35-36, 214, 238
Maranville, Rabbit, 29
Maravich, Pete, 165
Maris, Roger, 34-36
Marshall, Mike, 8
Martin, Billy, 30, 129, 225
Martin, J.C., 194
Martin, Jimmy, 168

Marvin, Lee, 165
Mathews, Eddie, 265
Matson, Randy, 48
Matuszak, John, 108
Mauch, Gene, 177, 214
Mauck, Carl, 187
Maye, Lee, 257
Mays, Jerry, 110-111
Mays, Willie, 3, 7, 165, 180, 248
Maysel, Lou, 161, 162
McAuliffe, Christa, 150
McCarver, Tim, 224
McClendon, Charlie, 199
McCray, Rodney, 75
McGee, Max, 108
McHale, Kevin, 77
McLean, Dude, 140
McMahon, Jim, 115-116
McMullen, John J., 9
McQueen, Steve, 218
Merchant, Larry, 50
Meredith, Dandy Don, 20
Michaels, Lou, 109
Michaels, Walt, 109
Micheaux, Larry, 81
Miller, Norm, 266
Mitchell, Johnny, 208
Mix, Tom, 245
Monroe, Earl ("The Pearl"), 78
Moon, Warren, 153, 184
Moore, Archie, 45
Moore, Bud, 205
Mora, Jim, 186
Morgan, Chesty, 174
Morgan, Joe, 8, 9, 16, 213, 214, 215, 256, 258, 261
Morgan, Stanley, 116
Morrall, Earl, 109
Morris, Mercury, 131
Motley, Marion, 90
Mungo, Van Lingle, 32
Murakami, Masanori, 257
Murphy, Bob, 198
Murphy, Calvin, 74-76, 81, 137
Murphy, Turk, 165
Murrell, Ivan, 266
Musburger, Brent, 113, 144
Musial, Stan, 214, 248
Muskie, Edmund, 48
Musso, Johnny, 199, 203

N

Naber, John, 226
Nagle, Kel, 32
Nagurski, Bronko, 31, 157
Naismith, James, 66
Namath, Joe, 109, 143, 202, 205, 229, 237-239, 262
Napoleon, Danny, 257
Navratilova, Martina, 150
Nealon, Clark, 210
Nelson, Byron, 32
Nelson, Lindsey, 12-13
Nelson, Willie, 133, 188
Newhouser, Hal, 3
Newman, Paul, 166, 218, 219

INDEX

Neyland, General Bob, 200
Niekro, Joe, 10, 14, 16, 68, 191
Nielsen, Gifford, 102, 104
Nielsen, Jim, 67
Nixon, Richard, 110
Norton, Ken, 42, 58
Nottebart, Don, 7

O

O'Brien, Jim, 110
O'Brien, Pat, 90
Ojeda, Bob, 23
Olajuwon, Akeem, 78, 79, 81, 83, 154
Olivares, Eddie, 248
Orosco, Jesse, 22, 23
Orr, Jimmy, 109
Ott, Mel, 33

P

Paige, Satchel, 25-27, 28, 230, 259
Pallone, Dave, 196
Palmer, Arnold, 32
Palmer, Jim, 174-175
Pardee, Jack, 133-134, 199
Parker, Gardner, 187
Parseghian, Ara, 200
Pasche, Alden, 83
Passe, Loel, xvii, 264-265
Pastorini, Dan, 102, 103, 108, 182
Patrick, Linnie, 207
Patterson, Floyd, 45, 46
Paultz, Billy, 137
Payton, Walter, 115
Pearl, Minnie, 78
Pepitone, Joe, 257
Perkins, D.D., 97
Perkins, Ray, 208
Perry, Gaylord, 25, 33, 213
Perry, William, 114, 115
Peterson, Bill, 177
Peychaud, Antoine, 119
Phillips, Bum, 92-94, 95-97, 184, 187, 199
Pinson, Vada, 177
Plunkett, Jim, 108
Powell, Boog, 191, 194
Puhl, Terry, 9-10, 19, 68, 191
Pyle, Ernie, 53

Q

Quarry, Jerry, 165

R

Rader, Doug, 9
Ramsey, Jones, 159, 161-162
Ranew, Merritt, 32, 247
Ratterman, George, 263
Raymond, Claude, 262
Reagan, Ronald, 128, 175, 205
Reed, Willis, 78
Reid, Robert, 75, 137
Resnik, Judith, 150
Reyes, Napoleon, 231
Reynolds, Craig, 10, 68
Reynolds, Debbie, 105
Reynolds, George, 66, 67
Rice, Grantland, 197

Richard, J.R., 2, 10, 16, 69, 191
Richards, Golden, 31
Richards, Paul, 9, 213, 249, 253, 257
Richardson, Micheal Ray, 131
Richardson, Spec, 264
Rickey, Branch, 241
Rickles, Don, 61
Ride, Sally, 150
Riggs, Bobby, 68, 148-151
Rizzuto, Phil, 32
Roberts, Morganna, 174
Roberts, Oral, 123
Roberts, Robin, 7, 8, 256, 258
Robinson, Brooks, 194
Robinson, Frank, 194
Robinson, Jackie, 27, 145-147
Robinson, Sugar Ray, 61
Rockne, Knute, 210
Rogers, Roy, xviii
Rose, Pete, 20, 33, 153, 174, 213, 214
Rosen, Al, 10
Rosenthal, Harold, 242
Rossman, Mike, 55
Rossovich, Tim, 94
Royal, Darrell, 86-88, 96, 97, 140, 159-162, 200
Rubinstein, Artur, 31
Ruhle, Vern, 10, 68
Runnels, Pete, 8, 260
Russell, Jane, 112, 164
Ruth, Babe, 28, 32, 34-36, 218, 238, 242
Ruth, Dr., 122
Ruthven, Dick, 20
Ryan, Nolan, 5, 9, 10, 14, 19, 20, 22, 24, 33, 68, 69, 190-192, 193-195, 196-198
Ryan, Ruth, 192, 194
Rymkus, Lou, 89-91, 98-101, 104

S

Sadecki, Ray, 224
Sambito, Joe, 10, 16, 20, 21, 68
Sampson, Greg, 181, 182
Sampson, Ralph, 75, 76, 77-78, 154
Sanders, Don, 68-70
Sanders, Red, 200
Savalas, Telly, 165
Schmeling, Max, 40
Schwarzenegger, Arnold, 198
Scott, George C., 165
Scott, Mike, 24
Sembera, Carroll, 3
Serling, Rod, 116
Shakespeare, 11, 152-154, 256
Shamsky, Art, 194
Shantz, Bobby, 6, 8, 259, 260
Sherrill, Jackie, 139, 141
Sherrod, Blackie, 160
Sherry, Larry, 265-266
Shor, Toots, 242, 263
Short, Chris, 33
Shula, Don, 89, 110
Simmons, Curt, 225
Simpson, O.J., 238
Sims, Billy, 133
Sims, Orland, 5
Slaughter, Enos, 33

271

INDEX

Sloan, Steve, 199, 239
Smith, Bubba, 234-236
Smith, Dave, 23, 197
Smith, Hal, 6
Smith, Red, 145
Smith, Reggie, 192
Smith, Tal, 10, 15
Smothers brothers, 218
Snider, Duke, 33
Snyder, Jimmy the Greek, 68, 112, 118, 125-127, 142, 144
Spahn, Warren, 225, 253, 257
Spain, Ken, 67
Spangler, Al, 6, 246, 250, 257
Speaker, Tris, 33
Spink, J.G. Taylor, 26
Spinks, Leon, 53-55, 58
Spinks, Michael, 56-57, 152
Spitz, Mark, 226-228
Stabler, Ken, 94, 102-104, 202, 209
Stagg, Amos Alonzo, 199-200, 204, 210
Stallings, Gene, 139-141, 202, 209
Stanky, Eddie, 265
Stargell, Willie, 213
Starr, Bart, 108
Staub, Rusty, 8, 32, 212-216, 251, 261, 262, 266
Staubach, Roger, 143, 175
Steckel, Les, 116
Stello, Dick, 174
Stengel, Casey, 2, 11-13, 147, 242, 257, 258
Stephenson, Jan, 173
Stirnweiss, George, 241
Stone, Dean, 6
Stooksberry, Milo, 112
Strawberry, Darryl, 31, 32, 198
Street, James, 160
Studley, Chuck, 183-184
Suman, Don, 100
Sutton, Don, 190-191
Swann, Lynn, 31

T

Tatum, Jack, 94
Tatum, Jim, 210
Tatupu, Mosi, 115
Taylor, Arlie, 232
Taylor, Elizabeth, 53, 105
Taylor, Ron, 257
Taylor, Ted, 220
Temple, Johnny, 8, 177, 260
Thomas, Duane, 94, 109-110
Thomas, Frank, 200, 258
Thomas, Pinklon, 44
Thomson, Bobby, 33, 162
Thon, Dickie, 10
Todd, Mike, 53
Tomjanovich, Rudy, 75
Torres, Hector, 266
Towle, Steve, 181
Traynor, Pie, 33
Trevino, Claudia, 174
Trevino, Lee, 174
Triandos, Gus, 32
Trillo, Manny, 20
Trucks, Virgil ("Fire"), 3
Trull, Don, 103

Truman, Harry, 206
Trump, Donald, 56
Tubbs, Tony, 45
Tyson, Mike, 44-46, 56-57

U

Uecker, Bob, 223-225
Unitas, Johnny, 105-107, 109
Unser, Del, 20

V

Valentino, Rudolph, 138
Valenzuela, Fernando, 33, 136-138
Vance, Dazzy, 33
Veeck, Bill, 25, 28-30
Virdon, Bill, 9, 16, 69

W

Waddell, Rube, 29-30
Wadkins, Lanny, 31
Wagner, Dick, 10
Wagner, Honus, 33
Walker, Doak, 31
Walker, Harry, 8, 214
Walling, Denny, 18, 19, 68
Walls, Lee, 248
Waner, Paul, 29
Ward, Danny, 215
Warfield, Paul, 110
Warner, John, 53
Warner, Pop, 200
Warren, Mike, 67
Watson, Bob, 8
Watson, Don, 205
Wayne, John, 19, 101
Weems, Ted, 118
Weis, Al, 194
Weissmuller, Johnny, 227
Weld, Tuesday, 40
Wepner, Chuck, 49
Wernz, Jack, 4
Wharton, Hogan, 100
Wilhelm, Hoyt, 36
Wilkinson, Bud, 200
Williams, Carl, 57
Williams, Doug, 125
Williams, Paul, 174
Williams, Ted, 214
Williams, Vanessa, 173
Williams, Walter ("No-Neck"), 3, 9, 260
Williamson, Fred, 108
Wilson, Don, 8
Wilson, Hack, 29
Wilson, John, 184
Wilson, Tim, 187
Winchell, Walter, 136, 254
Winkler, Henry ("The Fonz"), 148
Witherspoon, Tim, 45
Wolf, Wally, 246
Wooden, John, 65, 66, 80
Woodeshick, Hal, 6, 214, 248, 253, 257
Woolf, Bob, 72, 73
Worster, Steve, 160
Wouk, Herman, 105
Wray, Fay, 49, 164
Wright, Rayfield, 234

INDEX

Wussler, Bob, 143
Wynn, Jimmy, 8, 215, 250, 261, 262

Y

Yastrzemski, Carl, 213
Yeoman, Bill, 96, 97, 128, 129, 160
Yepremian, Garo, 110

Young, Bob, 95
Young, Brigham, 156
Young, Cy, 33, 192
Young, Michael, 81

Z

Zindler, Marvin, 122

GV 583.H48 1989

	DATE DUE		
OCT 2 4 1997			